SOUNDS OF ADVOCACY, LANGUAGE AND LIBERATION

SOUNDS OF ADVOCACY, LANGUAGE AND LIBERATION

PAPERS IN HONOUR OF HUBERT DEVONISH

EDITED BY

CLIVE FORRESTER
NICKESHA DAWKINS

FOREWORD BY

CAROLYN COOPER

The University of the
West Indies Press

The University of the West Indies Press
7A Gibraltar Hall Road, Mona
Kingston 7, Jamaica
www.uwipress.com

A catalogue record of this book is available from the
National Library of Jamaica.

ISBN: 978-976-640-894-7 (print)
978-976-640-946-3 (ePub)

Front cover photograph: The sonic blast from the Marroon's ancient
instrument reverberates across the moonlit landscape alerting all
who hear it, from the mountains to the sea, that freedom is at hand.

Cover and book design by Robert Harris
Set in Scala 11/14.5 x 24.

Printed in the United States of America

Contents

List of Figures and Charts

FIGURES

CHARTS

List of Tables

"Riispek Juu"

Collaborative Research in the Humanities

CAROLYN COOPER

I MET HUBERT DEVONISH IN 1980 WHEN I came to teach at the University of the West Indies, Mona, in what was then the Department of English, now Literatures in English, and soon to rebranded yet again to include film studies. Hubert was teaching in the Department of Linguistics and Use of English, which has evolved into Language, Linguistics and Philosophy. We soon discovered that we had shared interests in Caribbean languages and literature. But Hubert was a strict gatekeeper. Linguistics was a science and mere humanists needed to tread carefully and respectfully in the specialist field. Karen Carpenter wittily conceives her forays into Linguistics as "trespassing". I think of my own explorations into protected territory as "moonlighting" – with all the transgressive associations of secretive night work. My rather elementary study of Linguistics was a labour of love. And I felt completely entitled to follow where my heart led. Even if Hubert disapproved! And he certainly did.

In 1988, I experimented with Jamaican as a language of literary analysis. And I must thank Dr Velma Pollard, educator and creative writer, for inspiring that experiment. I was writing a paper on Sistren Theatre Collective's *Lionheart Gal: Life Stories of Jamaican Women*, edited by Honor Ford-Smith. One morning, I went over to Velma's house and began telling her about it. At that time, we both lived in College Common, just one house apart. University housing provides a distinct opportunity for cross-disciplinary conversations but not many academics seem to appreciate this fact. I said to Velma, "Mi feel seh Honor fix-up, fix-up wa di uman dem seh." Velma's laughing response went something like this: "You see you literature people, by the time you done write the paper it not going to sound nothing like that.I decided to take up Velma's challenge to write the paper in Jamaican. And because I had already written a fair bit in English, I tried to translate what I had into Jamaican. That was a big mistake. When I read my first attempt to both Velma and Hubert, who also lived in College Common, they stopped me in my tracks. The Jamaican translation sounded stilted, bearing the markings of its English genesis. What I needed to do was to think the paper through in Jamaican. And that's what I proceeded to do. The final version, which is published in *Noises in the Blood,* is bilingual. I was certainly not going to throw away the section I had already written in English.

For the *Lionheart Gal* essay, I asked Celia Blake, then a graduate student in the Department of Linguistics and Use of English, to convert my "chaka-chaka" writing system into Cassidy. My decision to use the specialist orthography, which Hubert certainly approved, marked a departure from conventional wisdom. Popular orthographies for Jamaican depend exclusively on English orthography: colonialism inscribed. With varying degrees of skill, amateur linguists adapt the notoriously irregular writing system of English to suit the sounds of Jamaican.

A year later, I collaborated more substantively with Hubert on another academic project. Long-time *Gleaner* columnist Morris Cargill had written one of his usual contemptuous articles with the mocking headline, "Corruption of Language Is No Cultural Heritage". He attempted to ridicule the lucid arguments made by Dr Mertel Thompson in support of bilingual education for Jamaican students, in an article also published in the *Gleaner.* For more than two decades, Dr Thompson taught Use of English at Mona. She certainly understood the complexities of language teaching and learning in Jamaica.

With typical disdain, Cargill argued that Dr Thompson "would like to see Patois retained as part of our cultural heritage, and believe that it can occupy that honourable place alongside the teaching of standard English". Cargill made his own position absolutely clear: "I, on the other hand, take the view that if it is what is called "our cultural heritage", it is a lousy heritage redolent of slavery and that if we keep on saying it is a great thing, it merely encourages its continued use until it will finally swamp what remains of standard English in Jamaica. Of necessity, most people have inherited Patois, but I see no reason to make a virtue of necessity." Making a virtue of necessity, I knew that it was imperative to respond to Cargill; and in the Jamaican language. Too often we defend the Jamaican language in English.

In addition to writing the response in Jamaican, I also decided to use the Cassidy orthography. This time, I asked Hubert to convert my "chaka-chaka" spelling into the specialist writing system which I was just beginning to learn. Hubert readily agreed. The headline I came up with for the article was, "Cho! Misa Cargill, Rispek Juu". It was primarily a reference to Cargill's disrespect for the Jamaican language but also for Dr Thompson. First, he assumed she was male and then when he was corrected, he made matters worse: "Miss Thompson (or is she Ms or Mrs?)." It did not seem to have occurred to Cargill that she could have been "Dr".

Unfortunately, there was Guyanese Creole interference in Hubert's rendition of my Jamaican Creole headline. "Rispek" became "riispek". But I had so much respect for Hubert's authority as the expert in the field, I didn't dare proofread his text and so I didn't pick up the error. And there were a couple of other errors that might have been made by the *Gleaner* proofreaders. There was English interference in the spelling of some words. For example, "bark" was not spelled "baak"; "to" was not spelled "tu"; and "of" was not spelled "aaf". But these spelling errors were relatively minor. The substance of the article was what really mattered. And it generated quite a bit of controversy.

This was the first time that the Cassidy orthography was being used in a newspaper article, as far as I could tell. And what irritated so many adults was that their children could easily read the text and they could not. Liberated from the vagaries of English orthography, the children easily decoded the unfamiliar text. And so did adult readers who were receptive to the new orthography. For example, Mr Andrew Sewell, a Rastaman who used to deliver mail in College Common, read and understood the article. He went straight to the heart of the matter: "It ful di spies af owa rial Afrikan langgwij" [It fills the space of our real African language].

The very strangeness of the orthography restores to Jamaican its integrity; it gives the language and its speakers presence. A political issue! Mr Sewell's "ful" the preferred Jamaican equivalent of the English "fill" fulfils an expectation of completion and closure in the transfer of culture across the Atlantic; fulling up the void of that "deep amnesiac blow" that was the Middle Passage – to cite the early Derek Walcott.

Hubert had written "Notes" to the orthography which should have been placed at the beginning of the article. Nonsensically, the notes were placed at the very end of the article with the original description intact: "Notes on the Jamaican Creole System used in the following statement". Clearly, nobody on the editorial team at the *Gleaner* was taking the article seriously. Nevertheless, that newspaper article, produced out of the collaboration between Hubert and me, played an important role in enabling me to write a bilingual newspaper column for the *Jamaica Observer*, starting in 1993. Much to the distress of the editors, I insisted that the Jamaican language was married to English, just like scarce and plentiful produce in the market. If they wanted a column at all, they would have to take it in both languages.

I called the column, "(W)uman Tong(ue)". I substituted a "u" for the "o" in woman and put both the "W" of Woman and the "ue" of Tongue in parentheses, to simultaneously signify English and Jamaican. Despite the constant attacks from readers who were angered by my use of Jamaican, the column was an important affirmation of the value of fi wi language.

In 1992, Hubert and I began collaborating on a truly innovative academic enterprise: Reggae Studies. In December that year, Olivia "Babsy" Grange, who was not a minister of government at the time, organized a seminar on Reggae Music as a Business, hosted by Specs-Shang Muzik, and Sandosa, in collaboration with the Eagle Merchant Bank, the National Commercial Bank and the Trafalgar Development Bank. The primary purpose of the seminar was to explore ways of establishing a venture capital fund for the industry. But attention was also paid to the culture of reggae.

I was invited to present a paper that I titled "Cultural Implications of Marketing Reggae Internationally". I focused on the mixed reception of Buju Banton's anti-homosexuality song, "Boom By-By". I prophetically argued that the fate of that controversial song in the "outernational" market, particularly in the United States and the United Kingdom. where highly politicized LGBT activists wield substantial power, was a test case of the degree to which local Jamaican cultural values could be exported, without censure, into a foreign market.

I asked a number of questions: How, then, should the reggae artist respond to this marketing problem? Adapt the message to suit the export market, sacrificing authenticity for air-play? Should the artist do one kind of song for the local market and another for export? Admittedly, in the age of the internet, the distinction between local and international markets is purely academic, in the worst sense of that word. Should the reggae artist risk censorship in order to maintain the cultural integrity of the Jamaican way of seeing the world? In my role of cultural critic, I assumed the burden of communal responsibility for the youthful DJ who had put himself at risk by running up his mouth. I concluded my presentation with a clear warning: the DJ must learn to censure himself, otherwise somebody else will do the censuring.

The reception of my presentation by the local Jamaican audience was so positive that on my way home from the Jamaica Conference Centre, it occurred to me that the reggae music industry would benefit from academic support that could be provided by the University of the West Indies. A proposal was submitted to Faculty board and approved. The Reggae Studies Unit was placed within the Institute of Caribbean Studies and launched in the 1994/1995 academic year. I was appointed as the Coordinator.

Twenty-two years later, the Institute issued a call for papers for a conference in which I was described as a "co-founder" of the Reggae Studies Unit. I immediately sent an email to the Director with the following recommendation: ". . . instead of designating me as "co-founder" of the Reggae Studies Unit, I'm suggesting that you just say that I conceived the Reggae Studies academic programme at Mona". One of the problems that arise within large institutions like the University of the West Indies is that latecomers do not always know the history of particular enterprises and so make unfounded assumptions. Even though there are countless minutes of meetings, these are not always consulted.

I sent an email to Hubert on the co-founder business and his initial response was most amusing:

Who is it claimed you "co-founded" it with[?]. I didn't see any duppy alongside you. It was your idea and you asked me to help you write it up. It was you who stood on the stage at the Creative Arts Centre, I think, and collected the first financial contributions for the centre. Didn't notice any shadows alongside you but then my eyesight has always been bad.

Hubert later sent me an even more explicit mail on the matter, copied to both the Director of the Institute and the Dean:

Dear All,

I hadn't up until now been privy to the discussion about the founding of the Reggae Studies Unit (originally conceived of as the International Reggae Studies Conference [Centre]). My recollection of the process is that Carolyn Cooper came up with the idea. I know I was subsequently drafted in to help with actually drafting the proposal, help which I rendered on Carolyn's front veranda in College Common. I gather that my name may have been attached to the draft. If that is so, this was most likely at Carolyn's insistence, given her stubborn determination to always call my name when she speaks of the origins of the Unit.

Carolyn was the advocate for the proposal right through the institutionalizing process, the person who presented it at the various levels of the university. She was both, therefore, the originator of the idea, and the driving force behind it being set up, arguing for it at all levels. If I played any role, it was as a willing conscript, carrying out functions which I was asked to perform to assist, helping as I would any colleague, in pushing forward with any ideas they may have. I am a little embarrassed that her generosity in acknowledging my role may be distorting history.

I can claim no paternity here, either natural or via in vitro fertilization. The Reggae Studies Unit is, as with many of Carolyn's ideas and projects, a product of immaculate conception. She is, as we all know, very very capable of coming up with bright ideas on her own and implementing them. Hope this clears things up.

Hubert's witty email does not indicate the full extent of his drafting. Even if he was not the baby-father, he certainly played an important post-conception role. He fleshed out my ideas, bringing a multi-disciplinary perspective to the enterprise. Of course, there was language and literature. And media and communications. But also physics for the study of sound technology! Our vision was rather grand. And Hubert remained a constant supporter of the Unit through all its ups and downs, like a good parent, whether biological or adoptive.

Another important collaborative project I did with Hubert was a news report for Mutabaruka's *Cutting Edge*programme on IRIE FM. In the late 1990s, Muta asked me to do a weekly report in Jamaican. Neither Muta nor I can remember the exact date; we are both senior citizens. I immediately invited Hubert to help implement the proposal. At the time, the *Gleaner* used to publish on Sunday, a summary of the big news stories from the previous week. I suggested that we translate that *Gleaner* summary into Jamaican. Hubert agreed and he recruited Mertel Thompson, Jean Wellington and Dhanais Jaggernaut to assist with translation. We called the resulting news programme, *Big Tingz Last Week*. It was very popular but ended because there was no funding to sustain the work of the enthusiastic volunteers.

That project may well have planted the seeds for the much later media work done by the Jamaican Language Unit to broadcast the news in Jamaican. Then in 2014, Hubert asked me to co-host with Tyane Robinson, a public affairs programme in Jamaican on *NewsTalk 93*. Again, it was very popular but it did not last.

Hubert also collaborated with me to co-author a chapter of my book, *Sound Clash: Jamaican Dancehall Culture At Large*. We called the chapter, The Dancehall Transnation: Language. Lit/orature and Global Jamaica. My writing style is quite different from Hubert's – I suppose he would say his is scientific and mine is metaphorical – so we had to negotiate with each other to end up with a language we would both consider representative.And I think we succeeded.

I must talk about some instances in which collaboration did not work out as I had expected. In 2013, I had the idea to establish at Mona, a multi-disciplinary, cross-faculty Centre for the Creative Industries and Cultural Enterprise. It was an outgrowth of the degree programme in Entertainment and Cultural Enterprise Management that the Reggae Studies Unit had established and offered for a year, before a former Dean of the Faculty appropriated it for the Institute of Caribbean Studies, refusing to give the Unit access to the funding earned from teaching summer school courses. But that's another story. Naturally, I shared the proposal for the new Centre with Hubert and later, Deborah Hickling whose expertise in the field enhanced the draft. When the proposal was submitted to the Campus Principal, I included both Hubert and Deborah as co-authors because of their input. The proposal did not receive the support of the principal who informed me that it was not supported by my faculty. It was sabotaged from within. In fact, I was asked by a faculty member, who must remain unnamed, if the Centre was a post-retirement project. It was not. I retired as soon as I could.

In October of 2018, Waibinte Wariboko, then Dean of the Faculty of Humanities and Education, asked Hubert to develop a new inter-disciplinary degree programme for the Faculty based on my proposal and his input in it. I thought Hubert could have asked me to collaborate. But he did not. And I should have learned from that experience that academic collaboration, like sex, must be consensual. But I did not. Last year, when I thought that the Jamaican Language Unit was turning 10 – it was actually 15 – I asked Hubert what he was going to be doing to mark the occasion. He said that because of resource constraints – both human and financial – it seemed unlikely that the anniversary would be marked.

I did not read the sub-text of that statement carefully enough and blithely offered to do a lecture. Hubert sent the following email:

> My Dearest Caroline[*sic*] C,
>
> Thanks for the offer which is eagerly accepted. The Cassidy-Le Page Distinguished Lecture Series – Special Lecture celebrating 15 years of JLU. Carolyn Cooper "'Disguise up the English': Louise Bennett's Anansi Poetics". Tentatively on Creole International Creole Day, Thursday 26 October 2017. Will try to get the Undercroft for 5:30 p.m.
>
> On *Big Tingz*, we had suspended waiting to restart when we got restored our slot on *Newstalk*. Still negotiating that one. Thanks again for all the support and solidarity through the years. You made the long journey of fifteen years seem short (10). We will be in touch with you in about a week, once planning for the lecture gets on the way.
>
> Hubert

To sustain my unscientific carnal metaphor, let me tell you that appearances can be very deceiving in academic matters as in sex. Remarkably, in his introduction of me at the lecture, Hubert outlined all of the many times I had trespassed in Linguistics. I was alarmed. But it served me right. I had forced myself on the Jamaican Language Unit and had to take full responsibility for my coercive actions. Despite this error of judgement on my part, I must state unequivocally, that the sustained pleasure of consensual collaboration with Hubert on so many projects for more than three decades is long-lasting.

One of the highlights of our academic intercourse was Hubert's unsolicited invitation for me to give the closing plenary lecture at the 21st biennial conference of the Society for Caribbean Linguistics held at Mona in 2016. I spoke on the topic, "'To Di Worl'": Reggae, Dancehall and the Globalization of Jamaican. I was definitely not trespassing at that conference. In retirement, I hope that in these golden years we will find other academic work on which to enthusiastically collaborate.

Big up, Hubert! Nof, nof riispek juu fi chruu.

Remarks

HUBERT DEVONISH

IIZII LESN GUD FO DONS (TAKE HEED)

I begin with the regularly quoted translated words of the Martinican anti-colonialist revolutionary, Frantz Fanon, that "Each generation must ... discover its mission, fulfil it, or betray it" (Fanon 1963, p.206). The quote captures many insights. It pushes us to feel that we can be agents and change the world around us. We open our eyes at birth, see an imperfect world and wonder why "they" haven't done anything to fix it. Over time, the realization should dawn on us that we should indeed be agents. But for many, that early light of "dee-kliin" never comes. The fact is, a generation that is involved in discovering and fulfilling its mission, recognizes that change is best achieved with collective effort.

It is easy to assume that all the good things around us came about by accident. Or, we think they are given to usbecause we are entitled to them, by virtue of our birth, our intellectual brilliance or that most deceptive of illusions, because "we worked hard". Whether driven by a false sense of entitlement or an equally false one about having worked hard, we enjoy the good fortune of what we have because of the efforts of others who came before us. A proper sense of history should keep us grounded, protected from the small-minded petty self-centred arrogance. This tells us that achieving academic and other status titles cannot be our goal in life as Caribbean people. A sense of history, of how those before us acted to create the privileges we now enjoy, empowers us to discover a mission beyond money, status and titles. We learn that we, our communities, countries and region, beyond being victims of our history, are authors of our futures. We discover our mission and hopefully fulfil it.

Wa Bin De Fos Taim (Background)

At present, for large parts of the Creole-speaking Caribbean, the desirability of official status for Caribbean Creole and indigenous languages is widely accepted. Within the formerly British Caribbean, notably Jamaica and Guyana, the way forward is a matter of ongoing public debate. The situation was not always so. The historical development of awareness of the Creole language issue and the way in which this became embedded in the practice of language education in primary and secondary schools, is ably documented in the work of Novelette McLean Francis (2021), in her PhD thesis on this question. The story of the planned insertion of Creole language awareness into higher education was thoroughly covered in the work of another PhD thesis, that by Caroline Dyche (2012). I won't repeat the stories here. And of course, no, there wasn't a single plan. It was a series of overlapping plans produced by individuals working within and outside institutions, that pushed the issue over time to where it is now. I will simply speak about the part of the story that I took part in once I came onto the scene.

My 1978 DPhil dissertation was on the creation of a standard variety of Guyanese Creole (Creolese) for use in public communication. This was a push back against portions of the then dominant doctrine amongst scholars of Caribbean Creole languages. The doctrine stated that the English-lexicon Creoles could not be used in official public communication nor as a formal medium of education, because of the existence of a "(post)-Creole continuum". Having completed my doctoral thesis the previous year, in 1979 I searched to find a place where someone with an assertive position on Creole languages might be able to make a contribution. This search included a short period in Grenada over May to August 1979, during the early days of the People's Revolutionary Government of Grenada. As well, it took the form of letters of inquiry to the government of the Republic of the Seychelles. Here, Seychellois French-lexicon Creole had been declared an official language after a left wing revolution in 1978. Another letter of inquiry went out to Nicaragua which had had a revolution just a few months after the March 1979 revolution in Grenada. The hope was that that approach would open a chance for me to engage in Creole language literacy work on the English-lexicon

Creole-speaking Caribbean coast of that country. But, as fate would have it, in October 1979, I ended up in Jamaica, where I have spent the rest of my professional academic life.

The idea of granting official status to Caribbean Creole languages was, for most linguistic scholars at the time, a romantic and unrealistic dream. The "people'" the very Creole speakers one was trying to help, would resist. This would come about given their own striving for social mobility through the acquisition of the European official language. Our role as linguists was to facilitate that progress they so wished for, through a process which came institutionalized on the name, "mono-literate transitional bilingualism" in education. Teachers would use the "home language as a bridge to the language of the school". The dominant "progressive" voices outside of linguistics in Jamaica talked about the role of "(the) dialect" as a mode of cultural expression. It should have its proper place in culture, but was no competitor with English for areas of modern life, knowledge and technology.

It No Hapm Jos So – Breen Jraa (Things didn't happen just like that – they were the product of serious thought)

It was clear that the only hope of changing the situation was the students in linguistics. They were, with the idealism and boldness of youth, willing to visualize a new linguistic order that their elders could not. The obvious path was to use time which was on my side, and the students who were learning linguistics. Investing in students was the way to ensure both a change in attitude across the society. They would spread progressive language ideas in their classrooms, offices and professional domains, years long after their time at the university had ended. The situation was clear. To have a shot at changing the language situation in Jamaica and beyond required patience, discipline and foresight.

The course, Language Planning, was approved and introduced in 1983 as my first explicit attack on the language policy consensus. This course was easily one of the first undergraduate courses covering this subject area. Language Planning was, at the time, just emerging as a sub-discipline of linguistics. I saw this course I had designed as the recruitment base for language advocates and activists who would carry the ideas of official status for Jamaican and Caribbean Creole languages with them for decades into the future and across the Caribbean. The number of students in this course grew steadily over the years from an average of ten to a high of ninety in 2004. To target the increase in student numbers in linguistics and by extension in the Language Planning course, a decision was taken around 1988 to teach the introductory linguistics courses in the evening slot of 5–6 p. m. This was to reach out to the many students who, by that time, were doing their Level 1 courses as part-time registrants. They had full-time day jobs and were available only in the evenings. The approach was expanded later to the holding of more advanced courses in the afternoons, again to cater for a similar market amongst the students at higher levels. Innovations, including semesterly field trips that took students in courses to Guyana, Suriname, Guadeloupe, Tobago, Belize, Aruba, Curacao and Bonaire, became the norm. Language activism in Jamaica could not take place in a context of narrow insularity.

Contrary to what has been commonly suggested, there was no funding set aside for the field trips for most of the period. Determined creativity and collaboration across campuses made these happen. When institutional funding was fought for and appeared, within three years it was taken away, with students made to face greater and greater hurdles to access that funding. The field trips started and continued, not because there was an institutional will or commitment to them taking place, but in spite of institutional efforts to block them. In addition, a successful postgraduate programme in linguistics was built, again with the view to providing the skills necessary to implement the use of Jamaican as an official language and as a formal language of education.

The MA degree programme in linguistics was pioneered by an Australian syntactician, Steve Johnson, who taught in the Department of Linguistics and Use of English at UWI, Mona, in the early 1980s. Steve's energy opened an opportunity to maintain extended and even career-long links with students beyond the completion of their first degree. One example, that of Celia Blake, illustrates this. She was in the first group of MA recruits in 1983. On completion, she was involved in a project, after the 1988 Hurricane Gilbert disaster, to develop technical terminology for weather in Jamaican and to pioneer broadcasting weather news in Jamaican. When, at the end of the 1980s, she returned to UWI as a first-year undergraduate in law, she did the course, Language Planning, which she had missed as an undergraduate student in linguistics. A decade later, in 2001, now a fully qualified attorney-at-law teaching business and commercial law at university level, we had need to rely on her legal training and background. She accompanied me to present the proposal for the inclusion of the right to freedom from discrimination on the ground of language, to the Joint Select Committee of Parliament on a Charter of Rights to the Jamaican Constitution. She was a key party to some of the subsequent background discussions coming out of this presentation.

The joint select committee did agree that the presentation was per-suasive but preferred to withhold a final decision on the language rights issue, subject to recommended action being taken. They proposed that an entity be set up at the UWI to support the popularization of a standard writing system for Jamaican language and to carry out a public education campaign on the language issue. That entity is now the Jamaican Language Unit, within the Department of Language, Linguistics and Philosophy.

Celia Blake had played, as already mentioned, a critical role in propos-ing that language make it into the constitutional legislation. Fittingly, therefore, she subsequently wrote her PhD thesis on the question of language rights in Jamaica and the granting of official status to Jamaican, the point of the law and the legal arrangements and protections to be put in place. We are ready for the next phase in establishment resistance, the cry that "We accept in principle but the legal arrangements are very complex and require careful and extended study". The Celia Blake case can be taken as merely representative of the decades-long association with former students, some links more active than others, that have served both to spread the message and to initiate bursts of collaboration around language – related activities in the institutions where they work.

Nof Han Ga fo Klap fo Mek Naiz (Alliances for Progress)

In the field of language rights activism, the linguist cannot go it alone. This is particularly so in my case, as I am a linguist not native to the Jamaican Creole-speaking community, even though I belong to a related Caribbean Creole-speaking country. Carolyn Cooper, elsewhere in this volume, has detailed some of the collaborations that have involved her with the linguist activists, notably myself, in Jamaica over the years. In her language activism, she brought a level of public visibility, starting at the beginning of the 1990s, with her Jamaican language newspaper articles. Using the still then relatively unknown Cassidy writing system for Jamaican, she wrote a weekly column in the *Jamaica Observer* and then later, the *Gleaner*. Her high visibility in the media and her insisting that the expertise on the issue lay with linguists, created for me numerous opportunities for public advocacy. The 1990s saw an opening up of "talk radio". I was a frequent guest on the programme, *Breakfast Club*, pitted gladiator style against a range of anti-Jamaican language proponents. It clearly was a format intended to grab listener attention. When a hot language issue flared up, like that of Ebonics in the United States in the late 1990s. I would find myself a guest on numerous radio programmes and on television as well, over a very short period.

The high visibility that Carolyn Cooper gave the language issue over the years had another effect. It made it easier for me to write articles for the print media on the language issue and get published. She, in a very direct way, frequently intervened to ensure that an article I sent to an unresponsive sub-editor would make it into print. Over three decades, but particularly during the 2000s and 2010s, I wrote a series of articles, in the main, for the *Sunday Gleaner*, on various aspects of the language question. One main topic has been language rights as they related to the need for the Charter of Rights to the Constitution of Jamaica to include a prohibition on discrimination on the ground of language. Another has been bilingual education with specific reference to the use of Jamaican as a language of education on an equal footing with English. The Bilingual Education Project, from 2004 to 2008, was the outcome of another collaboration, that with Karen Carpenter. Karen covered the education angle of the project as well as much of the teacher education. Meanwhile, completing undergraduate students in linguistics prepared Jamaican language teaching materials as linguistics interns with the Jamaican Language Unit. These interns contributed greatly to the Bilingual Education Project, even as they gained practical on-the-job experience applying their academic linguistics knowledge to the creation of teaching support materials in Jmaican.

There have been numerous other alliances struck up over the years, notably with sections of the Roman Catholic Church, the Wycliffe Bible

Translators and the Bible Society of the West Indies. The last was very central in the campaign to popularize the Cassidy-JLU writing system by adopting it in its translation of the New Testament of the Bible. It also, in visual terms in the printed version of the New Testament, ensured the linkage between the colours of the Jamaican national flag and the language and its writing system. All of this was done in a blaze of publicity, both local and foreign, that was linked to and coincided with the celebrations of the fiftieth anniversary of Jamaican independence in 2012.

Dis Taim Na Laang Taim (Things have changed)

Well, then, what happened to the finger I pointed at "them" for not making Caribbean society somewhere I considered just and fair for the majority within the Creole-speaking Caribbean? It produced the proverbial other three fingers pointing back at me. I am obviously grateful to the hundreds of people who have in one way or the other accompanied me on this journey. They have made what seemed impossible forty-three years ago very possible now. Back in the activist and radical 1960s, 1970s and early 1980s, resistance against oppression was organized around the categories of race, colour, culture, economic power, and the imperial power of the United States and its European allies. Language – related discrimination and oppression, welded into the complex of the preceding list of points of resistance, never received any specific attention. Not one march was ever staged, not one stone thrown in the defence of the language rights of the majority. Things and times have changed. There is now language consciousness across the Creole-speaking Caribbean, specifically in Jamaica and increasingly in Guyana where my understanding of the issue has its foundation.

The mass of the Creole-speaking population of the Caribbean speak their languages and have become increasingly assertive in doing so. There has been little language rights demand from the grassroots level, however, despite this assertiveness and national pride. The claim for these languages to be used to give free access, as a matter of right, to all domains of the state, including the education system, came from the language activists supported by linguists. That the 2018 National Standards Curriculum of the Ministry of Education and Youth of Jamaica, in its attainment targets for Grade 1, Unit 1, Writing: Communication, would include the following, is eye-opening.

- 'Communicate with confidence and competence for different purposes and audiences, using **SJE and JC** appropriately and creatively
- Recognize, value and make distinctions between **home language and SJE** to improve/acquire language and literacy competencies
- Explain and comment on speakers' use of language, including use of **SJE and JC**, and their use of vocabulary, grammar and other features' (National Standards Curriculum, 2018, p. 135, my emphasis)

The concept of teaching and practising literacy in the Creole mother tongues of children is, in fact, even now, opposed or at least thought impractical, even by some with formal training in linguistics. That Jamaica has got this far is spectacular. This is evidence of the effects of advocacy and agitation. Progress began before my generation and continued during the tenure of my generation. What is already done looks a lot easier than what is to be done. That is a fallacy. It was just as hard going forward then as it is going forward now. That is cold comfort to those accepting the task of identifying a generational vision and fulfilling it. It is not going to be difficult. In the words of the Trinidad and Tobago calypsonian, Black Stalin, we have to "... keep on jammin" in order to "... get a little something", since as "... ah done tell you already", Creole-speaking Caribbean people "... don't get nothing easy".

REFERENCES

Brown-Blake, Celia. 2011. "The Potential Impact of Language Rights on Language Policy in Jamaica". PhD diss., University of the West Indies Mona, Jamaica. Devonish, Hubert. 1978. "The Selection and Codification of a Widely Understood and Publicly Useable Language Variety in Guyana to be Used as a Vehicle for National Development". DPhil diss., University of York, UK.

Dyche, Caroline. 2012. "Demystifying Empiricism: Understanding English Language Education Policy-Making in a Commonwealth Caribbean University". PhD diss., University of the West Indies Mona, Jamaica. Fanon, Frantz. 2004. *The Wretched of the Earth*. New York: Grove Press.

McLean-Francis, Novelette. 2020. "Ring Road: Evolving Currents and Models in Official Education Policy in Jamaica 1947 to 2018". PhD diss., University of the West Indies, Mona, Jamaica.

Preface

THE IDEA FOR THIS VOLUME AROSE OUT of the Sounds of Advocacy, Language, and Liberation conference in October of 2018 at the University of the West Indies (UWI), Mona, to commemorate the retirement of Professor Hubert Devonish – Prof most who know the man would still find it hard to read the words "retirement of Hubert Devonish" seriously, but, as it turns out, even a great batsman must leave the pitch at some point, even if a frustrated bowler never managed to find the wicket during the long and accomplished spell. Such was the occasion for the meeting of Devonish's contemporaries, friends, graduate students, mentees, professional colleagues, and well-wishers to celebrate Hubert Devonish's service to the university and Caribbean linguistics; forty-two years of service not out!

When the call for papers went out, the organizers had to devise a way to keep it a secret from Prof, primarily because he would scoff at the idea of an entire conference to honour him as "chupidness" but also because the organizers knew he would somehow find himself meddling on the committee. And so it was that the plan was hatched to speak about the conference in hushed tones, send emails that he would never see, and most of all, to carry on as if his retirement was no big deal. The plan almost succeeded and would have, had it not been for the flurry of activities which picked up the week of the conference, not least of which were old friends of Prof's who "coincidentally" seemed to be converging on Jamaica the same week. The surprise factor was lessened by the time we had the opening of the conference, but by no means the impact. It was clear to everyone present that Prof's influence in areas such as applied and theoretical linguistics, language advocacy, university governance, and community organizing was more than what many could accomplish in two lifetimes.

If Prof were reviewing this preface to the volume, he would argue that the preceding sentence constitutes too much niceties and frivolity. This shouldn't be news to any of his graduate students. When asked to say a few words after my PhD defence, he could only offer, "It done!" Indeed, if I were to heap any more praise on Prof, he would sarcastically remark that I'm delivering a nice eulogy. In that spirit, I will shift gears at this point and talk instead about a call to action that I believe should be at the forefront of the agenda for his previous and current graduate students

Anyone who has spent enough time talking with Prof would've noticed that he can be fiercely protective of Caribbean linguistic identity, and the agency of Caribbean nationals in determining how this identity is researched, preserved, and marketed. For Prof, the long colonial legacy in the Caribbean makes it all too easy for the very nature of reality to be viewed through a Eurocentric lens, which could ultimately result in aspects of Caribbean culture being seen as lacking or inferior when compared with parallels which exist in Europe.

Himself a graduate student in England in 1978, Prof would've come face to face with the spectre of racism and the idea of Caribbean inferiority while at the University of York. And the audacity of him to be writing a PhD dissertation arguing for the standardization of his native Guyanese Creole! One can only imagine how he managed to pull off such a feat three decades before #blacklivesmatter and without a single black professor of linguistics in sight. It is precisely for this reason that the new generation of Caribbean linguists, myself included, cannot afford for the integrity and vitality of Caribbean languages to be judged from the perspective of foreign sources of epistemology. Our mandate and mission as Caribbean linguists must be to use our indigenous ways of interrogating reality to unlock the full potential of our linguistic heritage and give it back to our communities.

It is with this mandate in mind that these ten chapters here are compiled, not just to honour the work of Prof, but to showcase the diversity of ideas which are present in Caribbean linguistic thought. Topics as diverse as evaluating students' perception of English to determining how to interpret Jamaican speech in a Toronto murder case.

Admittedly, this collection is but half of the papers presented at the conference, and whether it was due to time commitments on the part of potential contributors or meeting deadlines on the part of the editors, all the papers did not make it into this volume. Nevertheless, the chapters presented here, from junior and seasoned academics, all represent topics on which Prof has either published, mentored a writer, lobbied the government, or done a public interview. And in some cases, all of the above. The contributions in this volume are as much a testament to the excellence and breadth of work carried out by Prof as much as they are a commitment from a generation of linguists, to ensure his legacy births several more legacies of excellence in Caribbean linguistic research. I have no doubt his influence and proclivity to inspire others will continue long into his post-retirement years.

Clive Forrester
Department of English Language and Literature
University of Waterloo, Canada.

Acknowledgements

AS WITH ANY PROJECT OF THIS MAGNITUDE, a number of key players were involved in the process and we would like to acknowledge their contribution here. Firstly, we would like to say a big thank you to the organizing committee of the Sounds of Advocacy conference who worked tirelessly and assiduously to coordinate all the moving parts to put the conference together. In particular, we would like to acknowledge the work of Kadian Walters, committee chair, Susanna Blagrove, Celia Blake, and Joseph Farquharson. The organizing committee benefited from assistance from the Jamaican Language Unit (JLU) and the UWI Mona Linguistics Club, LOUD, who provided a team of energetic and enthusiastic volunteers who ensured all the attendees were well taken care of for the duration of the conference. And, on the administrative front, the core organizing committee was also assisted by Ingrid McLaren, chair of the Department of Linguistics, Yvette Mundy-Whyte, administrative secretary in the Department of Linguistics, and Waibinte Wariboko, then Dean of the Faculty of Humanities and Education. The editors would like to express heartfelt thanks to the core and extended organizers of this memorable conference. Indeed, it was a job well done!

Turning now specifically to this volume, we would also like to thank our chapter reviewers, all of whom agreed without hesitation to serve as peer reviewers simply because the project was associated with Professor Devonish. In no particular order, we would like to thank Jason Seigel, Tasheney Francis, Andre Sheriah, Dalea Bean, Sandra Evans, Kathy Depradine and Ingrid McLaren. After the blind peer review process concluded, and the manuscript was nearing completion, Professors Ian Robertson and Nicolas Faraclas were selected by the UWI Press to complete the mammoth task of reviewing the entire manuscript. We extend our profuse thanks for all the hard work done here, no doubt amidst the burden of additional university work.

Finally, we would like to thank the UWI Press for seeing this project all the way through to completion, in particular, Althea Brown, who has been in contact with us at every step of the process, and former director of the UWI Press, Joseph Powell, who showed a keen interest in the work from the outset. Sadly, Joseph passed away before the publication of this manuscript, and though not with us to celebrate the final product, would no doubt have been proud the editors stuck with the project to the end and allowed the UWI Press to bring it to the world. We thank each and everyone involved in this publication – it is as much for you, as it is for Prof.

Introduction

THE CHAPTERS IN THIS VOLUME ARE ARRANGED in three broad categories, corresponding with three of the major research areas in which Devonish has published his work and continues to exert influence; (i) linguistic theory, (ii)
language, education, and culture, and (iii) politics and the law. Rather
than constituting an exhaustive representation of the research areas in
which Devonish has done work, the chapters instead represent topics
under which all the papers from the Sounds of Advocacy, Language
and Liberation conference could be grouped. Of the twenty-two papers
presented at the conference, the ten chapters which follow also give a
good proportional representation of the subject types which were on
display at the conference, that is, most of the presenters did a topic in
the language, education and culture sub-area, then politics and the law,
and finally, linguistic theory.

LINGUISTIC THEORY

The two papers in this area deal with linguistic theory pertaining to Creole
languages in two different yet very interesting ways. Gooden attempts
to provide acoustic evidence for the existence of implosives in Jamaican
Creole (JC) while Thomas delivers a mathematical conjecture used to
judge allowable sentences in Guyanese Creole. It is significant that these
chapters should tackle these questions, given that Devonish is a native
speaker of Guyanese Creole but is probably more internationally known
for his decades – long advocacy work in the promotion of JC. These first
two chapters demonstrate both Devonish's versatility in carrying out academic work in different Caribbean Creoles as well as the diversity in the
kinds of theoretical interests that preoccupy his research. Interestingly,
both chapters in this section use aspects of DeCamp's (1971) discussion

on the creole continuum as a starting point for their analyses even though the theses in each of the chapters are so divergent.

Thomas's contribution straddles the line between mathematics and Creole studies and simultaneously demonstrates the importance of inter-disciplinary research in the area of linguistics, as well as the necessity for linguists to be versed in analytical tools not ordinarily found in the humanities. Thomas – himself a native speaker of Guyanese Creole and a trained mathematician – gives an intriguing explication of a conjecture proposed by Devonish which seeks to express the number of allowable English or Creolese lexemes in a given Guyanese Creole sentence as a mathematical formula. The premise for the conjecture originates from DeCamp's development of the "creole continuum" idea where DeCamp demonstrates that the idiolect of each speaker in a community moves between variations which are unmistakably Creole in their structure (the basilect) to varieties which are recognized as Standard English (the acrolect) with a range of *mesolectal* varieties existing between the opposite ends. Though DeCamp indicated that the varieties along the continuum aren't simply a strewing together of random Creole and English fea-tures, he stopped short of giving an empirical reason which constrains the acceptability of variations along the continuum. Thomas, by use of speaker intuition as well as statistical modeling in R, demonstrates that it is at least possible to represent this constraint as a mathematical formula correlating the acceptability of a continuum sentence to the length of the sentence. Thomas's conclusions are fascinating for the mere fact that he attempts to statistically explain a linguistic phenomenon that is usually governed by speakers' subjective intuition.

Gooden's chapter is grounded in the long-held analysis of voiced stops in JC being realized exclusively as eggressive pulmonic consonants. While the data for the study comes from the Moore Town Maroons, collected by DeCamp in 1971, the analysis makes use of tools that would not have been readily available to earlier Caribbean researchers carrying out pho-nological investigations, in particular, the spectrogram. Gooden uses both waveform and spectrographic analyses on the data set collected in this community to interrogate whether there are sociological factors which could cause the eggressive voiced stops [b, [d], [g], to be realized as their ingressive counterparts [ɓ], [ɗ], [ɠ]. The chapter concludes with a discussion of the role of "pre-voicing" in the production of these consonants and evaluates the likelihood that this could either have a historical-substrate source, or a purely context-based explanation. Gooden sets the stage for a far deeper phonological analysis of the Moore Town data with the use of modern technology such as spectrography and forced alignment.

LANGUAGE, EDUCATION AND CULTURE

Advocating for language rights as it pertains to the speakers of creole languages by giving them access to education and other services in their language (specifically Jamaican Creole) and recognition of the rich culture derived from these languages has been an essential part of Devonish's work. Some of these endeavours consist of establishing the Jamaican Language Unit at the University of the West Indies, Mona, which is dedicated to projects that give recognition and potential status to the Jamaican Creole language. One such project is the partnership with the Jamaican Bible Society in translating the New Testament Bible into JC (Bible Society of the West Indies 2012), which is now the largest body of printed work in that language. In addition, via the Jamaican Language Unit, Devonish established the Bilingual Education Programme, which involved the use of the Jamaican Creole language as a medium of instruction alongside Jamaican Standard English, in two primary schools in Kingston, Jamaica (Devonish and Carpenter 2007).

In keeping with the work of Hubert Devonish, the papers in this chapter examine language, education and culture of minority languages, with the exception of the article by Jules, which advocates for the best practice in listening instruction in English as a Second Language. The first chapter in this section is by Montoya-Stemann, who evaluates the oral performance skills of Jamaican students at the Edna Manley College of the Visual and Performing Arts, who aspire to become drama in education teachers or theatre art professionals and the challenges they face when presenting an oral performance of a poetical text written in Standard English (SE). On the contrary, she outlines that presentation of a JC poetical text to their audience does not represent a major challenge for these student-performers, which is displayed by an appropriate level of confidence in their oral skills in JC. Montoya-Steman posits that written and oral competencies complement each other; however, the educational system focuses on written assessments and the oral competencies are disregarded. This causes a lack of relationship with written text and ultimately affects the communicative competence of students.

Abu El Adas, McAllister and Washington's paper investigates production variability in children acquiring Jamaican Creole and English, an understudied language pairing characterized by similar phonologies and extensive cognate overlap between the languages. They argue that research examining bilingual development in children has focused mostly on English and Spanish speakers and that other language contexts are understudied in the literature. One such context is bilingual acquisition of English and JC, whose speakers represent approximately 20 per cent of the Caribbean-born immigrant group in the United States (U.S. Census Bureau, 2015). Their study focuses on bilingual acquisition in this under-represented population, in addition to providing direct guidance for clinical management of this group.

Tomlinson, in her article, argues for the use of a culturally responsive teaching (CRT) and pedagogy in the Jamaican language/literacy classroom as the use of culturally relevant material stands at the forefront of students' language learning. Tomlinson suggests that language programmes should be developed to assist Jamaican students in acquiring the standardized variety by taking into account the students' home language and culture. Such a programme would therefore, introduce teachers and students to a culturally responsive pedagogy which incorporates students' language and cultural background, and as such, challenge language ideologies that have negatively shaped how Creole language varieties and features are perceived and positioned in Jamaica's educational system and wider society.

The penultimate chapter in this section, by Jules, examines the best practice in listening instruction in English as a Second Language. She initially outlines that the increased demand for studies in English as a Second Language is a worldwide phenomenon with a widening of the market within the Anglophone Caribbean associated with learners' extrinsic and intrinsic needs. This applied research suggests that while learners are exposed to the application of some best practice principles with particular attention to "Student-centredness", "Challenging" and

""Reflection" during listening instruction, it is necessary to also deal with the interrelation of other principles such as "Authentic", "Holistic"and "Cognitive".

Blake and Dawkins support the advocacy work of Hubert Devonish as shown in their paper's commitment to understanding the larger global impact of Jamaican and African American Languages. The paper honours Devonish and his critical body of work on the impact of technologized Jamaican orality through dancehall in the creation of new national ideologies and identities for the Jamaican masses, both locally and "tu di worl" in the age of advanced technologies. Their paper extends Devonish's linkage, arguing that the seemingly parallel and intersecting technological and spoken innovations in the art forms of dancehall and rap are, in fact, historically connected at the nexus of Jamaican reggae and African American soul music.

POLITICS AND LAW

A considerable portion of Devonish's public advocacy has been spent navigating the political and legal arenas. Whether it involves lobbying parliament to entrench freedom from linguistic discrimination in the constitutional charter of rights, or consulting with lawyers defending a Creole speaker, Devonish has embraced this aspect of his role as a public intellectual. The chapters in this section explore three separate aspects of politics and the law. Belgrave looks at the persuasive element in political cartoons in Barbados, Irvine-Sobers assesses the language rights provisions in the constitutions of territories in the Organization of American States, and Forrester recounts his time as an expert witness in a Toronto murder trial interpreting JC idioms.

Belgrave takes aim at the political cartoons leading up to the general elections of Barbados in 2008. The data for the study is comprised of fifteen political cartoons that deal with the usual hot-button issues during a campaign season – leadership, political corruption, and cost of living. Belgrave uses analytical techniques made popular in critical discourse analysis, as well as techniques commonly used in the analysis of visual rhetoric. What emerges is an in-depth analysis of the ways in which cartoonists deploy a mixture of enthymemes, rhetorical caricature, and

Creole dialogue to deliver powerful commentary on the sociopolitical status of Barbados. While it might be uncertain how impactful political cartoons in the print media might be today, the situation leading up to the 2008 general electionduring the infancy of social media, would have been significantly different. Belgrave manages to explain how the linguistic and visual persuasive elements overlap in these rhetorical artefacts, and how they could have ultimately swayed the election in favour of the winning party.

Irvine-Sobers investigates the extent to which member countries to the Organization of American States include clauses in their respective constitutions which seek to provide citizens with linguistic rights. This is particularly important for Caribbean territories – the dominant representation in the Organization of American States – given that many of these territories are signator to the Universal Declaration of Human Rights yet lack constitutional provisions that seek to protect linguistic human rights. Though Irvine-Sobers describes the chapter as a "preliminary investigation", the study is quite revealing, bordering on grim; of the thirty-five member states in the Organization of American States, only five have explicit constitutional provisions that prohibit discrimination on the grounds of language. The study consequently reveals that constitutional protection against linguistic discrimination is unevenly applied in several member states which, not surprisingly, has a greater negative impact on speakers of Creole languages.

Forrester's chapter closes with a retelling of his experience serving as an expert witness in a Toronto murder trial, that had him working as a consultant for the defence team on interpreting police wiretap recordings. The experience was an intriguing one, given that despite the proliferation of Jamaican language in the Greater Toronto Area, there are still multiple opportunities for misinterpretation. This is problematized in Forrester's discussion when he explains that JC, Afro-Canadian vernacular, and English can all be present in a single wiretap recording, and though they all make use of the same lexicon of English, their interpretations are context as well as language dependent. Ultimately, Forrester reveals that his expert testimony assisted in the reduction of the defendant's verdict from first-degree to second-degree murder in a case which was at least partially reliant on linguistic evidence.

REFERENCES

Bible Society of the West indies (BSWI). 2012. *Jamaican Diglot New Testament (King James Version Bibles)*. Kingston: Bible Society of the West Indies.

DeCamp, David. 1971. "Toward a Generative Analysis of a Post-Creole Speech Continuum." In *Pidginization and Creolization of Languages*, edited by Dell Hymes, 349–70. Cambridge: Cambridge University Press.

Devonish, Hubert, and Karen Carpenter. 2007. "Towards Full Bilingual Education: The Jamaican Bilingual Primary Education Project". *Social and Economic Studies* 56 (1–2.): 277–303. Accessed 25 July 2022. https://www.jstor.org/stable/27866504)

U.S. Census Bureau. 2015. Quick Facts: United States. Census Bureau Quick Facts. United States Census Bureau. Accessed 25 July 2022. https://www.census.gov/quickfacts/fact/table/US/PST045217

List of Abbreviations/Acronyms

BEP	Bilingual Education Project
BLP	Barbados Labour Party
CAPE	Caribbean Advanced Proficiency Examination
CDA	Critical Discourse Analysis
CEC	Caribbean English-Lexicon Creoles
CLT	Comunicative Language Teaching
CRP	Culturally Responsive Pedagogy
CRP	Culturally Relevant Pedagogy
CRT	Culturally Relevant Teaching
CRT	Culturally Responsive Teaching
CSEC	Caribbean Secondary Examination Certificate
DARLA	Dartmouth Linguistic Automation
DEAP	Diagnostic Evaluation of Articulaataion and Phonology
DEAP WIA	DEAP Word Inconsistency Assessment
DLP	Democratic Labour Party
EGG	Electroglottograph
EMCVPA	Edna Manley College of the Visual and Performing Arts
ESL	English as a Second Language
GCE	General Certificate of Education
GFLT	Grade 4 Literacy Test
GSAT	Grade 6 Achievement Test
JC	Jamaican Creole
JLU	Jamaican Language Unit
MOEYC	Ministry of Education, Youth and Culture
NEI	National Education Inspectorate
OAS	Organization of American States
PTONI	Primary Test of Non-verbal Intelligence
SE	Standaaard English
SJE	Standard Jamaican English
SOD	School of Drama
SP	Student-Performers
UNDHR	Universal Declaration of Human Rights
UNICEF	United Nations Children's Fund
UWI	The University of the West Indies
UWI Press	The University of the West Indies Press
VDCLO	Voiced Closure
VLCLO	Voiceless Closure
VOT	Voice Onset Time

CHAPTER 1

Devonish's Conjecture Relating the Number, A_n, of "Allowable" Sentences in a Creole/English Speech Community to n, the Length of the Sentences

EWART THOMAS

INTRODUCTION

One of the many interests of Professor Hubert Devonish, whom we honour at this conference, is "Creole Linguistics." It is the last of the eleven entries listed in the *Call for Papers* that Dr Farquharson sent us, and even though it may be the least of his interests, it is the one that I'll discuss in this paper. We are meeting on the 50th anniversary of a seminal conference held here at Mona in 1968 on Pidginization and Creolization of Languages. (The proceedings of this conference can be found in Hymes 1971.) So, my choice of topic, as well as the overall theme of the present conference, belong to the rich tradition established by that 1968 conference and an earlier one at Mona in 1959 on Creole Languages (Le Page 1961).

However, the main reason for my choice is that Devonish and I have worked intermittently over the last two decades on a regularity he discovered when examining the "allowability" of sentences within the Guyanese Creole speech community. (Some of this joint work was presented in Thomas and Devonish 2008.) Consider, for example, the following sentences.

(1a)　　I (am) reading.
(1b)　　Mi a riid.

(2a)   I was reading.
(2b)   Mi bin riiding.

Sentences (1a) and (1b) have $n = 2$ slots, the 1st slot containing the subject pronoun, the first-person singular variable, represented by the Creole variant, *mi*, or the English variant, *ai*; and the 2nd slot containing the continuative/progressive marker variable, represented by the Creole variant, preverbal *a*, or the English variant, post-verbal *–in*. Sentences (2a) and (2b) have $n = 3$ slots, two being the same as in Sentences (1), and the 3rd slot corresponding to the tense marker variable, represented by the Creole variant, *bin*, or the English variant, *woz*. Devonish used his intuitions as a native speaker of Guyanese Creole to judge that all 4 sentences above are allowable in his speech community. In these sentences, the variants in each slot are either all English (E) or all Creole (C). What, then, is the allowability of mixed sentences with both E and C variants? In the case of Sentences (1), there are two such sentences:

(1c)   I a read.
(1d)   Mi riiding.

Sentence (1d), but not Sentence (1c), was judged as allowable.

More generally, for a given number, n, of slots, (i) how many sentences, pure or mixed, are allowable that express a given meaning, and (ii) what linguistic constraints on co-occurring C and E variants within a sentence might be posited to account for the observed relationship between n and the number, A_n, of allowable sentences? To address these questions, Devonish (personal communication, and summarized in Thomas and Devonish 2008) judged the allowability of each sentence in 38 structured sets of sentences, such as Sentences (1). Across these sets, the number, n, of slots in each sentence varied from 2 to 9, with a median of 4. For each n, he counted the number, A_n, of allowable sentences. For example, when $n = 2$, as in Sentences 1 above, only 3 of the 4 possible sentences are allowable; that is, $A_2 = 3$. When $n = 3$, as in Sentences 2 above, only 4 of the 8 possible sentences are allowable; that is, $A_3 = 4$. Rather remarkably, Devonish noticed that this pattern held for most of the 38 sets of sentences he studied, and this led him to state his *conjecture* that $A_n = n + 1$, the so-called *(n + 1)-rule*.

This rule, albeit with somewhat different referents, was introduced into linguistics by David DeCamp at the 1968 Mona conference; it was derived as a property of implicational scales (DeCamp 1971). In DeCamp's model, the Creole *variants* of the *n* linguistic variables under consideration are assumed to be ordered on a continuum that can be interpreted as relative "Creoleness". Importantly, this model implies that the *lects* or *speaker-categories* predicted by this ordering can also be ordered on the same continuum. Also, this model predicts that $n + 1$ lects will be observed in speech corpora from the community. (See, for example, Rickford 2002, for an accessible description of the development, applications and critiques of implicational scales.) In the present paper, I will retain (i) the simplifying assumption of DeCamp's (1971) model that each linguistic variable is binary with values, (C)reole or (E)nglish, and (ii) DeCamp's focus on the *number* of, say, E variants in sentences of a given length, *n*. Of course, sentences of a given length can always be ordered with respect to the number of E variants, but there will be no requirement in the present work that, for example, the C *variants* themselves be ordered.

I will examine general mechanisms by which allowable sentences of length *n* might be extended into allowable sentences of length $n + 1$ by the addition of a C or an E variant. This extensional approach is motivated partly by the way Devonish constructed his sets of sentences, such as, Sentences (1) and (2) above, and partly by analogy with dynamic models of language evolution in heterogeneous populations. These latter models typically start by specifying how the distribution of speakers across 2 or more grammars changes from *time n* to *time n + 1*. From these local dynamics, one can then derive the equilibrium (or steady-state) distribution within the population (for example, Niyogi and Berwick 2009). The present approach allows for (i) the identification of a class of mechanisms that can account for the linear *(n + 1)-rule*, and (ii) the specification of *non*-linear relationships between A_n and *n* that might be derived from other classes of mechanisms. I will comment on the plausibility of the general mechanisms, and try to interpret the derived relationships between A_n and *n*. In particular, I outline a set of constraints under which, as *n* becomes large, the number of allowable language varieties tends to 2, "English" and "Creole"

INTRODUCTION OF FORMAL MODELING

Allowability as a Probabilistic Concept

Modeling the linguistic reality of a social community requires the assumption of shared rules about, for instance, what forms of speech are allowable. However, even with these shared rules, there will be variability in linguistic intuition. This is why I will treat the *number* of allowable sentences as a *random variable,* and consider a probabilistic $(n + 1)$-rule, $A_n = n + 1$, in which A_n is the *average* number of allowable n-sentences.

Extending an allowable n-sentence to an allowable $(n + 1)$-sentence

In order to constrain probabilistically the co-occurrences of variants, focus is placed, not on the co-occurrences among the variants within a given n-sentence, but rather on the possible co-occurrences between these n variants and the English or Creole variant that might be added as the $(n + 1)$th variant to form an $(n + 1)$-sentence. Not all additions to an allowable n-sentence result in allowable $(n + 1)$-sentences, and we need to specify how the probability of an allowable extension depends on the sentence and on the additional variant. I will assume that the only relevant aspects of a sentence are its length, n, and the number, e, of English variants in it. A sentence, therefore, is no more than a 'string' of n codes, e of which are E's, and $n - e$ of which are C's. Such strings are denoted by $S(n, e)$. Many sentences can be represented by a given string, and a string is said to be allowable if at least one of the sentences it represents is allowable. Further, pure strings with all E variants or all C variants are unique, and presumably always allowable. An informal examination of sentence extensions suggests an interesting asymmetry: the probability that adding a C variant to a pure English sentence (for example, EE extended to EEC) results in an allowable sentence is not necessarily equal to that resulting from adding an E variant to a pure Creole sentence (for example, CC extended to CCE). In other words, the "compatibility" of a new E variant with a pure or mostly Creole sentence may be different from that of a new C variant with a pure or mostly English sentence. I allow for such asymmetry in the present models.

As examples of extensions, Sentence (1a), denoted by (EE), can be extended to:

(3a) I am reading the books (EEE).
(3b) I am reading di book dem (EEC).

And Sentence (1b), denoted by (CC), can be extended to:

(3c) Mi a riid di book dem (CCC).
(3d) Mi a riid the books (CCE).

Sentences (3a), (3c) and (3d), but not Sentence (3b), would likely be judged as allowable.

An Iterative Procedure

I now construct an iterative procedure for calculating the average number of allowable sentences of a given length. The procedure is simplified by the fact that there are, at most, 2 ways in which an $(n + 1)$-string, $S(n+1, e)$, can be generated from an n-string, $S(n, e)$. Let us denote by $m_{n,e}$ the average number of allowable n-strings with e E variants. Our assumption, stated above, that pure strings are unique and allowable leads to the constraints: (i) for pure C strings, $m_{n,0} = 1$; and (ii) for pure E strings, $m_{n,n} = 1$. Then, for a given n, adding these $m_{n,e}$, for $e = 0, 1, ..., n$, would yield the average number, A_n, of allowable n-strings:

$$A_n = m_{n,0} + m_{n,1} + ... + m_{n,n} = 1 + m_{n,1} + ... + 1 \geq 2. \qquad (1)$$

One way of generating an $(n + 1)$-string with e E variants by adding 1 variant (or slot) is to add a C variant to an allowable n-string with e E variants, $S(n, e)$, for $e = 0, 1, ..., n$. The average number of these n-strings is $m_{n,e}$, which, therefore, is the average number of $(n + 1)$-strings with e E variants resulting from this extension. Some proportion, denoted by $P_C(n, e)$, of these $(n + 1)$-strings will be allowable, implying that the average number of allowable $(n + 1)$-strings resulting from this extension is $m_{n,e} \times P_C(n, e)$. The other way of generating an $(n+1)$-string with e E variants by adding 1 variant (or slot) is to add an E variant to an allowable n-string with $(e - 1)$ E variants, $S(n, e - 1)$, for $e = 1, 2, ..., n$. The average number of these n-strings is $m_{n,e-1}$, which, therefore, is the average number of $(n + 1)$-strings with e E variants resulting from this second extension. Some proportion, denoted by $P_E(n, e-1)$, of these $(n + 1)$-strings will be allowable, implying that the average number of allowable $(n + 1)$-strings resulting from this extension is $m_{n,e-1} \times P_E(n, e-1)$. On adding the numbers of allowable strings resulting from these 2 extensions, we get the average number, $m_{n+1,e}$, of allowable $(n + 1)$-strings, S$(n+1, e)$, with e E variants:

$$m_{n+1,e} = m_{n,e} \times P_C(n, e) + m_{n,e-1} \times P_E(n, e-1), e = 1, 2, ..., n; n = 1, 2, ...;$$

$$m_{1,0} = m_{1,1} = 1; m_{n+1,0} = m_{n+1,n+1} = 1. \tag{2}$$

Provided the functions, $P_C(n, e)$ and $P_E(n, e)$, are specified, these equations allow us to calculate the set, $\{mn_{+1,e}\}$, from the set, $\{m_{n,e}\}$, and, using Eq. (1), to calculate A_n for all n. We refer to these functions as 'compatibility functions', because they index the ease with which a new variant can combine with an existing string to form an allowable string.

Specifying the compatibility functions, $P_C(n, e)$ and $P_E(n, e)$

We wish the compatibility functions to satisfy certain boundary and monotonicity conditions.

Adding an English variant (E) to a string consisting of a single Creole variant, (C), to get a 2-string, (CE), is *sometimes* allowed, otherwise mixed strings, such as Sentence (1d), would never be allowed. Formally, this is equivalent to requiring that $P_E(1, 0) > 0$. Interchanging E and C and arguing similarly, we require that $P_C(1, 1) > 0$.

Adding E to pure (and, therefore, allowable) E strings is *always* allowed. Formally, this is equivalent to requiring that $P_E(n, n) = 1$. Analogously, we require that $P_C(n, 0) = 1$.

For a given string length, n, the probability that adding E to an allowable S(n, e) is allowable increases as e increases. Formally, we require that $P_E(n, e)$ be an *increasing function* of e. By the same token, comparing strings of different lengths but with the same number, e, of E variants, the probability that adding E to an allowable S(n, e) is allowable decreases as n increases. Formally, we require that $P_E(n, e)$ be a decreasing function of n.

Using the same intuition that underlies the above, and replacing E by C, the probability that adding C to an allowable S(n, e) is allowable increases as the number, $n - e$, of C variants increases. This leads to the requirements that, for fixed n, $P_C(n, e)$ be a decreasing function of e; and that, for fixed $(n - e)$, $P_C(n, e)$ be a decreasing function of n.

$P_E(n, e)$ and $P_C(n, e)$ linear

The simplest form for $P_E(n, e)$ that satisfies three of the four conditions listed above is the proportional form, $P_E(n, e) = e/n$. This function, which is intuitively appealing, is increasing in e (n fixed) and decreasing in n (e fixed), and it equals 1 when $e = n$. However in this specification, $P_E(1, 0) = 0$, in violation of the 1st condition. It can be modified to be strictly positive when $e = 0$ by introducing a strictly positive *compatibility* parameter, p_E, and writing:

$$P_E(n, e) = \frac{(p_E + e)}{(p_E + n)}, \ p_E > 0. \tag{3}$$

By analogy, we model $P_C(n, e)$ as:

$$P_C(n, e) = \frac{(p_C + n - e)}{(p_C + n)}, \ p_C > 0. \tag{4}$$

which also satisfies the four conditions. As long as $p_E \neq p_C$, there will be an asymmetry between the effect of adding a C variant to a pure English sentence and adding an E variant to a pure Creole sentence.

$P_E(n, e)$ and $P_C(n, e)$ nonlinear

The compatibility functions in Eqs. (3) and (4) are linear in e. In contrast, a class of nonlinear (in e) compatibility functions is obtained by assuming that, if a variant, E or C, is added to an allowable n-string, (a) the resulting $(n+1)$-string is allowable if and only if the added variant can co-occur with *all* of the n variants in the n-string, (b) these n co-occurrence events involving the added variant are statistically independent, and (c) an added E variant can co-occur with every E variant in the n-string, and an added C variant can co-occur with every C variant in the n-string. Let us denote by q_E the probability that an added E variant can co-occur with a randomly selected C variant in the n-string, and by q_C the probability that an added C variant can co-occur with a randomly selected E variant in the n-string. It follows from these assumptions that:

$$P_E(n, e) = q_E^{n-e}, \tag{5}$$

which increases exponentially as e increases from 0 to n, and which satisfies all four conditions identified above. Arguing similarly, $P_C(n, e)$ is defined as another exponential function,

$$P_C(n, e) = q_C^e, \tag{6}$$

which satisfies all four conditions identified above.

RESULTS

We used the computing and graphics package, R, for our model-derived calculations and for plotting the relationship between A_n and n. Starting with the initial conditions, $m_{n,o} = 1 = m_{n,n}$, and the definition of $P_E(n, e)$ and $P_C(n, e)$, we calculated the $\{m_{n,e}\}$ iteratively, using the recurrence relation in Eq. (2). Then, for each n, we calculated the average number of allowable n-strings as the sum of the $\{m_{n,e}\}$, using Eq. (1). Our interest was in finding conditions under which the $(n+1)$-rule is satisfied, and in describing the other relationships between A_n and n that were observed.

The numerical results, when the compatibility functions are linear and symmetric (that is, $p_E = p_C = p$), are shown in figure 1.1. The average number of allowable n-strings always increases as n increases. The rate of this increase in A_n depends on the compatibility parameter, p: the $(n+1)$-rule obtains only when $p = 1$; and, when p is greater (less) than 1, the rate increases (decreases) as n increases. This result shows that there exists a set of conditions under which the $(n+1)$-rule would be observed, but it says nothing about the likelihood of obtaining this set of conditions in a speech community. Nevertheless, it is tempting to suggest that, if p were regarded as a fixed parameter of the speech community, then perhaps the condition, p is equal to 1 (rather than any other positive number!), should be regarded as unlikely, that is, as a "knife-edge". If, however, p were regarded as a random *variable* with a *mean* close to 1, and if the range of

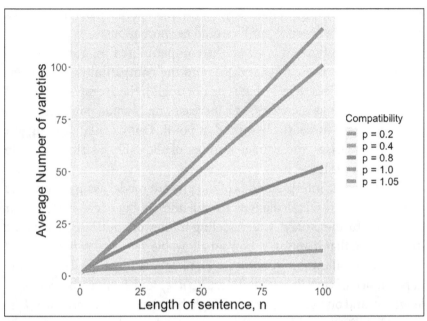

Figure 1.1. Plots showing the average number of allowable n-strings versus n, the string length, for the linear compatibility functions. For simplicity, it is assumed that $p_E = p_C = p$, and plots are shown for different values of p.

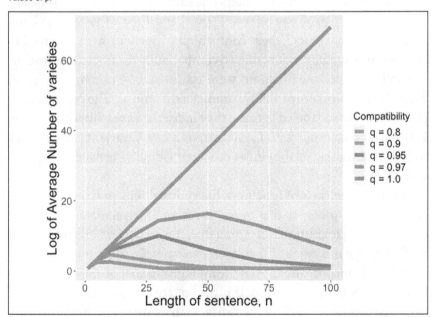

Figure 1.2. Plots showing the average number of allowable n-strings versus n, the string length, for the exponential compatibility functions. For simplicity, it is assumed that $q_E = q_C = q$, and plots are shown for different values of q.

n used in a study were 'small' (say, 1 to 6), then perhaps the finding of a linear relation between A_n and n would be more robust.

As shown in figure 1.2, when the compatibility functions are non-linear, as given in Eqs. (5) and (6), and the compatibility parameter, q $(= q_E = q_C)$, is less than 1 (that is, is not 'high'), the average number of allowable n-strings increases, as n increases up to some point, and then decreases, as n increases beyond that point. Our calculations suggest that, in these cases, the average number of allowable n-strings tends to 2, as n becomes large.

The linguistic interpretations of the present model assumptions and of the model-derived calculations are still unclear, but a few issues appear to warrant further study. The modeling framework outlined is dynamic in the sense that it specifies how an allowable sentence can be derived from shorter allowable sentences. The key relationships describe the dependence of certain probabilities, $P_E(n, e)$ and $P_C(n, e)$, on sentence length, n, and on the number, e, of English variants in the sentence. P_E is the probability that adding an E variant to an allowable n-sentence results in an allowable $(n+1)$-sentence, and P_C is the probability that adding a C variant to an allowable n-sentence results in an allowable $(n+1)$-sentence. For this reason, we refer to $P_E(n, e)$ and $P_C(n, e)$ as compatibility functions. In one model, these compatibility functions were assumed to be linear in e and dependent on two compatibility parameters, p_E and p_C. In another model, the functions were assumed to be nonlinear in e and dependent on two compatibility parameters, q_E and q_C. The compatibility parameters are so labeled because they index the ease with which a new E variant can co-occur with C variants, or a new C variant can co-occur with E variants, that is, they index the "compatibility" between "English" and "Creole".

For the linear class of functions, the compatibility parameters can be any positive number, so that $p_E = p_C = 1$ is an 'intermediate' value. Our results can be paraphrased as stating that, if p_E and p_C are less than 1, that is, if language mixing is 'difficult' or, equivalently, if the two languages are relatively incompatible, then the average number of allowable n-sentences is less than $n + 1$. Also, if p_E and p_C are greater than 1, that is, if language mixing is "easy" or the two languages are relatively compatible, then the average number of allowable n-sentences is greater than $n + 1$.

The $(n + 1)$-rule is valid only on the 'knife-edge', $p_E = p_C = 1$. If one were to assume that no value of these parameters is special *a priori*, then one might conclude that observing the $(n + 1)$-rule should be a relatively rare occurrence. Thus further empirical work is warranted on, for example, whether the $(n + 1)$-rule is valid for 'large' n, and on what other relationships between A_n and n are possible, empirically and theoretically.

For the nonlinear class of functions, the compatibility parameters lie between 0 and 1, and the model-derived calculations differ markedly from those associated with the linear class. When $q_E = q_C = 1$ ("high" compatibility), the average number of allowable n-sentences increases exponentially as n increases, corresponding to completely random mixing of variants, that is, to the absence of constraints on the co-occurrence of E and C variants. However, when q_E and q_C are less than 1, the average number of allowable n-sentences increases, as n increases up to some point, and then decreases, as n increases beyond this point. We do not yet have an analytical solution for this nonlinear model, but our calculations suggest that, as n becomes very large, the average number of allowable n-sentences tends to 2. The dynamic interpretation of this conjecture is that, if by a 'speech sample' is meant a 'very long sentence', then the nonlinear model predicts that, as long as compatibility between E and C is not high, there will be only *two* language varieties!

ACKNOWLEDGEMENT

I am grateful to Hubert Devonish for teaching me the basics and the intricacies of Creole Linguistics, and for generously sharing his ideas, which are as inspirational today as they were when we started collaborating in 1995.

REFERENCES

DeCamp, David. 1971. "Toward a Generative Analysis of a Post-Creole Speech Continuum". In *Pidginization and Creolization of Languages*, edited by Dell Hymes, 349–70. Cambridge: Cambridge University Press.

Hymes, Dell,ed. 1971. *Pidginization and Creolization of Languages*. Cambridge: Cambridge University Press.

Le Page, Robert. 1961. *Creole Language Studies II: Proceedings of the conference on Creole Language Studies, held at the University College of the West Indies, 28 March–4 April 1959*. London: Macmillan.

Niyogi, Partha and Robert C. Berwick. 2009. "The Proper Treatment of Language Acquisition and Change in a Population Setting". *Proceedings of the National Academy of Sciences* 106 (25):10124–29. Accessed 26 July 2022. https: //doi.org/10.1073/pnas.0903993106.

Rickford, John R. 2004. "Implicational Scales". In *Handbook of Language Variation*, edited by J.K. Chambers, Peter Trudgill, and Natalie Schilling-Estes, 142–67. Malden, MA, Oxford: Blackwell Publishing.

Thomas, Ewart, and Hubert Devonish. 2008. "Mathematical and Empirical Studies of English/Creole Language Variation". In *Proceedings of the 16th Caribbean Academy of Sciences Biennial Conference on Science and Technology: Vehicles for Sustainable Economic Development in the Caribbean*, 1–19.

Phonetic Variation in Voiced Stops in Moore Town

SHELOME GOODEN

INTRODUCTION

While earlier descriptions of Jamaican Creole (JC) describe the voiced stops [b] [d] [g] as pulmonic egressive stops (Cassidy and LePage 1967), more recent work shows that some JC speakers produce implosives as allophonic variants of the pulmonic voiced stops (Devonish and Harry 2004; Harry 2006; Gooden and Donnelly 2008, 2009). However, precise acoustic characteristics and associated constraints on the variation have not yet been discussed. Research on the phonological systems of Caribbean English-lexicon Creole languages (CECs) is crucial to achieving a wholistic view of their structural properties and historical development (Clements and Gooden 2009). Devonish (1989, 2002) and Klein (2006), for example, proposed that the phonological system of Creole languages can shed light on their diachronic development and on the nature of Creole genesis itself. Thus, there is a longstanding need to understand the synchronic and diachronic roles of phonetic cues in supporting phonological contrasts. Moreover, the phonological systems in JC bear strong socio-indexical loads for speakers and listeners alike, delineating the stigmatized versus the prestigious and differentiating between the JC and the Jamaican English speaker (Wassink 1999; Wassink and Dyer 2004; Irvine 2004; Irvine 2008). While there is a growing body of research on CEC phonology, this area has remained relatively underexplored compared to other areas of language structure. In fact, the phonological identity of Creole languages continues to be a subject of debate at both the segmental and prosodic levels.

Currently, there are few acoustic-phonetic analyses of CEC phonological systems, and even fewer studies on the voicing qualities of stops in Creoles (Lamy 2016; Stewart et al. 2018). As such, there is less information on the acoustic correlates of voicing in Creoles, a feature which is known to be highly variable cross-linguistically (Abramson and Whalen 2017), and thus highly susceptible to sociolinguistic influences. In addition, our understanding of the phonological category [voice] in CECs is likely shrouded by implicit assumptions about the analogous category in English.

The fact that these typologically rare implosives occur in at least some contexts also raises the question of how the sounds developed in JC. The answer, however, is not clear-cut. If we are to think in terms of substrate effects, several challenges emerge. The first challenge is the indelible fact that these languages are the result of multi-language contact, often with typologically different phonological structures in play. It is well known that intense contact can lead to varying degrees of transfer from a source language to a recipient language (Van Coetsem 1998; Thomason and Kaufman 1988). However, since transfer is not an absolute, even in these contexts, a recurrent question is whether the phonological grammar of the emergent contact language consists of separate or coexistent linguistic systems, a single merged system or other patterns of hybridity, or other contact-induced changes that are devoid of influence from input languages (Clements and Gooden 2011). (See also Gooden et al. (2009) for a discussion of contact effects on prosody). Currently, we still lack sufficient knowledge about precisely what aspects, if any, of the prosodic system of the input languages were transferred to Creole languages and, most importantly, whether these features have been retained in their synchronic phonologies.

Second, JC, for example, has been shown to have multiple substrate languages with varying degrees of influence (Farquharson 2013; Kouwenberg 2008), making it difficult to assess the relative strength of their influences. Even when a dominant substrate is identified, documentation of implosives and their phonetic quality is variably reported in the putative substrate languages (Heine and Nurse 2008). In some cases, 19th and 20th century grammars of the putative substrates, show plosives to the exclusion of implosives. Third, if implosives are a substrate feature, we might reasonably expect them to be strongly represented in more conservative varieties like Maroon Creoles which are known to preserve substrate language structure. Yet, it is also quite possible that there are pronunciations (compare lexical Africanisms) that are restricted to these Maroon communities that have not been attested in non-Maroon speech (Farquharson 2013).

This current project contributes to an emerging body of work that provides empirical evidence needed to assess contact effects on the synchronic phonological systems of CECs (Klein 2006; Lesho 2013; Lamy 2016). With this, we gain a better understanding of how CECs developed or changed over time, how these changes are reflected in the synchronic systems (Devonish 1989; Clements and Gooden 2009), and the endeavour simultaneously encourages evaluation or reassessment of theories of Creole formation (Cassidy 1961; Cassidy 1967; DeCamp 1974; Devonish 1989; Singh and Muysken 1995; Klein 2006). This also impacts the extent to which we can make empirically based typological arguments, whether parametric or non-parametric (Klein 2006). While I make the suggestion, I am not implying that this is a simple task. Notwithstanding the lack of early recordings with which to conduct acoustic analyses, the effects of social factors and ideological stances of speakers can result in widely varying sociophonetic differences (Wassink 1999; Wassink and Dyer 2004; Irvine 2004; Irvine 2008), and these are also nearly impossible to reliably recover. More recent perception based studies on Australian Creoles, suggest that consonant production and perception can show language contact influence (Stewart et al. 2018) which will influence how they are learned. Further, even where the phonological system of a Creole language bears resemblances to its input languages, the phonetic implementation could yield significant differences from these source languages (Lesho 2013).

This study shows how factors such as speech context and phonetic environment affect the realization of voiced stops as either plosives ([b], [d], [g]) or implosives ([ɓ], [ɗ], [ɠ]) and also discusses the implications for phonological development in JC and for Caribbean English-lexicon Creoles, more broadly (Smith and Haabo 2007). This paper is part of a larger investigation aimed at a broader discussion on sociophonetic variation in voiced stops in JC, which incorporates several linguistic and sociolinguistic factors that might influence voicing variation.

BACKGROUND

Previous work

Devonish and Harry (2004) and Harry (2006) were the first published studies on JC to identify implosive stops [ɓ], [ɗ], and [ɠ], which occur as allophonic counterparts of voiced plosives /b/, /d/, and /g/ respectively. Implosives are said to occur in the onset of prominent syllables, but in coda position or the onset of a non-prominent syllable, voiced stops are instead realized as non-implosives (as shown in 1). The single example of an implosive in intervocalic position in the word, [ɓreɗa] "brother/friend", begs the question of whether or not there are other instances of implosive quality sounds in other than word-initial position. The variation is also said to be sociolinguistically conditioned due to differences between Western and Eastern varieties of JC. In terms of phonetic quality, Harry (2006) notes an increased amplitude throughout the closure portion of word-initial stops but gave no indication of whether these were in word lists or longer stretches of speech. So, it is not clear if speech style/context plays a role in the realization of stops. The analysis was based on the speech of two younger females who spoke conservative Eastern varieties of JC, which brings up the issue of age-related variation as well.

1. Jamaican Creole

| biit | 'beat' | daag | 'dog' | ɠud | 'good' |
| tiɐbul | 'table' | fiid | 'feed' | maaga | 'slim' |

Distribution of implosives and plain stops (Harry 2006, 127).

In a preliminary qualitative study, Gooden and Donnelly (2008; 2009) analysed a small sample of speech from three different sources (Harry 2006; Gooden 2003; DeCamp 1958), representing different speech contexts (word list, word elicitation task, spontaneous speech) and speakers of different ages, gender, and geographical backgrounds. The study considered presence of increasing amplitude during the closure, intensity throughout the closure, and differences in the spectral properties of the burst release. The results suggested that: implosives were more likely found in the speech of older speakers than younger speakers (age-related variation); there were only bilabial implosives, none at the alveolar and velar places of articulation; there is intra-speaker variation based on phonetic environment and speech context; and finally, that inter-speaker variation was also present. In addition, implosives were most likely to be produced in word-initial position in word list contexts. In spontaneous speech, however, the phonetic realization of stops was less clear, hence the need for a re-examination here.

These results provide a good starting point for the current study but must be treated with some caution. Given the purely qualitative nature of this preliminary study, we are unable to draw any strong conclusions about the phonetic properties of stops, in general, or about the distribution of plain stops versus implosives.

Phonetic Properties of Implosives

Voice Onset Time (VOT) has traditionally been defined as the interval between the release of closure of a stop consonant and the onset of vocal fold vibration (Lisker 1964). By this, voicing differences can be grouped into three categories, namely, voicing lead (around −30 ms or less), zero-onset or short-lag (from 0 to ~30 ms), and long-lag (~50 ms or longer). Implosives fall into the voicing lead category being pre-voiced. A more recent discussion (Abramson and Whalen 2017) suggests that there is much phonetic variability in the temporal relation between release of a stop closure and the onset of glottal pulsing, so divisions are not discrete and must go beyond laryngeal timing. Relevant to this discussion is that "fully voiced" stops, like implosives, show voicing lead through much or all of its closure whereas "partially voiced" stops, as seen in many English varieties, do not. Implosives are typically characterized by increasing voicing amplitude during closure, shorter closure duration and/or creaky phonation of the following vowel by means of harmonic amplitude differences such as H_1-H_2 (Keating et al. 2010; Tanaka 2016). At the same time, their actual phonetic realization shows much variation across languages (Ladefoged and Maddieson 1996; Lindau 1984). It is important to note, however, that the discussions of pre-voicing duration are not configured purely in terms of VOT, since I am only looking at voicing during the closure.

From an articulatory perspective, implosives can be viewed as strongly emphasized versions of the more regularly occurring pulmonic sounds (Hayward 2000). Cross-linguistic variability in voicing across languages in producing these sounds, makes it challenging to define a rigid set of criteria by which to circumscribe their collective properties (Cho and Ladefoged 1999; Hussain 2018). Nonetheless, despite different physical manipulations, robust acoustic effects are commonly seen in the closure portion of the stops and is often characterized by increasing or sustained amplitude throughout the closure portion as seen in figure 2.1 (shaded portion).

During the production of implosives stops, an oft cited strategy is for the larynx to be lowered resulting in an expanded oral cavity, which allows vocal fold vibration to be maintained during the entire closure portion of the stop (Hayward 2000; Reetz and Jongman 2011; Ladefoged and Disner 2012). More precisely, it is the maintenance of voicing that often results in an increase in amplitude throughout the closure or at

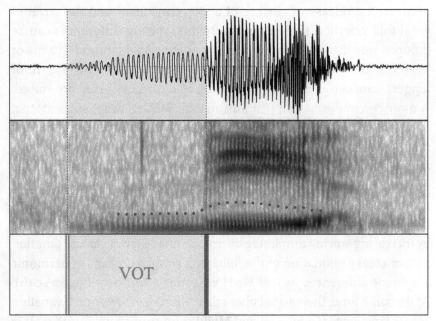

Figure 2.1. Waveform Showing Voiced Closure in an Alveolar Stop [diet] "Date" from Harry (2006) Word List

least remaining constant, (Lindau 1984), not dying off towards the end of the closure. At the same time, Ladefoged and Maddieson (1986, 82) suggest that implosives can be produced with modal voice, with a more tense voice setting, and with complete glottal closure. This means that producing a stop with implosive qualities of increased closure amplitude, does not necessarily mean changing the type of airstream mechanism, but rather can result from manipulating the flow of air in the oral cavity or other physical manipulations during speech production. Voicing maintenance can also be achieved with other articulatory manipulations such as cheek-puffing, tongue-lowering, advancing the tongue root, jaw-lowering (Eddington and Turner 2017; Hussain 2018). These articulatory changes can also differ, based on place of articulation such that we can observe differences in the duration of closure voicing based on place of articulation. Hussain (2018) explains that due to aerodynamic constraints, the intraoral pressure behind the constriction rapidly increases for voiced velar stops, which leads to small voicing lead VOTs, compared to labials and sounds at other places of articulation.

Sociophonetic variation in implosives

Distributionally, implosives are typologically rare sounds and might be considered "exotic" sounds from an English perspective (Hayward 2000). Voiced implosives are found in many languages in South and South-East Asia, for example, Indo-Iranian, the Americas and in Africa (Niger-Congo, Nilo-Saharan, Afro-Asiatic languages) (Catford 1988; Ladefoged and Disner 2012), representing approximately 13 per cent of the world's languages (Maddieson 2011). These languages also show lots of variation in allophonic versus phonemic status and in phonetic realization of implosive qualities (see for example, discussions in (Hussain 2018). In addition, Stuart-Smith et al (2015), and the references cited therein show that speakers can manipulate VOT as a social-indexical marker, suggesting that the lead VOT quality (that is, pre-voicing of implosives) is similarly variable and susceptible to sociolinguistic variation.

Implosives in Related Creoles and Substrates

The research on implosives in CECs hints of sociolinguistic variation.

Smith and Haabo (2004, 2007) for example, identify implosive stops in Saramaccan. Although, none of the significant input languages have implosives, they do note variation in the distribution of plain and implosive stops based on source language and status of the initial consonant in a word. For example, Kikongo derived words have [ɓ] in word-initial position, but Portuguese and English-derived words vary between plain and implosive stops even in the same phonological context. Based on elicitation from two Saramaccan speakers and visual inspection of acoustic displays of a sample of words, McWhorter and Good (2012) suggest that the contemporary variation (plain/implosive) is quite likely due to dialectal differences. They also note that word-initial voiced stops (b, d, g) are more "consistently voiced" than in English. Voorhoeve (1959), cited in McWhorter and Good) described Saramaccan labio-velar stops as implosives and other descriptions of the language list a plain stop and pre-nasalized stop. These latter descriptions are consistent with the other reports on the consonant inventory of Saramaccan, as both labio-velars and pre-nasalized stops have sustained voicing during the closure.

For JC, a transfer solution is not one that is easily constructed by connecting the dots of putative substrate languages that were spoken by enslaved Africans. Following the substrate trail for a moment, though the contemporary varieties of the substrate languages do not have implosives, they belong to language families which do (Smith and van de Vate 2012; Farquharson 2013). Farquharson argues that, during the formative period, the bulk of enslaved Africans were taken from, in ranked order, the Bight of Benin >Bight of Biafra >West Central Africa and spoke languages such as Gbè, Ijo and Yoruba, and other Kwa languages, areas where implosives and labio-velars are prevalent. It has also been suggested that the doubly articulated labiovelar stops [k͡p, ɡ͡b] which are common in the Gbè branch of Niger-Congo languages, are a likely source of implosives in JC (Kouwenberg 2018). These sounds, like implosives, are quite rare among the world's languages and their articulatory properties suggest that they have implosive components (Connell 1994; Ladefoged and Maddieson 1996). In fact, Ladefoged and Maddieson argue that labial implosives in one variety of Igbo developed from doubly articulated stops. In other languages, like Yoruba, [k͡p] appears to be voiced, so that voicing influence on implosives could come from both voiced and "voiceless"labiovelar stops.

Grawunder et al. (2011) provide electroglottograph (EGG) data from Yoruba showing that both voiced and voiceless labiovelar stops are characterized by pre-voicing, although [k͡p] has a comparatively shorter duration of pre-voicing. The Gx movement component of the EGG is taken as a rough indicator for larynx displacement, and given the results, they note that all voiced stops in Yoruba seem to have a voicing enhancement mechanism, which they suggest might involve lowering of the larynx. As noted in section 2.2, larynx lowering is a well-known characteristic of implosives as it enhances the speaker's ability to sustain voicing. If labiovelars are indeed the precursors to CEC implosives, then the articulatory manipulations, rather than the phone itself, could have been retained in the synchronic voiced stops.

Another issue is that importation of enslaved Africans to Jamaica from other Caribbean territories (presumably already speaking varieties of Proto-Atlantic English-based Creole) (Farquharson 2013, 27–28), also came from areas with implosives. Farquharson presents historical data supporting a decent Surinamese influence in the linguistic situation in Jamaican in the 1660s and 1670s, which could be another source of influence on voiced stop production. If we are to suggest a substrate retention effect in JC, we must also allow for the possibility that the influences are likely not all due to direct input from its putative substrates, but may have been filtered through other sources, such as Saramaccan and/or other emerging CECs.

English varieties

Arguments for a substrate effect (or even development from a Proto-Creole) are further complicated by the fact that some English varieties have been argued to have implosives. Voiced stops in English varieties do not typically have voicing throughout the closure portion and in fact may be partially voiced or completely voiceless until after the release of the closure (Abramson and Whalen 2017). However, non-pulmonic/glottalic sounds like implosives (and ejectives) reportedly occur non-contrastively in English varieties due to variability in pre-voicing rather than simultaneous release. The variation can be also attributed to both sociolinguistic differences such as idiosyncratic properties of idiolects, stylistic or regional variation (Jacewicz et al. 2009; Foulkes, Docherty and Jones 2011, 59) or phonological differences such as positional variation and prosody (Ladefoged and Johnson 2015). For example, Herbert Stahlke (2009), in a Linguist List post claims that many varieties of Southern American English use implosives voiced stops initially in stressed syllables, (that is, Nebraska, Oklahoma, North Carolina, Mississippi) and Stewart (1971 cited in Eddington and Turner 2017) suggests the same for African American Language. Jacewicz et al. (2009) provide further sociophonetic evidence for voiced implosive stops in North Carolina and Wisconsin dialects and, Eddington and Turner (2017) for Western varieties (Utah and New Mexico). Where voiced stops in English varieties show pre-voicing, this depends on the presence and/or the degree of vocal fold vibration during closure (Stuart-Smith et al. 2015). In addition to the phonetic factors discussed, researchers treat the variation as a matter of dialectal differences.

Research questions

Under ideal conditions, a researcher investigating the implosive quality of voiced stops would undertake different laboratory techniques, such as measurement of intraoral pressure and laryngographic studies, to check the exact acoustic properties involved (Ladefoged and Disner 2012). However, these techniques are unavailable for pre-existing data. Following, Grawunder et al. (2011), I take the presence and duration of pre-voicing in stops as a proxy for assessing the "ease"of vocal fold vibration before the release of the stop closure, and the extent to which voicing might be maintained throughout the closure. Duration differences based on place of articulation can point to differences in articulatory efforts to maintain voicing of the different stops. In addition to these phonetic differences, the earlier Saramaccan and JC studies suggest that there are linguistic and/or sociolinguistic constraints on their occurrence. As noted above, to sort out this puzzle, this paper is narrowly focused on one particular dimension of the voiced stops, lead VOT (pre-voicing) as a cue to implosive quality and addresses the following research questions: (a) Is pre-voicing a feature of voiced stops in JC? and if so (b) what linguistic factors affect pre-voicing of stops? and finally (c) what does this tell us about the status of implosive qualities of stops?

METHODOLOGY

Data

The analysis provided here is based on a 42-minute sample of recorded interviews by David DeCamp (Dec 1958) in Moore Town (Eastern dialect region). I focus on the interview with Mr Harris, an older man of Maroon heritage. He spoke a conservative variety of JC as evidenced, for example, by the prevalence of TH-stopping, zero copula, use of plural marker *dem*, and *min*, a rare variant of the PAST anterior marker found predominantly in Eastern varieties (Farquharson 2013, 26).

The Moore Town data are important for several reasons. Moore Town is built on land granted by the British government to Maroon leader turned national heroine "Granny Nanny" in 1740 and so, is one of the oldest settlements of Creole speakers. Also, as an Eastern dialect area, it is putatively more conservative than non-eastern varieties of JC and has remained relatively isolated, placing it among the most conservative varieties (Smith and van de Vate 2012).

Annotation and transcription

Visual inspection of a sample of waveforms and spectrograms suggests that voiced stops vary between having short lag VOT, where the onset of voicing and the release of the closure are basically simultaneous, and having lead VOT, where the voicing precedes the release of the closure. In order to gauge the prevalence of these different productions, voiced stops were segmented from the onset of the closure to the release burst as shown in figure (2.2). All transcriptions and acoustic analyses were done using Praat 6.029 (Boersma and Weenik 2017). The data was annotated using a five-step semi-automatic process using an online forced alignment tool and automatic VOT measurements followed by manual correction at each stage. Note deriving VOT measurements from spontaneous speech has been tagged as being "more difficult and time-consuming than from read speech or citation forms", Stuart-Smith et al. (2015, 507). Given the procedures used, another contribution of this paper is its commentary on the use of computing technologies for speech analysis in CECs. Although manual transcription remains the gold-standard for transcribing audio files for speech analysis, it is notoriously laborious (Babinski et al. 2019). Forced alignment, a lucrative alternative, is a technique that takes an orthographic transcription and an audio file as input and generates a time-aligned output using a pronunciation dictionary to look up phones in words. In the past decade, forced alignment tools have become publicly available and have been used by sociolinguists to process large amounts of phonetic data for variation analysis, but has not yet enjoyed similar usage in research on Caribbean Creole languages.

With a variety of modifications, the data discussed here were processed using the semi-automated alignment option in DARLA (Dartmouth Linguistic Automation) (Reddy and Stanford 2015), which is an online forced alignment and extraction system that makes use of automatic speech recognition using the Carnegie Mellon University Sphinx system. The most recent version of DARLA uses the Montreal Forced Aligner (McAuliffe et al. 2017). The system creates time-aligned Praat text grids as outputs and these were then manually checked and adjusted as needed. Although correction time was still a lot, it was somewhat reduced with this approach, compared to a completely manual transcription. The relative success of processes like this, have the potential to have a positive and transformative impact on our ability to take on large-scale empirically based investigations. It also underscores the importance of computational methodologies in data analysis in Creole studies (Bakker et al. 2011).

The extraction of all acoustic measurements was automated using Praat scripts (based on interval tiers), thus improving the reliability and consistency of measurements. The script prepopulate.praat[1] was used to automate the creation of new annotation tiers (Phone) with VOT labels inserted for every stop, (that is, VDCLO = voiced closure, VLCLO = voiceless closure, ASP = aspirated and REL = release). Given the requirements of the Praat interval tier, REL was the only obligatory label. All other labels were deleted or manually adjusted as needed, which again eased the labour of transcribing. The getvot.praat script[2] was used to generate another annotation tier (VOT), from which all duration measurements were extracted using an extraction script, Get_duration_2.0.praat.[3]

Acoustic measurements

These analyses and measurements relied on inspection of both the wave-form and spectrogram. Following (Jacewicz et al. 2009, Abramson and Whalen 2017), several acoustic landmarks were identified as shown in figure 2.2. The onset of the stop closure (also word beginning for stop initial words) was located on the waveform at a zero-crossing where acoustic energy was reduced or low, cued by a drop in amplitude in the waveform. The end of the closure (stop release) was visually identified from the waveform.

The start of voicing in the closure was located at the first visible zero crossing of vocal fold vibration and the voice bar in the spectrogram; the end of closure voicing was located at the onset of the stop release. An abrupt energy rise after the closure marked the burst release. However, where there was no evidence of a burst release (usually where the closure was voiced throughout), the end of the closure was located at the vowel onset, where the amplitude increased significantly. Word ending was located where the waveform activity ceased after the word final phone.

With these locations marked, several acoustic measures were calculated as follows. The duration of vocal fold vibration during stop closure, *closure voicing duration*, measured as closure release (burst location) minus onset of closure voicing; the duration of closure voicing relative to the total

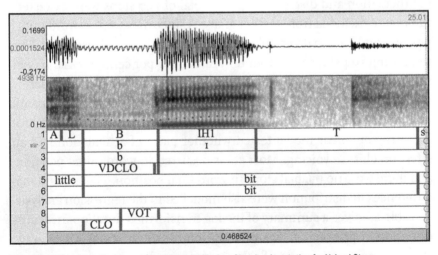

Figure 2.2. Waveform, Spectrogram and Textgrid Markup Showing Annotation for Voiced Stops

closure duration, *proportion of voicing*, (Jacewicz et al. 2009, Eddington and Turner 2017); duration of the entire closure (*closure duration*) and *word duration*.

Statistical methods

The data were analysed in R (R Development Core Team, 2013), employing a linear multiple fixed effects model using the lme4 package (Bates et al. 2015) in R Studio (R Studio Team 2015). The statistical analysis modelled closure voicing duration (response variable) as a function of the following predictors (fixed effects): place of articulation – *segment* (labial, alveolar, velar); position in the word – *position* (initial, medial, final); discourse topic – *topic* (land, 1903, whenboy) and word duration (*wordur*). All the duration measurements were log-transformed to reduce or eliminate skewing in their distribution and thus reduce the effect of any outliers, (Baayen 2008, 92), a procedure that is reportedly commonplace in phonetic studies (Rosen 2005).

RESULTS

In this section, I discuss durational evidence for enhancement of voicing in JC stops, and further whether there are differences based on place of articulation and discourse topic. A total of 197 stops were extracted, three were excluded from further analysis since they were in word initial position and had no detectable closure portion, just a release burst. The remaining 194 stops were found in initial (80 per cent), medial (11 per cent), and final (9 per cent), positions (table 2.1). The most frequently occurring stop was [d] (51.4 per cent) followed by [b] (27.84 per cent), then [g] (20.62 per cent). Given that [d]s contributed just over half of the data, the linear model tested whether place of articulation had an effect on closure voicing. Most stops occurred in word initial position, and there were no bilabial stops in word final position. These positional differences in distribution were also modelled in the regression analysis.

Table 2.1 gives a summary of the log transformed duration measures (duration of prevoicing, closure duration, word duration). On average stop closure duration was 3.81 (log-transformed) or 45.2ms. Only 13.92

Table 2.1. Distribution of Stops by Place of Articulation and Word Position

	labial [b]	alveolar [d]	velar [g]	Total
initial	46 (85%)	77 (77%)	32 (80%)	155 (80%)
medial	8 (15%)	10 (10%	3 (8%)	21 (11%)
final	0	13 (13%)	5 (13%)	18 (9%)
Total	54 (27.84%)	100 (51.54%)	40 (20.62%)	194 (100%)

Table 2.2. Summary Statistics (durations)

Statistic	N	Mean	St. Dev.	Min	Pctl(25)	Pctl(75)	Max
closure duration	194	3.811	0.592	2.400	3.393	4.107	5.740
prevoicing	167	3.722	0.565	2.320	3.370	4.045	5.360
word duration	194	5.296	0.570	4.240	4.863	5.670	6.720

per cent (27) of the 194 voiced stops lacked voicing during the closure. This means that the majority of stops were fully voiced. In fact, 16 of the remaining 167 stops had a proportion of voicing that was greater than or equal to 70 per cent, and another two showed 64 per cent and 54 per cent proportion of voicing respectively. Pre-voicing in these contexts was therefore not trivial and means that in a future analysis I will need to revisit the cut off for a partially versus a fully voiced stop. For purposes of this analysis, all 167 stops were included.

Figure 2.3 shows that alveolar stops had the longest pre-voicing duration, followed by bilabials, then velars.

Neither the linear data nor the log-transformed data for total closure duration met the assumptions for normality (Shapiro-Wilks) and, as such, these measures were excluded from the regression analysis. The linear model of voicing during the closure (pre-voicing) as constructed, was statistically significant (F (7, 159) =12.45, p <0.001) (see table 2.3). Three of the fixed-effects considered were found to be significant (that is, POA, word duration, topic), and I will discuss the results for each in turn.

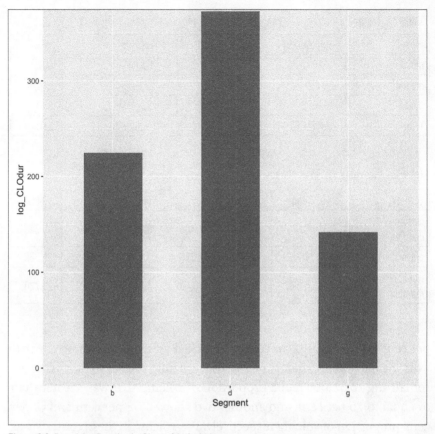

Figure 2.3. Prevoicing Duration by Place of Articulation

Place of Articulation

I examined whether the duration of voicing during the closure is affected by place of articulation of the stops. The model indicates that all voiced stops were found to be significant and are further differentiated by place of articulation. More specifically, the results of the model indicate that the duration of pre-voicing in alveolar stops is shorter than bilabials ([d] $\beta = 0.264$, $t = -2.75$, $p = 0.007$), and shortest in velar stops, ([g] $\beta = 0.495$, $t = -4.295$, $p < 0.001$). That is, both factors contributed less to pre-voicing duration than bilabials.

Table 2.3. Linear Regression Results

	Dependent variable:
	Duration of closure voicing
alveolar	-0.264*** (0.096)
velar	-0.495*** (0.115)
Harrisboy	0.291*** (0.101)
Harrisland	0.254*** (0.097)
wordPositionI	0.104 (0.128)
wordPositionM	-0.248 (0.159)
log _ wordur	0.434*** (0.078)
(Intercept)	1.401*** (0.493)
Observations	167
R^2	0.354
Adjusted R^2	0.326
Residual Std. Error	0.464 (df = 159)
F Statistic	12.455*** (df = 7; 159)
Note:	*p< 0.1;**p<0.05;***p<0.01

Word Duration

The regression model showed a clear influence of word duration, (β = 0.43, t = 5.54, p < 0.001). The overall mean word duration was 5.296 (log-transformed) or 199.54ms. There were 4 words that were produced with narrow focus and the stops in these words were longer than stops in non focused words. With log transformation, these did not skew the data distribution; however, a future paper could investigate the effect of stress or prosodic focus on pre-voicing as this has been shown to affect stop voicing.

Topic

Finally, Mr Harris's conversation with DeCamp was chunked in three groups roughly separated by the main topic of discussion. These were reports of "when he was a boy"; "happenings in 1903" and a discussion of "land ownership and farming". The latter produced the most stop tokens. In listening to the conversation, it appeared that Mr Harris was more passionate and animated when discussing certain topics. In the spirit of Labov's danger-of-death stories, I expected Mr Harris to have even more conservative pronunciations when discussing topics he was passionate about, so coding it in the statistical model provided a way to check for effects. Topic had a significant influence on pre-voicing of the stops. Topics discussing when Mr Harris was a boy and land ownership had longer pre-voicing, than discussions about happenings in 1903, i.e. [harrisboy] ($\beta = 0.29$, $t = 2.88$, $p < 0.01$); [harrisland] ($\beta = 0.25$, $t = 2.62$, $p < 0.01$).

Word Position

Recall that implosives were said not to occur in coda position, and it was not clear whether they reliably occurred in word medial position. Visual inspection of the box plot in figure 2.4 suggests that word initial and word medial positions had the most impact on stop voicing duration. Word position, however, was not significant (table 2.3).

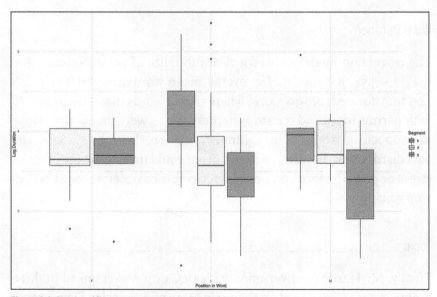

Figure 2.4. Boxplot of Pre-voicing Duration by Place of Articulation

DISCUSSION AND FUTURE DIRECTIONS

We started out querying whether there was phonetic evidence for implosive-quality sounds in JC, using these Moore Town data. We looked at several duration metrics that might reveal whether the stops have sustained voicing and thus enhanced voicing mechanisms during production. The focus was on the presence and duration of voicing during the closure rather than on increased amplitude throughout the closure as this is not ubiquitous in implosives (Hussain 2018).

These data showed that most voiced stops in these data had pre-voicing, and the duration of pre-voicing was influenced by place of articulation, (reflecting the cross-linguistic pattern bilabial > alveolar > velar [Lisker and Abramson 1964]) and was linked to longer word durations. Discourse topic also affected the duration of pre-voicing in stops in Mr Harris's speech.

Regarding the roots of implosives in JC, I am hesitant to suggest that this was a case of verbatim transfer/substrate retention, when this has not been the case for many other properties in the language. As discussed above, the voicing properties of plain, pre-nasalized and doubly articulated stops in putative substrates would have had sustained voicing, thus using some form of enhanced voicing mechanisms. All of these sounds could have converged to influence how listeners heard and reproduced voiced stops in the emerging Creoles. Thus, the articulatory phonetic *mechanism* for enhancing voicing (rather than the phone itself) might have been transferred in the learning process.

This study contributes to research on sociophonetic variation of voiced stops in naturally-occurring spontaneous speech. More narrowly, studies such as this are important for a better understanding of synchronic phonological variation in Creoles (Lesho 2013; Lamy 2016). There is much more of DeCamp's recordings and as analyses of these data continue, perhaps using the forced alignment techniques described here, this will increase the body of data by which to support claims regarding variation and change in the phonological system of JC.

We will also be better positioned to be able to say more about sociolinguistic factors affecting variation. The Harry and the Gooden data, for example, are from different regions and the preliminary findings from these suggested that pre-voicing is more widespread in JC, that is, beyond

Moore Town, but what sociolinguistic features are associated with this variation and what socio-indexical meanings it could be associated with, remains to be investigated.

NOTES

1. https://github.com/HaskinsLabs/get_vot/blob/master/prepopulate.praat
2. https://github.com/HaskinsLabs/get_vot/blob/master/get_vot.praat
3. https://www.acsu.buffalo.edu/~cdicanio/scripts/Get_duration_2.0.praat

REFERENCES

Abramson, Arthur S., and Douglas H. Whalen. 2017. "Voice Onset Time (VOT) at 50: Theoretical and Practical Issues in Measuring Voicing Distinctions". *Journal of Phonetics* 63 (July): 75–86.

Baayen, R.H. 2008. *Analyzing Linguistic Data: A Practical Introduction to Statistics using R.* Cambridge, Cambridge University Press.

Babinski, Sarah, Rikker Dockum, J. Hunter Craft, Anelisa Fergus, Dolly Goldenberg, and Claire Bowern. 2019. "A Robin Hood Approach to Forced Alignment: English-trained Algorithms and Their Use on Australian Languages". *Proceedings of the Linguistic Society of America* 4 (3): 1–12.

Bakker, Peter, Aymeric Daval-Markussen, Mikael Parkvall, and Ingo Plag. 2011. "Creoles are Typologically Distinct From Non-Creoles". *Journal of Pidgin and Creole Languages* 26 (1): 5–42.

Bates, Douglas, Martin Mächler, Ben Bolker, and Steve Walker. 2015. "Fitting Linear Mixed-effects Models Using lme4". *Journal of Statistical Software* 67 (1): 1–48. https://doi.org/:10.18637

Boersma, Paul, and David Weenik. 2017. "Praat: Doing Phonetics by Computer [computer program] version 6.029". https://www. praat. org/.

Cassidy, Frederick. 1961. *Jamaica Talk:Tthree Hundred Years of the English Language in Jamaica.* London: Macmillan.

Cassidy, Frederick, and Robert LePage. 1967. *Dictionary of Jamaican English.* Cambridge: Cambridge University Press.

Catford, John Cunnison. 1988. *A Practical Introduction to Phonetics.* Oxford: Clarendon Press.

Cho, Taehong, and Peter Ladefoged. 1999. "Variation and Universals in VOT: Evidence from 18 Languages." *Journal of Phonetics* 27(2): 207–29.

Clements, J. Clancy, and Shelome Gooden. 2011. *Language Change in Contact Languages: Grammatical anPprosodic Considerations.* Vol. 36. Amsterdam: John Benjamins Publishing.

Clements, J. Clancy, and Shelome Gooden. 2009. "Language Change in Creole Languages: Grammatical and Prosodic Considerations – An Introduction". *Studies in Language* 33 (2): 259–76.

Connell, Bruce. 1994. "The structure of labial-velar stops". *Journal of Phonetics* 22 (4): 441–76.

DeCamp, David. 1974. "Neutralizations, Iteratives, and Ideophones: The Locus of Language in Jamaica". In *Pidgins and Creoles: Current trends and prospects*, edited by David DeCamp and Ian F. Hancock, 46–60. Washington, DC: Georgetown University Press.

Devonish, Hubert. 1989. *Talking in Tones: A Study of Tone in Afro-European Creole Languages*. Kingston, Jamaica: Karia Press. Caribbean Academic Publications.

_____. 2002. *Talking Rythm Stressing Tone:Tthe Rrole of Prominence in Anglo-West African Creole Languages*. Kingston, Jamaica: Arawak Publications.

_____. and Otelemate G. Harry. 2004. "Jamaican Creole and Jamaican English: Phonology". In *Handbook of Varieties of English vol.1,The Americas and the Caribbean*, 450–80. Berlin: De Gruyter.

Eddington, David, and Michael Turner. 2017. "In Search of Cowboy b: Bilabial Implosives in American English". *American Speech* 92 (1): 41–51.

Farquharson, Joseph Tito. 2013. "The African Lexis in Jamaican: Its Linguistic and Sociohistorical Significance". PhD diss., University of the West Indies, Mona, Jamaica.

Gooden, Shelome A. 2003. "The Phonology and Phonetics of Jamaican Creole Reduplication". PhD diss., Ohio State University.

_____. and Erin Donnelly. 2008. *Phonetics of Implosives Consonants in Jamaican Creole*. Department of Linguistics Colloquium. University of Pittsburgh.

_____. 2009. *Phonetics of Implosives in Jamaican Creole*. Paper presented at the Meeting of the Linguistic Society of America/ Society for Pidgin and Creole Linguistics. California.

Gooden, Shelome, Kathy-Ann Drayton, and Mary Beckman. 2009. "Tone Inventories and Tune-text Alignments". *Studies in Language* 33 (2): 396–436.

Grawunder, Sven, Bodo Winter, and Joseph Atoyebi. 2011. "Voicing of Labiovelar Stops in Yoruba". In Online Proceedings of the International Congress of Phonetic Sciences, XVII, 767–70.

Harry, Otelemate G. 2006. "Jamaican Creole". *Journal of the International Phonetic Association* 36 (1): 125–31.

Hayward, Katrina. 2000. *Experimental Phonetics: An Introduction*. London: Pearson Education.Heine, Bernd, and Derek Nurse. 2008. *A Linguistic Geography of Africa*. Cambridge: Cambridge University Press.

Hussain, Qandeel. 2018. "A Typological Study of Voice Onset Time (VOT) in Indo-Iranian Languages".*Journal of Phonetics* 71: 284–305.

Irvine, Alison. 2004. "A Good Command of the English Language: Phonological Variation in the Jamaican Acrolect". *Journal of Pidgin and Creole Languages* 19 1): 41–76.

_____. 2008. "Contrast and Convergence in Standard Jamaican English: The Phonological Architecture of the Standard in an Ideologically Bidialectal Community". *World Englishes* 27 (1): 9–25.

Jacewicz, Ewa, Robert Allen Fox and Samantha Lyle. 2009. "Variation in Stop Consonant Voicing in Two Regional Varieties of American English". *Journal of the International Phonetic Association* 39 (3): 313–34.

Klein, Thomas. 2006. "Creole Phonology Typology: Phoneme Inventory Size, Vowel Quality Distinctions and Stop Consonant Series". In *The Structure of Creole Words: Segmental, Syllabic and MorphologicalAspects*, edited by Parth Bhatt and Ingo Plag, 3–21. Tubingen: Max Niemeyer Verlag.

Ladefoged, Peter, and Sandra Ferrari Disner. 2012. *Vowels and consonants*. Hoboken, NJ: Wiley.

Ladefoged, Peter, and Keith Johnson. 2015. *A Course in Phonetics*, 7th edition. Stamford, CT: Cengage Learning, Ladefoged, Peter, and Ian Maddieson. 1996. *The Sounds of the World's Languages*. Hoboken, NJ: Wiley-Blackwell.

Lamy, Delano S. 2016. "A Variationist Account of Voice Onset Time (VOT) Among Bilingual West Indians in Panama". *Studies in Hispanic and Lusophone Linguistics* 9 (1): 113–41.

Lesho, Marivic. 2013. "The Sociophonetics and Phonology of the Cavite Chabacano Vowel System". PhD diss., Ohio State University.

Lindau, Mona. 1984. "Phonetic Differences in Glottalic Consonants". *Journal of Phonetics* 12(2): 147–55.

Lisker, Leigh, and Arthur S. Abramson. 1964. "A Cross-language Study of Voicing in Initial Stops: Acoustic Measurements". *Word* 20 3): 384–422.

Maddieson, Ian. 2011. "Consonant Inventories". In *The World Atlas of Language Structures Online*, edited by Matthew Dryer and Martin Haspelmath, 10–13. Munich: Max Planck Digital Library.

McAuliffe, Michael, Michaela Socolof, Sarah Mihuc, Michael Wagner, and Morgan Sonderegger. 2017. "Montreal Forced Aligner: Trainable Text-Speech Alignment Using Kaldi". Proceedings, *Interspeech 2017*: Conference of the the the International Speech Communication Association 498–502.

McWhorter, John, and Jeff Good. 2012. *A Grammar of Saramaccan Creole*. Berlin/Boston:De Gruyter.

R Core Team. 2013. *R: A Language and Environment for Statistical Computing*. R Foundation for Statistical Computing. Vienna, Austria. http://www.R-project.org/.

Reddy, Sravana, and James Stanford. 2015. *A web application for automated dialect analysis*. In Proceedings of the 2015 Conference of the North American Chapter of the Association for Computational Linguistics: Demonstrations, 71–75. https://

doi.org/10.3115/v1/N153015

Reetz, Henning and Allard Jongman. 2011. *Phonetics: Transcription, Production, Acoustics, and Perception*. Hoboken, NJ: Wiley.

Rosen, Kristen M. 2005. "Analysis of Speech Segment Duration with the Lognormal Distribution: A Basis for Unification and Comparison". *Journal of Phonetics* 33:411–26.

RStudio Team. 2015. *RStudio: Integrated Development Environment for R*. Boston, MA: RStudio http://www.rstudio.com/.

Singh, Rajendra, and Pieter Muysken. 1995. "Wanted: A Debate in Pidgin/Creole Phonology". *Journal of Pidgin and Creole Languages* 10 (1): 157–70.

Smith, Norval, and Vinije Haabo. 2004. "Suriname Creoles: Phonology". In *Handbook of Varieties of English; 2: The Americas and the Caribbean*, edited by Edgar W. Schneider, 525–66. Berlin: De Gruyter.

_____. 2007. "The Saramaccan Implosives: Tools for Linguistic Archaeology?" *Journal of Pidgin and Creole Languages* 22 (1): 101–22.

Smith, Norval, and Marleen van de Vate. 2012. "Population Movements, Colonial Control and Vowel Systems." In *The Structure of Creole Words: Segmental, Syllabic and Morphological Aspects* (Linguistische Arbeiten), edited by Parth Blatt and Ingo Plag, 59–82. Berlin: DeGruyter.

Stahlke, Herbert. 2009. "Linguist List Ask-A-Linguist Message Forum". https://linguistlist.org/ask-ling/message-details2.cfm? asklingid=200437585#.

Stewart, Jesse, Felicity Meakins, Cassandra Algy, and Angelina Joshua. 2018. "The Development of Phonological Stratification: Evidence from Stop Voicing Perception in Gurindji Kriol and Roper Kriol". *Journal of Language Contact* 11(1): 71–112.

Stuart-Smith, Jane, Morgan Sonderegger, Tamara Rathcke, and Rachel Macdonald. 2015. "The Private Life of Stops: VOT in a Real-time Corpus of Spontaneous Glaswegian". *Laboratory Phonology* 6 (3–4): 505–49.

Tanaka, Yu. 2016. "Implosives in Jakarta Indonesian". *Journal of the Acoustical Society of America* 140 (4): 3112–3112.

Thomason, Sarah, and Terrence Kaufman. 1988. *Language Contact, Creolization and Genetic Linguistics*. Berkely, CA: University of California Press.

Van Coetsem, Frans. 1998. *Loan Phonology and the Two Transfer Types in Language Contact*. Dordrecht, The Netherlands: Foris.

Wassink, Alicia Beckford. 1999. "Historic Low Prestige and Seeds of Change: Attitudes Toward Jamaican Creole". *Language in Society* 28 (1): 57–92.

_____, and Judy Dyer. 2004. "Language Ideology and the Transmission of Phonological Change: Changing Indexicality in Two Situations of Language Contact". *Journal of English Linguistics* 32 (1): 3–30. https://doi.org/10.1177/0075424203261799

CHAPTER 3

School of Drama Students' Perceptions of Standard English

The Impact of Background on Confidence Levels
in the Use of Language

ELIZABETH MONTOYA-STEMANN

INTRODUCTION

In theatre, oral performance is one of the main skills of expression. Jamaican college students who aspire to become drama teachers or theatre art professionals encounter challenges when presenting an oral performance of a poetical text written in Standard English (SE). This situation is commonly observed in the Voice and Speech classes that I teach at the School of Drama (SoD) at the Edna Manley College of the Visual and Performing Arts (EMCVPA) in Kingston.

This chapter is based on empirical research carried out with students representing all four years in the SoD programmes. The general objective is to understand the reasons why these students present a low level of confidence (LoC) when performing a poetical text in SE to classmates and the SoD audience. I will argue that this is due to the students' lack of a direct relationship with SE. This in turn means that they lack the skills to analyse and transform a text written in SE into an oral performance.

The reasons given by the student-performers (SPs) for their self-reported low level of confidence (LoC) when performing a poetical text using SE, are the focus of this chapter. The research assessed the SPs' oral performance of the poem "Flowers" (Craig 1999) in order to establish possible correlations between the different aspects that emerged from the data analysis. The reasons that explain their self-reported low confidence levels when performing in SE, along with their oral performance assessments were found to be linked to their relationship with SE, which in turn derives from their degree of SE exposure. At the end of this paper, I will put forward suggestions for a future intervention in the EMCV-PA-SoD programmes. But I will first survey the literature relevant to this research and the background of the students before I present and analyse the data.

LANGUAGE AND EDUCATION IN JAMAICA

Language Context in Jamaica

The linguistic situation in Jamaica is complex, so it is difficult to define in exact terms. Jamaica is considered a de facto bilingual society (Shields 1989, Alleyne 1989 as cited in MOEY&C 2001) with two dominant forms of language, namely, Standard Jamaican English (SJE) (Alleyne 1989, 132) and Jamaican Creole (JC), the latter commonly known as Patwa (Cassidy 2007, DeCamp 1968). However, the reality is that different individuals display different levels of proficiency when using SJE and JC. In Jamaica, "the factors which determine the range of linguistic forms produced by an individual are his dominant code and his degree of bilingualism" (Akers 1988, 8). A study conducted in 2006 by the Jamaican Language Unit (JLU) (JLU 2007) collected information from one thousand Jamaican respondents and found that 46.4 per cent of the speakers consulted were able to alternate between JC and SJE. English monolinguals (17.1 per cent) were mainly highly skilled persons and professionals. JC monolinguals (36.5 per cent) were concentrated in the western rural parishes and were unskilled or unemployed (JLU, 6). This gives us an idea of the relationship between levels of bilingualism and social variables such as geographical location and level of skills and education. We could say that in Jamaica, only bilingual speakers can decide fully on the choice of variety according to different social situations (Carrington 1988).

Language Status

Languages record different prestige among their users according to different sociocultural features (Mühleisen 2002, 25). The draft elaborated by the Ministry of Education, Youth and Culture (MOEY&C) in November 2001 of the Language Education Policy, recognizes SJE as the official language (MOEY&C 2001) and the language to impart education in Jamaica. SJE has the status of the standard in Jamaica; it is used by educated people in leading positions in society. SJE has been related to the high status that is given to English as an international language (Kachru 1992). JC is the most spoken language and the language of the "overwhelming majority" (MOEY&C 2001, 7) and is acknowledged by the MOEY&C as the "home language" (2001, 2). Most Jamaicans prefer JC (Patwa) to talk to friends and family and reserve SJE to conduct business and talk to strangers or at work (JLU 2005, 8) even though JC is considered the non-prestigious variety and does not have official recognition. People have long held negative attitudes towards JC (Cassidy 1971; Alleyne 1985). In acquisitional terms, SJE is the first language (L1) for some of the population and a second language (L2) for the majority.

Language Attitudes and Notion of Standard and Non-Standard

The notion of "standard language" in Jamaica then, is informed by the perception of the person who is using the language in a given speech community; standard and non-standard speech varieties are thus related to specific groups of speakers and derive their prestige from the social status of those speakers. Language prestige interlinks with the cognitive, affective and conative/behavioural components of the theoretical construct of Attitude (Mühleisen 2002, 29). Speakers with high educational levels, who use more of the prestige variety's features, are considered to speak "Good English" (Irvine 2005, 317).

Attitudes are the ideas and feelings that people have about a language (Crystal 2008, 266). The standard language is perceived as proper language, and JC speakers are perceived as speaking English "but doing so badly" (Christie 2003, 4). This perception aligns with a standard view of language attitudes in a creole continuum,[1] which considers that "the standard is good and the non-standard (including the Creole) is bad" (Rickford 1985, 146). However, Rickford, whose research was conducted in Guyana, has issues with this view that "assumes a positive orientation toward the standard variety alone". (Rickford 1985, 146). He found evidence that language attitudes are multidimensional, and that while basilectal speakers attached positive socio-economic value to the use of the standard (overt prestige), they do not identify themselves with it on an affective level (covert prestige) (Rickford 1985, 153), or use it in everyday social interactions.

The attitudes towards SJE and JC in Jamaica could similarly be described as ambivalent since the factors determining overt and covert prestige interact. People may present ambivalent attitudes towards SJE because some see it as the language of the dominant social class or elite, but also as the medium of "upward social mobility" (Alleyne 1989, 133; Patrick 2000, 16). JC is the language Jamaicans associate positively with trust and use to talk to their friends and family. These different values are echoed in drama students' reflections on their own levels of confidence when using SE or JC (46–53).

Educational Context

The level of education of a speaker is "judged from the degree of his/her proficiency in English" and their use of JC (Christie 2003, 39). Nevertheless, JC is the language of the "overwhelming majority" (MOEY&C, 7); most Jamaicans prefer Patwa to talk to friends and family and reserve SJE to conduct business and talk to strangers or at work (JLU 2005, 8). Children enter the Jamaican school system with different levels of competency in SE; JC dominant students graduate from secondary school unable to perform with the expected "ideal" competency level in SJE (Evans 2001, 108).

In sum, educational policies and programmes are detached from the linguistic reality (Pollard 1978, 17). The result is, as highlighted by different authors, that children from low-income homes that are not frequently exposed to SJE, in written or spoken form, attain poor assessment scores in school (Shields-Brodber 1997, 61; Christie 2003, 40; Craig 2006, 25;

Devonish and Carpenter 2007, 34). These assessment scores derive from written standardized tests: Grade Four LiteracyTest (GFLT) presented upon ending grade 4 (primary school); Grade Six Achievement Test (GSAT), presented at the end of primary school (grade 6). At the end of high school, students sit the Caribbean Secondary Education Certificate (CSEC). Oral performance assessments are not included in the Jamaican primary and secondary educational system; all English language assessments are written.

Educational Outcome of the Student-performers

Of the forty primary schools attended by the SPs in the SoD programmes, thirteen are included in the National Education Inspectorate (NEI.) reports, of which seven are categorized as urban (Kingston, Portmore, Spanish Town, Brown's Town, Bridgeport, Linstead, and Grange Hill P.O.), and six are rural (Trelawny, Hanover (2), Manchester, St Catherine, and Westmoreland). Analysing the NEI, reports available, the common characteristics of the urban and rural schools include middle to low socio-economic background of the students. The areas surrounding some urban schools also present high levels of violence and, more so in rural than urban schools, middle to high unemployment levels. The NEI reports show patterns of unsatisfactory performance in the GFLT and GSAT. Nine schools obtained unsatisfactory results on the GFLT, one school obtained good in the GFLT, and three schools, satisfactory GFLT results in the national and regional English assessments. The NEI recommends, in the reports on almost all the schools that further action should be taken to improve the level of performance in the Language Arts and to tackle teaching and learning pedagogical strategies in general.

With literacy and language testing being mainly centred on the use of the written form, development of oral communication skills is largely disregarded. SJE is the language of instruction in schools, but the competencies targeted in education do not include students' capacity to use the language to verbally communicate their thoughts within their immediate social and familiar environment. In this way, students' relationship with the written form of SJE is almost "cosmetic" in the sense that by adopting the correct language forms, it is expected that, in practice, the targeted written text will be improved externally, but the internal relation with the spoken language is not established from school.

STUDENT-PERFORMERS' LANGUAGE COMPETENCE

Language Expectations at the School of Drama

The SoD offers programmes that expect proficiency in the English language. The SoD offers the following programmes that include voice and speech classes, as listed in the EMCVPA 2017–2018 Student Handbook, and at www.emc.edu.jm, (1) BA Drama in Education (4 years), (2) BFA Theatre Arts (4 years), and (3) BA Drama EMCVPA/University of the West indies (UWI) joined programme (3 years) (EMCVPA 2017–2018).

As part of the application process, prospective students are required to present different combinations of the following examinations, Caribbean Secondary Education Certificate (CSEC) and Caribbean Advanced Proficiency Examination (CAPE), administered by the Caribbean Examinations Council (CXC), and the UK General Certificate of Education (GCE). The CSEC examination offers English A and English B. The English A examination explores drama, poetry and prose, and fiction and "emphasizes the development of oral and written language skills among students through a variety of strategies" (CXC 2011). Also, "The skills to express ideas and gather information clearly and creatively in written form are assessed" (CXC 2010, 18–20). Applicants to the SoD programmes should present (1) five specific subjects in different CSEC, CAPE and GCE combinations, including CSEC English A; (2) an audition where applicants perform a dramatic piece in SE, and another in JC; (3) an interview, and (4) a passing grade on the SoD English proficiency test (EMCVPA 2017–2018).

The forty-six SPs who participated in this research graduated from public primary and high schools; few of them graduated from high-scoring schools. In the CSEC English A examination, seventeen obtained grade 2 (Very Good), twenty-one, grade 3 (Good) and eight obtained grade 1 (Excellent) [2]. The correlation between the SPs' LoC and CSEC English A will be analysed later in this chapter (54–55).

This study is centred on the oral performance of a cohort of SPs enrolled in BA programmes at EMCVPA SoD who were attending or had attended voice and speech classes. Throughout the programme, SPs are expected to develop, not just in their use of language, but in their oral performance of different kinds of SE and JC texts as well. However, my direct class experience with SPs suggests that the development of oral language skills in SJE poses a challenge for many of them.

VOICE AND SPEECH CLASSROOM EXPERIENCES

Voice and speech classes IA & B (V&S IA-B) and V&S IIA & B are taken in the first two years of the BA programmes at SoD. As part of V&S IA-B that I teach, SPs must read, select, analyse, prepare and present to an audience, texts ranging from informative (for example, newspapers articles) to poetical JC and SJE texts. For V&S IB, in the second semester, the tasks are: sight-reading of a narrative text, presenting a Shakespearean sonnet and telling a story that they create individually out of a given set of drawings using JC and SJE. SPs present different weaknesses on these tasks. When selecting a poetical piece from a recommended list, SPs may feel burdened by having to read different poetry books in order to find a text of their liking, for example, a poem or sonnet. Some SPs sometimes find poems in JC difficult to decode, since different authors use their own self-designed orthographies.

Analysis and Presentation of Poems

Interpretation and oral performance depend significantly on the level of understanding that the SPs have of the meaning and purpose of the piece. Meaning in drama is explained as an understanding of the context of the text: who is saying it, under which circumstances and why these words are said. Also, the literal and metaphorical aspects of words and sentences are sources to understand the meaning of a poetic text. In practice, when performers understand the meaning of a text, they can interpret it and convey it to an audience with clarity, after a rehearsal period.

Developing the physical and prosodic capacity of SPs' voices is not the mere objective of this class; combining vocal power and verbal communication craft is part of our standards. Beyond these skills, the qualities of language should be explored, drama students should aim for words to come alive as they speak (Carey and Clark Carey 2010, xx).

SPs struggle, first, with the literal significance of words, second, the interconnection of meaning between the different lines/stanzas of the poem, and third, the fact that the analysis of meaning should go beyond the initial response to the poem; in other words, SPs need to "have more than an initial reaction. [They will] need to develop an understanding of the poem" (Arp and Johnson 2002, ix). Where this process is not completed, the partial analysis will bring a superficial orality that shows a lack of confidence and SE performance competence.

Assessment Criteria

For V&S IA-B classes, there are four criteria to assess SPs' oral performances of SJE and JC texts: voice production, (audibility, use of pitch and vocal tone), speech clarity (articulation, enunciation and pronunciation of words, use of rhythm and rate), interpretation, and presentation of the text. In the interpretation criterion, phrasing of the text is assessed, as well as the skill to create the mood of the text with conviction and believability. Presentation assesses use of gestures, physical energy, composure and eye contact with the audience.

The standards for this course, as described in the 2014 course outline states"students should be able to demonstrate a fair awareness of how the voice works and a practical process of systematically and consciously shaping a fair oral delivery of a poem in dialect and another in SE" (EMCVPA 2014). On completion of V&S II A & B, students should have a full degree of comfort in using breath control, fluency of phrases, sound proficiency of vowel and consonant formation, and intelligent use of projection (EMCVPA 2014).

Some SPs can perform SE texts with proficiency, but others need to tackle the use of intonation, avoiding being repetitive or monotonous in their interpretation. Some students state that they feel they cannot express themselves freely using SE and that they get *stiff* (without physical expression). Although JC performances also pose some challenges, specifically related to interpretation of the written text, it is important to highlight that the focus of this study is not comparing SPs' JC and SJE oral performances. The general goal of this research is analysing SoD SPs' SJE perceptions when performing a poetical text in SE. In this paper, as will be elaborated, SPs express that they have challenges analysing and performing texts in SE, and reported low LoC in the use of SE.

The low LoC is explained by the SPs as gradations of feeling uncomfortable or unease, or experiencing specific personal challenges with the language. The complete data related to the level of confidence when performing in SE will be presented (50–53).

METHODOLOGY AND DATA COLLECTION INSTRUMENTS

This research required data that could serve to assess 46 SPs' oral performance and their levels of confidence when performing a poem using SJE. The method adopted was, first, collect SPs' metadata and audio data and then analyse them to establish correlations between the SPs' self-declared LoC when performing in SE and JC and their (actual) SJE oral performance. Recordings of a JC poem were considered unnecessary since this research focuses on SPs' SJE oral performance.

Questionnaires were designed to collect the SPs' (1) individual assessment of their LoC when performing in JC and SJE, (2) explanations for their selection, and (3) language background.

The oral performance of a selected SE poem was used to assess and qualify the SPs' oral performance in SJE. The poem "Flowers" by Dennis Craig (1999) was selected for its lexicon, phonological and morphosyntactic characteristics that can be classified as moderately challenging for the SPs who are JC dominant. Consent Forms were signed by all SPs collaborating in this research.

Consultants. Two independent consultants were selected to analyse SPs' phonological data and to assess SPs' oral performance. They were two female Jamaican bilingual (JC and SE) post-graduate students in the Linguistics programme at UWI Mona. When doing the phonological analysis of segmental features, they received a copy of the poem with lexical test items marked, SPs' standard features analysis form, and SPs' oral recordings that were distributed in two batches.

The consultants received written detailed instructions and workshops on how to judge the SPs' oral performance, along with the following forms: (1) Criteria to judge the Level of Understanding (LoU) and (2) Criteria to judge the Use of Prosody (UoP) and (3) Quality Control form. The latter, designed to maintain the standards of the consultant's judgements, assisted consultants and researcher to do weekly evaluations of the problems, improvements and development of the judging task.

To identify the SPs' production of fifty-five standard phonological features contained in the poem, the consultants received a list of test items (some had several instances in the poem). Some examples of test items are: (1) /h/ deletion, (2) /h/ insertion, (3) Final /t/ deletion, (4) final /d/ deletion, (5) presence of postvocalic /r/ in stressed syllables, (6) voiceless dental fricative variation.

The Oral Assessment Criteria for the recordings were based on the V&SIA-B assessment criteria used for oral examinations. The forms assessed individually the Level of Understanding (LoU) and Use of Prosody (UoP) of each SP. LoU and UoP criteria were graded on a Likert scale from 1–5 where 1 was assessed as Poor, 2 as Acceptable, 3 as Good, 4 as Very Good and 5 as an Outstanding oral performance. The assessment was carried out over a period of six months.

In the context of this article, the oral assessment performance process will not be elaborated but SPs' performances, irrespective of the year in the SoD programmes, were mostly assessed as Acceptable (2). Table 3.1 illustrates the results of the oral assessment elaborated by the independent consultants.

The assessment results in table 3.1 support my classroom experiences. These results will be analysed to find correlations (53–54) between the

Table 3.1. First to Fourth Year SPs' Oral Assessment

Assessment Value	SPs' LoU					SPs' UoP				
	1st	2nd	3rd	4th	Total	1st	2nd	3rd	4th	Total
Poor (1)	6	3	3	1	13	6	1	1	0	8
Acceptable (2)	9	3	6	8	26	9	6	8	10	33
Good (3)	0	1	2	1	4	0	1	2	0	2
Very Good (4)	0	2	1	1	4	0	1	1	1	3
Outstanding (5)	0	0	0	0	0	0	0	0	0	0

SPs' oral performance assessment and their LoC when performing using SE. Tthe analysis of their reasons will be explained first.

SPS' SELF-REPORTED LOC IN THE USE OF SJE AND JC

SPs participating in this research represent 80 per cent of the total number of SPs enrolled at SoD, with 15, 9, 12 and 11 SPs from years 1, 2, 3 and 4, respectively. All of them filled out the following form that requested their LoC when using JC and SJE.

(1) How do you feel performing in **Jamaican (Patwa)?** Please select the level of confidence between 1 and 5.

Min. 1   2   3   4   5   Max. Confidence.
Explain the reason for your answer.

(2) How do you feel performing in **Standard Jamaican English?** Please select the level of confidence between 1 and 5.

Min. 1   2   3   4   5   Max. Confidence.
Explain the reason for your answer.

SPs also had to state their LoC when speaking in JC and SJE in a Likert scale from minimum 1 to 5 Maximum and had to give explanations for their selection.

The analysis of the data collected from the forms mentioned above showed that, on average, SPs' reported a LoC of 4.4 when performing in JC and 3.5 for SJE. When speaking, the LoC for JC was 4.6 and 3.6 for SJE. When speaking and performing in JC, the LoC is self-reported as higher in comparison with the values given for SJE. SPs reported themselves with higher values for speaking in both JC and SJE than when performing. We could infer from the data that SPs perceive performing as more demanding than speaking. The averages given above were expected, given the SPs' SJE competence when graduating from high school and the predominant use of JC in social interaction.

An analysis of the reasons given by the forty-six SPs, in writing, helped to gather their perceptions of the JC/SJE languages and identify the elements contributing to the self-reported LoC when performing. The ones stated for self-reported LoC performing in JC will be analysed first.

Analysis of the Reasons Given for Self-reported LoC When Performing in JC

All SPs, except one, provided reasons for their self-reported LoC. In this section we will analyse the reasons given by forty-six SPs for their self-reported LoC 5 to 2 in JC. The SPs' reasons were grouped by LoC.

Table 3.2 summarizes the number of SPs by year and their self-reported LoC-JC.

Table 3.2. SPs' LoC Performing in JC Yearly

LoC in JC	First	Second	Third	Fourth	Total SPs
5	8	5	7	5	25
4	3	3	4	5	15
3	3	0	1	1	5
2	0	1	0	0	1
1	0	0	0	0	0
Total	14	9	12	11	46

In table 3.2 levels of confidence 4 and 5 are predominant when SPs perform in JC. As will be explained in the following sections, there are five recurring elements grouped as affective that SPs used to explain their self-reported high LoC in JC, for example, 1) ease or comfort, 2) JC as their L1, 3) expressivity, 4) identity & culture, and 5) love for the language. These elements are more recurrent at LoC 5 and lessfrequent at LoC 4.

Self-reported LoC 5 and 4 in JC

When performing in JC, twenty-five of the forty-six SPs self-reported LoC 5. SPs declared feeling comfortable and confident, their explanations relate to SPs' relationship with the language, oral competence, competencies related to the written form and general performance demands. These reasons were analysed and then grouped as: 1) affective, 2) linguistic, 3) technical, 4) related to general performance. Some examples of reasons, as given by the SPs, are shared below.

Affective: "Jamaican patois is my mother tongue, I grew up speaking that way [*sic*] that is one of the reasons why it is so easy for me to perform in Jamaican patois and I have absolutely no challenges performing in Jamaican patois because it is something I love to do and I do it well" (M-3-2).

Linguistic: "And if it is written so that I can read it, it is much easier to recite" (F-1-3).

At LoC-5-JC they affirm identifying themselves with JC at a deeper level and connecting with the audience.

In chart 3.1, almost all the reasons given at LoC-5-JC are positive or affective. At LoC 5 there are no problems with the use of JC, SPs have a genuine connection with the L1 language, many call "mother tongue".

LoC 4 in JC. At this level there are fifteen SPs. Although, the reasons here are slightly different from LoC-5-JC, most frequent reasons are affective, that is, JC is their L1 (eight) and feeling at ease (six). Some of the remaining elements are present but, in less proportion, for example, identity and culture (three), and greater expressivity (two). Love for the language is not expressed at this level.

At LoC-4-JC, SPs also experience linguistic and performance challenges, for example, "Patio [*sic*] poems are somewhat hard to deliver based on the diverse amount of interpretation of words, how they are

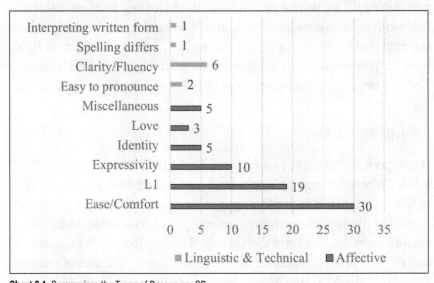

Chart 3.1. Summarizes the Types of Reason per SP

pronounced, etc." (M-3-4), "because it is [*sic*] in a different form from how I write it" (F-2-4), "The Jamaican Patwa is our native language it is what we are accostume [*sic*] to and what we as Jamaicans were born to speak. Although it [sic] much easier to present in a performance, preparation in terms of reading may challenge me at times." (F-1-7). Some SPs express mixed reasons associated to technical ability challenges, for example, "[I] feel almost perfect however I still call some words incorrectly" (F-1-8).

At LoC-4-JC a majority of SPs gave affective reasons but also linguistic and technical reasons related to interpreting the written form, mixing up the grammar, pronunciation and use of tone challenges and some reasons related to the general demands of performance.

Self-reported LoC 3 and 2 in JC

One SP out of five self-reported at LoC-3-JC gave one affective reason; other SPs' explanations reveal linguistic challenges related to interpreting the written form. Some examples of their reasons are:

Affective: "ok. Speaking Jamaican Patwa allow[s] me to be expressive" (F-3-6). "I do not like Jamaican Creole poems so performing then [*sic*] get a little difficult for me." (F-3-5).

Linguistic: "often times it is a little uncomfortable for me to read it and perform it" (F-0-5).

At LoC-3-JC SPs express affective matters, and linguistic challenges. *LoC 2 in JC*. One SP is self-reported at LoC 2-JC and explains having problems with the interpretation of the written form of JC.

To summarize, JC is the language most appreciated by forty of the forty-six SPs, and expressivity is a recurrent positive element at LoC 3-5-JC. The most recurrent negative reasons given at LoC 2-4 relate to linguistic difficulties making the connection between the JC written form and its pronunciation.

Analysis of the Reasons Given for Self-reported LoC When Performing in SJE

SPs' reasons that express positive and negative perceptions when performing in SJE, will be discussed in this section. Table 3.3 summarizes years 1-4 SPs' self-reported LoC values.

Table 3.3. SPs' LoC Performing in SJE Yearly

LoC in SJE	First	Second	Third	Fourth	Total SPs
1	0	0	0	0	0
2	3	1	1	0	5
3	6	3	4	8	21
4	3	3	5	1	12
5	2	2	2	2	8
Total	14	9	12	11	46

In table 3.3, most of the SPs in each year in the SoD programmes self-reported LoC-3-SJE and roughly a third at LoC-4-SJE.

Self-reported LoC 5 in SJE

The eight SPs at LoC-5-SE provided different reasons from those given at LoC-5-JC. The explanations relate to a technical level of comfort that is based on an ability or skill that they believe they have when analysing and delivering the text. Following, some representative examples of SPs' given reasons are listed below.

Affective: "This is my first language and I ma [sic] quite comfortable reading and performing in Standard English." (F-0-5).

Linguistic (positive): "Jamaicans including myself are bilingual people and so I have learned and gravitated to [sic] SJE and is now just as familiar as my mother tongue language." (F-2-1).

Technical abilitys: Three SPs declared that they find easier to interpret, memorize, analyse and deliver when using SE, for example, "It is easier for me to analyze and deliver [sic] text written in Standard English". (F-0-5).

Demands of performance: One SP (M-3-1) related his LoC to the process of preparation and performance: "i [sic] tend to be confident when i rehearse my piece when the piece is rehearsed". One SP feels undecided: "Performing in Standard English makes me very self-conscious. I constantly watch how I pronounce a word and how it may come across to people. I am confident in my delivery when people see me but deep down I am always checking myself." (F-2-7).

There are positive reasons at LoC-5-SJE related to the benefits of the written form but SPs find difficulties with pronunciation, and language self-consciousness when presenting to the audience.

Self-reported LoC 4 in SJE

At LoC-4-SJE there are twelve SPs expressing some affective, linguistic (positive and negative) and comparative reasons. They feel comfortable and confident, and as for LoC-5-SJE, SPs feel that they have technical competence in SJE and can articulate well, and love reading in SJE. A new aspect that emerges is that four SPs acknowledge that SJE was imparted and one, that SJE was enforced at school and they became comfortable using it.

Some examples of reasons given at LoC-4-SJE are:

Linguistic and technical: "[the] rhythmic pattern is challenging but can be done" (F-1-10).

Demands of performance: "I feel relaxed performing Standard J.E., but only when I am well prepared or else I would have the critics castrating me, worse, if I'm a nervous wreck" (F-1-4)

Comparative: "I am somewhat confident in my performance but its [*sic*] just not as good as me performing using Patwa. I feel like I am holding my true feelings sometimes when using SJE (F-1-5).

At LoC-4-SJE SPs identify some oral and language competence skills that they state have to develop to reach full confidence.

Self-reported LoC 3 in SJE

The largest number of SPs – twenty-one out of forty-six – self-reported at this LoC-SJE, but only three express positive reasons. Seventeen new negative reasons related to affective, linguistic and technical challenges appear here. There are eleven SPs expressing few negative reasons related to expressivity and the majority reporting pronunciation difficulties that go from simple mistakes to becoming a major issue for them. Several SPs spoke more generally of their competence levels using SJE and said that they find several challenges related to grammar, enunciation and pronunciation. They explain that this is related to the fact that they do not use SJE daily. Some reasons given at LoC-3-SJE are:

Affective: "[SJE] is closer to our dialect. So it is not so hard performing because it is natural for me" (F-9-1), "when performing it creates a sense of status that I enjoy." (F-2-5).

Linguistic and technical: "English to me is a very complex language and can be difficult especially when an individual is just being introduced to it. It's grammar way of nunciation [*sic*] & pronunciation can be very tricky." (M-2-1).

Demands of Performance: "I believe it takes to [*sic*] much energy to express myself, especially bringing across the emotions that I want to express while speaking." (F-0-6).

Comparative: "I express myself with words [*sic*] performing better than when using "patwa." (M-0-2).

At LoC-3-SJE SPs use the following elements to explain their reasons: L1, expressivity, comfort, fluency.

Chart 3.2 shows that most of the reasons given by twenty-one SPs at LoC-3-SJE are negative, and most are related to being insecure about pronunciation and interpreting the written text.

Self-reported LoC 2 in SJE

Five SPs at this level gave negative reasons related to pronunciation struggles (4), more preparation time needed (1), self-consciousness and

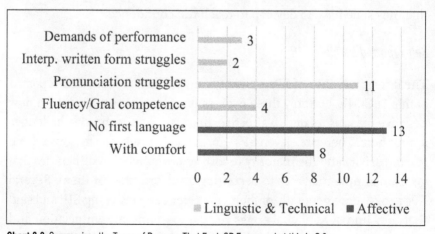

Chart 3.2. Summarizes the Types of Reasons That Each SP Expressed at this LoC 3

nervousness about making mistakes (2), lack of competence in SJE (1). One SP states: "I don't like it, but I have to do it. I get really nervous as am afraid to make mistakes." (F-1-8). "Nervousness" and "feeling insecure when performing" become acute at this level. A high level of self-consciousness related to linguistic and technical hurdles makes them become apprehensive and linguistically insecure. They consider overcoming SJE pronunciation demands as important.

To summarize, feeling at ease or comfortable was a common reason used to explain the LoC 5-4 in JC but at LoC-5-SJE the reasons differ as comfort is not related to being at ease but with a level of skill when using the language. As observed before (46–53), for LoC-JC, in SJE there is no pattern associated with the years in the programme for LoC.

In the following section, I will explore the relationship between the issues noted by the SPs and their unfamiliarity with SJE at the communicative and oral performance level.

Self-reported LoC and Oral Performance Assessment

The oral performance assessment assessed the SPs' level of understanding (LoU) and use of prosody (UoP) (44–46), to convey the images, meaning and ideas contained in the poem. In this correlation it is expected that higher LoC-SJE will obtain corresponding higher value for the oral performance assessment using SJE. This correlation is shown in figure 3.1.

Figure 3.1 shows that low-LoC reporting SPs have, on average, low

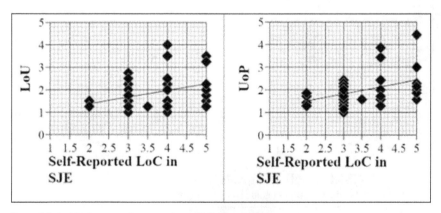

Figure 3.1. Oral Performance Assessments and Self-Reported LoC

values on LoU and UoP. The averages for LoU and UoP for LoC 2, 3, 4 and 5 are correspondingly: 1.3 and 1.6 (LoC 2), 1.6 and 1.7 (LoC 3), 2.2 & 2.3 (LoC 4) and 2.4 and 2.7 for self-reported LoC 5. On average, when performing in SJE, SPs convey a better understanding of the poem when self-reporting high LoC.

Self-reported LoC and CSEC English A Grade

This correlation can show how the SPs' CSEC English A grades relate to their self-reported LoC in SJE. The CSEC English A examination is the only national test that assesses the level of English language competence in the written form. Figure 3.2 shows this correlation.

Figure 3.2 shows a positive correlation between the self-reported LoC and the SPs' CSEC English A test. The CSEC English A average for the highest self-reported LoC values (4 and 5) is 2.0; for LoC 3 is 2.4 and for LoC 2 is 2.6.

Most of the SPs self-reported LoC-3-SJE, also most of them obtained grade 3 in the CSEC examination. Majority of the SPs who obtained CSEC English A grade 1 (highest passing grade) also reported a high LoC. The positive correlation between the self-reported LoC and the CSEC English A grade clearly suggests that the CSEC English A grade has an influence on the SPs' LoC.

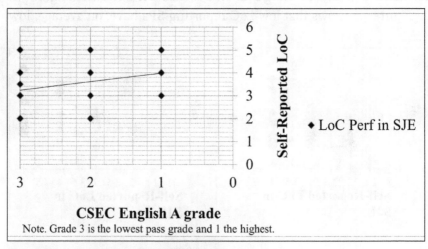

Figure 3.2. Self-reported LoC and CSEC English A Grade

However, at the individual level, the correlation holds only when observing the average for self-reported LoC 2; there are outliers at LoC 4 and 2 at LoC 5 that raise the average value for these levels. In sum, the averages are slightly higher at higher self-reported LoC.

FINDINGS AND IMPLICATIONS

Requesting the SPs to self-assess their LoC and provide comments on their LoC, helped to relate language competence to the SPs' perception of SJE as a language in which to communicate or express meaning.

Most of the SPs are self-reported at LoC 3 and 4-SJE and LoC 5 and 4-JC. At each LoC, SPs reveal an acknowledgement of the personal challenges when performing in SJE; as the level of LoC in SJE decreases, the number of positive or affective reasons given decreases. It is also noteworthy that through the different years in the SoD programmes, the reasons given by the SPs do not become more positive regarding performing using SJE.

The confidence level for JC relates to a linguistic relationship stated as LI or mother tongue. SPs' given reasons for their LoC-SJE explained from a JC perspective, are closely related to the experience when performing in JC rather than in SJE. In all, the reasons given for confidence in JC confirm the dominant status of JC in SPs' lives. In contrast, for SJE, the LoC is related to a technical level of competence and that, SPs acknowledge, requires personal effort to attain. Technical competence plays a role in LoC-JC in the more limited sense of an ability to read the diverse written forms of JC.

Almost all the SPs' comments explaining their LoC-SJE, even at self-reported LoC 5, are related to pronunciation, insecurity about grammar, and not being fluent in SJE. It is worth noting that the pronunciation issues reported by SPs are mostly unfounded. My research of SJE also revealed that SPs' articulation generally achieved standard targets. SPs' difficulties in interpreting the written SJE form orally, are part of a broader set of challenges. As noted earlier, the background to these difficulties includes the following:

1. SPs whose environment is JC dominant, lack exposure or opportunities to interact with fluent SJE speakers.

2. As a result of the focus on standardized written tests at primary and secondary levels of the educational system, SPs' SJE competence is largely based on the written use of the language and this does not equip them to use the language with confidence, orally.
3. JC remains the language of oral competence.
4. The limited use of SJE in the classroom where JC and SJE interact does not contribute to the development of SJE's oral competence across the same range as JC.Thus, the sociolinguistic and educational background and language exposure are linked directly to their SPs' LoC and prevent them from developing a satisfactory level of SJE language performance. In contrast, SPs relate their high JC LoC to a close, experiential relationship when performing in JC. SJE is an external language which is not usually used to speak to family and friends and to express feelings and personal ideas. SPs are aware that SJE is not their L1 and that it takes time and effort to target and master the "model" that they were taught at school.

In the oral performance (44–46) that assessed LoU and UoP, on average, SPs did not obtain values beyond *Acceptable*, evidencing a lack of ability to interpret the written text. The poetical text demands a deeper knowledge of different aspects of the SE text, including linkages between morphosyntax and semantics and an ability to deal with unfamiliar lexical items. The level of understanding of the meaning expressed in the poem would have to go along with the use of prosodic skills and vice versa. Thus, successful delivery requires a direct relationship with SJE.

In this paper, even though the assessments were chiefly based on subjective criteria, all pointed to the fact that language confidence is not perfectly correlated to communicative or linguistic competence as measured through the oral performance assessments: some SPs reporting higher LoC in SJE did not perform better. However, language proficiency and the way a language is imparted has an impact on students' confidence when using SJE to communicate.

Their self-assessed LoC when performing the text derives from their confidence in the linguistic and technical skills that allow them to analyse and deliver a text.

Approaching a Communicative Relationship with SJE

Students could benefit from educational programmes that seek to establish a close relationship with the language that SPs do not consider their L1 and that is taught in JC-SJE environments.

SPs at the EMCVPA-SoD receive voice and speech classes in first and second years only. Through the four years in the SoD programmes, on average, the SPs who participated in this study showed an increase in their LoC between second and third years, but lose the impetus in the final year. Overall, they do not show significant progress in their self-reported LoC, in their standard feature production, or in their oral performance assessments. The programmes at the EMCVPA-SoD need to be reoriented to address the level of linguistic competence and performance as well as SPs' self-confidence that can support the oral performance.

A system is needed to reinforce the relationship with the standard, not just in voice and speech courses but ideally in every subject of the performing arts at the SoD. The voice and speech course should also include workshops facilitated by experts related to the language situation in Jamaica, JC and SJE linguistic differences and JC orthography.

This research pointed to specific aspects of the oral performance of the SPs that should be considered in a future intervention, but which also speak to a national problem. Written and oral competencies go together but the educational system focuses on written assessments and the oral competencies are disregarded. This causes a lack of relationship with the written text and ultimately affects the communicative competence of students. SPs need to develop a more communicative relationship with SJE that empowers them to interpret meaning and sense with skill. It is crucial that administrators and lectures are trained to identify the linguistic background of the SPs and develop programmes linked to their linguistic reality.

NOTES

1. This situation, initially described by Le Page (cited in DeCamp, 1957) and DeCamp (1968) as post-Creole Continuum, is a "socio-economically oriented linguistic continuous spectrum of speech varieties" with a range of intermediate varieties between the extremes which are not mutually intelligible (DeCamp).

The varieties considered standard are the acrolect and at the other extreme basilect varieties. The intermediate varieties are called the mesolect. For the purpose of this research, basilect and mesolect are not distinguished. Thus, JC covers both.

2. The labels associated with the pass levels are those used by the Caribbean Examination Council http://www.cxc.org/examinations/csec/

REFERENCES

Alleyne, Mervyn C. 1985. "A Linguistic Perspective on the Caribbean". In *Caribbean Contours,* edited by Sydney Mintz and Sally Price, 155–79. Baltimore,MD: John Hopkins.

_____. 1989. *Roots of Jamaican Culture.* London: Pluto Press.

Akers, Glenn A. 1981. *Phonological Variation in the Jamaican Continuum.* Ann Arbor, MI: Karoma Publishers.

Arp, Thomas R. and Greg Johnson. 2002. *Perrine's Sound and Sense: An Introduction to Poetry,* 10th ed. Boston, MA: Heinle and Heinle.

Carey, David and Rebecca Clark Carey. 2010. *The Verbal Aarts Workbook.* London, UK: Methuen Drama.

Caribbean Examinations Council. 2010. *English syllabus.* http://cxc.org/SiteAssets/syllabusses/CSEC/CSEC_English.pdf

_____. 2011. *English A.* http://www.cxc.org/node/669

Carrington, L.D. 1988. *Creole Discourse and Social Development (Manuscript Report 212e).* Ottawa, Canada: International Development Research Centre (IDRC).

Cassidy, Frederic G.1971. "Tracing the Pidgin Element in Jamaican Creole". In *Pidginization and Creolization of Languages.* Proceedings of a Conference held at the University of the West Indies, Mona, Kingston, Jamaica, April 1968, edited by Dell Hymes, 203–21. Cambridge: Cambridge University Press.

_____. 2007. *Jamaica Talk: Three hundred Years of the English Language in Jamaica.* Kingston, Jamaica: University of the West Indies Press.

Christie, Pauline. 2003. *Language in Jamaica.* Kingston, Jamaica: Arawak Publications.

Craig, Dennis. 1999. *Near the Seashore: Collected poems 1996.* Georgetown, Guyana: Education and Development Services.

_____. 2006. *Teaching Language and Literacy to Caribbean Students.* Kingston: Ian Randle Publishers.

Crystal, David. 2008. *A Dictionary of Linguistics and Phonetics.* Oxford,UK: Blackwell Publishing.

DeCamp, David. 1968. "The Field of Creole Language Studies". *Latin America Research Review* 3(3): 25–46.

Devonish, Hubert, and Karen Carpenter. 2007. "Full Bilingual Education in a Creole Language Situation: The Jamaican Bilingual Primary Education". *Occasional paper. Society for Caribbean Linguistics (SCL)*. 35 (February). Document.

Devonish, Hubert, and Otelemate Harry. 2004. "Jamaican Creole and Jamaican English: Phonology". In 1 *The Americas and the Caribbean, Varieties in English*, edited by Edgar.W. Schneider and Kathryn Burridge et al. Berlin: de Gruyter.

Edna Manley College of the Visual and Performing Arts. 2014. *Course Outlines*. Unpublished document EMCVPA-SoD.

Edna Manley College of the Visual and Performing Arts. 2017–2018. *Student handbook*. EMCVPA.

_____. 2018. *Application Requirements*. http://emc.edu.jm/admissions/application-requirements/

Evans, Hyacinth. 2001. *Inside Jamaican Schools*. Kingston, Jamaica: University of the West Indies Press.

Irvine, Alison G. 2005. "Defining Good English in Jamaica: Language Variation and Language Ideology in an Agency of the Jamaican State". PhD diss., University of the West Indies, Mona, Jamaica .

Jamaica. Ministry of Education, Youth and Culture. 2001. *Language Education Policy*. Kingston, Jamaica: Ministry of Education, Youth and Culture.

Jamaican Language Unit (JLU), Department of Language, Linguistics and Philosophy. 2007. *The Language Competence Survey of Jamaica: Data Analysis*. Faculty of Humanities and Education, University of the West Indies, Mona. Kachru, Braj B.1992. "Teaching World Englishes". In *The Other Tongue: English Across Cultures*, edited by Braj Kachru, 355–65. Urbana,IL: University of Illinois Press.

Mühleisen, Susanne. 2002. "Defining Language Prestige: The positioning of Creole in Linguistic and Social Parameters". In *Creole Discourse: Exploring Prestige Formation and Change Across Caribbean English-Lexicon Creoles*, 23–52. Amsterdam: John Benjamins Publishing.

Patrick, Peter. 2000. "Social Status and Mobility in Urban Jamaican Patwa". http://74.125.155.132/scholar?q=cache:xDQiM9LYaA4J:scholar.google.com/+social+status+and+mobility+in+Urban+jamaican+patwa&hl=en&as_sdt=2000&as_vis=1

Pollard, Velma. 1978. "Code Switching in Jamaican Creole: Some Educational Implications". *Caribbean Journal of Education* 5 (1): 16–31.

Rickford, John R. 1985. "Standard and Non-Standard Language: Attitudes in Creole Continuum." In *Language of Inequality*, edited by N. Wolfson and J. Manes, 145–60. New York: Mouton.

Shields-Brodber, Kathryn. 1997. "Standard English in Jamaica: A Case of Competing Models". *English World-Wide* 10(1), 41–53.

CHAPTER 4

Variability Across Repeated Productions in Bilingual Children Acquiring Jamaican Creole and English

A Pilot Study

SANDY ABU EL ADAS, TARA McALLISTER AND KARLA WASHINGTON

INTRODUCTION

The term developmental speech sound disorder (Shriberg et al. 1997) refers to a class of impairments affecting articulation and phonological processing that can have a negative effect on social and academic performance (Felsenfeld, Broen, and McGue 1994; Hitchcock, Harel, and McAllister Byun 2015). Speech-language pathologists (SLPs) often face particular challenges in connection with the assessment and diagnosis of speech sound disorders in bilingual children. Two primary factors can be identified as contributing to these challenges. First, despite the fact that approximately 21 per cent of the population living in the United States speaks a language other than English (U.S. Census Bureau 2015), only 8.3 per cent of SLPs that are members of the American Speech Language Hearing Association (ASHA) identify as bilingual service providers (ASHA 2023). Second, most diagnostic criteria and assessment instruments that SLPs use are based on characteristics of monolingual English speakers, which often differ from the characteristics of typical bilingual speakers (Skahan, Watson, and Lof 2007). This is primarily due to the lack of diagnostic tools available to clinicians to assess these populations. This lack of clear criteria for bilingual children may lead to both under-diagnosis, where children with speech sound disorders are mistakenly characterized as typically developing, and over-diagnosis, where typical children are misclassified as disordered.

Research examining bilingual development in children has focused mostly on English and Spanish speakers (Fabiano-Smith and Barlow 2010; Fabiano-Smith and Goldstein 2010), leaving other language contexts understudied in the literature. One such context is bilingual acquisition of English and Jamaican Creole (JC), whose speakers represent approximately 20 per cent of the Caribbean-born immigrant group in the United States (US Census Bureau 2015). The current study will focus on bilingual acquisition in this understudied population. In addition to providing direct guidance for clinical management of this group, this line of research can be considered important for broader reasons. Bilingual development may proceed differently, depending on the nature of the typological relationship between the two languages being acquired. If we arrive at an understanding of bilingual speech development that is based on a narrow range of language pairings, we run a risk of making clinical recommendations that will not necessarily generalize to the full range of bilingual populations represented in the SLP caseload. For instance, there is evidence that the degree of similarity between two languages can influence the course of bilingual acquisition (Bosch and Ramon-Casas 2011). The close relationship between JC and English, its lexifier language, is quite distinct from that between Spanish and English, the pairing that has formed the focus for most previous literature examining bilingual speech development. The present research is thus well-positioned to broaden our understanding of bilingual development, with particular implications for other language pairings that share similar phonologies and extensive cognate vocabulary, for example, Spanish and Catalan, other pairings of a Creole and its lexifier, for example French and Haitian Creole, and may even be extended to the acquisition of divergent dialects of a single language, such as African American English and Mainstream American English.

Diagnostic Markers

Previous studies have used different types of diagnostic markers when assessing phonological development in bilinguals. One common type of analysis involves phonemic accuracy measures, such as Percent Consonants Correct (PCC), which has been found to be strongly correlated with intelligibility in the speech of monolingual children (Shriberg et al. 1997). Fabiano-Smith and Hoffman (2018) reported that PCC can serve as a sensitive measure of phonological ability in both monolingual and bilingual children at the age of 5;0, but it shows lower sensitivity with younger bilingual children, where there is a higher risk of misdiagnosis. Another diagnostic approach involves measuring token-to-token variability across repeated productions, which has been identified as a potentially useful tool for diagnosing speech sound disorders in bilingual children (Holm, Dodd, Stow, and Pert 1999; Preston and Seki 2011).

The main advantage of using variability measures is that the child is compared against him or herself over repeated productions, rather than being compared against the adult target, where influences from one language to another could come into play. However, use of this measure rests on the assumption that variability will be similar across the two languages a child speaks. This has been asserted in previous literature (Holm et al.1999; Preston and Seki 2011), but it has not been rigorously established in large-scale studies. In Holm et al. (1999) one of two bilingual children acquiring English and Mirpuri made inconsistent errors (indicating a high degree of speech variability) in both language contexts, suggesting a phonological deficit that spanned language contexts. Preston and Seki (2011) also argued for the use of token-to-token production variability in assessing speech sound disorders in bilingual children. They examined the productions of a bilingual child acquiring Japanese and English and argued that in this case study, token-to-token variability did not show an influence of transfer from one language to the other, or of proficiency with a given language. However, there is need for further study to substantiate this claim. In addition, there is debate over what degree of token-to-token variability should be considered typical even in monolingual development; we discuss this debate in the next section.

Token-to-token Variability in Child Speech

Previous studies disagree on whether variability across repeated productions is a normal characteristic or a sign of disorder in speech development.
Holm, Crosbie, and Dodd (2007) reported low rates of variability over
typical children's repeated productions of the same word. For instance,
they found that children aged 3;0-3;6 showed variability in 13 per cent of
repeated productions (words elicited three times each), and older children
aged 6;0-7;0 showed variability in only 3 per cent of productions. They
thus suggested that higher rates of variability are suggestive of disordered
speech development (Holm, Crosbie, and Dodd 2007). However, Sosa
(2015) and Macrae and Sosa (2015) reported higher rates of variability in
typically developing children, with children aged 2;6-4;2 showing variability in approximately 70 per cent of repeated productions elicited in
the same manner described by Holm et al. (2007). These authors argued
that variability is common in typical child speakers and may in fact be a
sign of progress to a new stage of phonological development. One possible explanation for the discrepancy across studies may be related to the
method of transcription, since Holm et al. (2007) had a single listener
transcribe the productions in an online fashion, whereas Macrae and
Sosa (2015) followed a more elaborate procedure in which two listeners
independently generated an offline transcription and then compared
their responses to arrive at a consensus transcription.

Apart from the disagreement over what level of token-to-token variability should be considered typical in monolingual speakers, it is unclear
whether elevated levels of token-to-token variability should be seen as
a sign of a deficit in phonological planning, motor planning, both, or
neither (Bradford and Dodd 1996; Dodd and McCormack 1995). Some
studies have highlighted variable error patterns as a hallmark of Childhood apraxia of speech (CAS), a developmental motor planning disorder
(Iuzzini-Seigel, Hogan, and Green 2017). On the other hand, Goffman,
Gerken, and Lucchesi (2007) showed that transcription-based measures
of token-to-token variability do not always align with measures of movement inconsistency derived from instrumental tracking of the articula-
tors, suggesting that transcribed token-to-token variability may not be
a reliable index of a motor planning problem. This is compatible with
work by Dodd and colleagues, who argued that high variability across

transcribed tokens reflects issues with phonological rather than motor planning. While this debate remains unresolved, it appears that obtaining acoustic or articulatory as well as transcription-based measures of variability would be optimal to make a claim about differences in motor control.

Factors that Influence Variability

Previous studies have described different factors affecting token-to-token variability. Some of these factors are speaker-specific, such as age (Macrae, 2013) and expressive vocabulary size (Macrae 2013; Sosa and Stoel-Gammon 2012), while others are stimulus- or context-specific, such as word frequency and density (Sosa and Stoel-Gammon 2012), or the degree of acoustic overlap in the input (Bosch and Ramon-Casas 2011; Sundara and Scutellaro 2011). Age and expressive vocabulary are two speaker-level factors that have also been reported to affect production variability. Holm et al. (2007) found that variability tends to decrease with age, such that older children exhibit lower rates of variability compared to younger children. However, findings regarding the effect of age on variability have been inconsistent across studies. Some have argued that age plays an important role in determining variability (Holm et al. 2007), while others either did not find an effect of age (Sosa and Stoel-Gammon 2012) or have argued that the effect of age disappears when controlling for expressive vocabulary (Macrae and Sosa 2015). In Macrae and Sosa's (2015) study, children with larger vocabularies exhibited lower rates of variability in production. The purported effect of vocabulary size on variability has a theoretical basis in the lexical restructuring hypothesis (Metsala and Walley 1998), which argues that children's representations transition from more holistic to more segmental as their vocabulary size grows larger, and that variability decreases as representations become more specified at the segmental level.

Lexical characteristics such as word frequency and neighborhood density have also been described as factors affecting variability in production (Sosa and Stoel-Gammon 2006, 2012). Sosa and Stoel-Gammon (2012) examined the influence of phonological neighborhood density, phonotactic probability, and age of acquisition of words on variability across repeated productions in monolingual children ages 2;0–2;5. The results revealed an effect of phonological neighborhood density, such that children were less variable when producing words in dense phonological neighbourhoods. These results align with older work by Sosa and Stoel-Gammon (2006), showing that both word frequency and phonological neighborhood density have an effect on variability in children's productions.

Lastly, it has been argued that the nature of the input also plays an important role in shaping variability in production. This factor forms the main focus of the present paper. Central to this line of thinking is the idea that exposure to a wide range of exemplars can affect how bilinguals acquire phonemic contrasts, and this influence may be further modulated by the degree of overlap between phonological categories across languages. Due to the greater variability in their input, bilingual children might be expected to show greater variability in production than monolingual children (Byers-Heinlein and Fennell 2014). The effects of input become more complex when taking into consideration the type of language pairings involved.

When the two languages to which the bilingual child is exposed are phonologically similar and share many cognate words, phonological representations may become less precise due to shared influences from one language to the other. To address the effects of language pairing on production variability, Bosch and Ramon-Casas (2011) examined acoustic measures of vowels produced by bilingual adult speakers of Catalan and Spanish, two languages that share extensive cognates and phonological overlap. Their results revealed high levels of variability in production of mid-front vowels that are similar but not identical across Catalan and Spanish, supporting the idea that bilingual input and pairing of two phonologically related languages can play an important role in shaping production variability.

The Catalan-Spanish case may extend to other cases of bilinguals speaking different pairs of phonologically related languages, such as Creole languages and their associated lexifier languages (for example, JC and English, Haitian Creole and French). However, we are not aware of previous research systematically investigating this question in the creole context. The current study examines token-to-token variability in single-word productions by bilingual children speaking JC and English.

Given the close phonological and lexical ties between JC and its lexifier language, English (Devonish and Harry 2008; Harry 2006; Washington 2012), bilingual children acquiring these languages present an ideal test case for hypotheses about the impact of variable and overlapping input on children's token-to-token variability in production. Since token-to-token variability has been proposed as a diagnostic marker for speech sound disorders in bilingual children (Preston and Seki 2012), the present study may also have implications for clinical decision-making with this underserved population.

Research Questions

This study addresses the following questions. (1) Do bilingual children speaking JC and English differ in token-to-token variability relative to monolingual children in the same age range (Macrae and Sosa 2015)? (2) Does token-to-token variability differ across repeated productions in JC versus English? We hypothesize that variability will be higher in bilingual than monolingual children due to the greater variability in their input. We additionally hypothesize that variability will be higher in JC than in English. This latter hypothesis is based on the diglossic status of JC and the notion that language exists in a continuum spanning from basilectal JC (most distinct from Standard English) to acrolectal JC (most similar to Standard English) (Kouwenberg and Singler 2008). While this is a pilot investigation, this line of research can ultimately be expected to assist SLPs in making diagnostic decisions when working with bilingual clients, especially in the context of acquisition of a Creole and its lexifier.

METHODS

Participants

The pilot study included a convenience sample of bilingual children acquiring JC and English and also drew on data from a previously collected sample of monolingual English-speaking children (Macrae and Sosa 2015). All children provided verbal assent and parents provided written consent for their child's participation in the study. The bilingual sample included nine children (eight females and one male) ages 3;0 to 6;0 (M = 4;4, SD = 1.5). The bilingual children were recruited from a preschool located in New York City (Queens borough). Children were classified in the bilingual group based on parental report (Pearson et al. 1997) and were required to have a minimum of 20 per cent reported input and output in each language to be considered bilingual in the languages of interest. Parent report was also required to reveal no history of speech, language and hearing disorders, and participants additionally passed a pure tone hearing screening at 25 dB HL for octave frequencies of 1000, 2000, and 4000 Hz. The Primary Test of Nonverbal Intelligence (PTONI; Ehrler and McGhee 2008) and the oral motor subtest of the Diagnostic Evaluation of Articulation and Phonology (DEAP; Dodd et al. 2009) were administered to ensure that all the children had nonverbal IQ scores within the normal range and no major anomalies in the oral mechanism. All children performed within the average range on the PTONI and met the age-based criterion on the DEAP Oral Motor subtest.

The monolingual sample was selected from Macrae and Sosa (2015), which originally included a total of forty-three monolingual children (twenty-four females and nineteen males) ages 2;6 to 4;2. The children were recruited from university speech and hearing clinics based in Arizona and Florida. Because the mean age in the monolingual sample was substantially lower than in our bilingual pilot sample, we selected the oldest children from the original study to achieve a better-matched sample for statistical comparison. This resulted in a final sample of eleven children aged 3;6-4;1 (six females and five males). Even after hand-selecting the oldest participants from Macrae and Sosa (2015), the mean age of the monolingual sample remained lower than that of the bilingual sample; we return to this point in the Discussion section. All monolingual children passed a hearing screening and scored less than one standard deviation below the mean on an array of standardized tests measuring language skills and speech development, including the Goldman–Fristoe Test of Articulation, Second Edition (GFTA-2; Goldman and Fristoe 2000), Expressive Vocabulary Test, Second Edition (EVT-2; Williams and Williams 2007), and Peabody Picture Vocabulary Test, Fourth Edition (PPVT-4; Dunn and Dunn 2007). A summary of demographic information across the two groups is presented in table 4.1.

Table 4.1. Participant Demographics across the Two Group Samples

	Bilingual sample	Monolingual sample
Male	1	5
Female	8	6
Total	9	11
Age	M = 4;4, SD = 1.2	M = 3;6, SD = 0.3
Site	New York City (Queens)	Arizona, Florida

Note: Age is listed as years; months
NB: Convenience sampling resulted in more females than males being included in this pilot investigation. Please see the discussion for implications of this imbalance.

Protocol

Participants completed the DEAP Word Inconsistency Assessment (WIA), which has formed the basis for previous studies evaluating children's consistency across repeated productions of the same word (Dodd et al. 2009; Macrae and Sosa 2015). The DEAP WIA consists of twenty-five words (for example, *fish*, *watch*, *zebra*) that are elicited three times; the standard testing procedure specifies that the three repetitions should be spaced out over time, with other activities intervening between each elicitation of the twenty-five target words. The present study differed from the standard administration of the DEAP WIA in two ways. First and foremost, it is a unique feature of the present study that repeated productions were elicited in both JC and English. Language-specific assessors (bilingual speakers of JC and English and monolingual speakers of English) elicited items in a given language by first reminding the child to speak in JC or English and then prompting the target item by saying, "What is this?" for English or, "Wa dis?" for JC. Elicitation was blocked by language, and the order of language elicitation was counterbalanced across participants. Second, in a deviation from the standard WIA protocol, each item was elicited in three consecutive productions in the present sample. We return to this difference in our discussion below, since it has the potential to impact our primary measure of interest, token-to-token variability. Finally, the present study analyzed eleven of the twenty-five words on the DEAP WIA. These eleven words were previously validated for the Jamaican context for the age group of children included in this study (Washington et al. 2017).

All productions were recorded using a ZOOM H4N portable recorder with a MOVO LV4-C XLR cardiod lavalier microphone. The microphone was attached on a fitted vest worn by the child in an effort to optimize acoustic quality by controlling for extraneous noise from movement and clothing. Samples were digitized with a sampling rate of 22KHz and 24-bit encoding.

Measurement

All repetitions of the eleven DEAP WIA words that were validated for use with JC-speaking children were isolated from session-level audio recordings using Praat acoustic software. Acoustic and orthographic information for these words were then read into Phon (Rose and Hedlund, 2016), a software designed to facilitate transcription and analysis of speech samples. Broad transcription of each item was then completed following a consensus procedure detailed below, based on that adopted by Macrae and Sosa (2015).

Four undergraduate and graduate students in the Communicative Sciences and Disorders department at New York University underwent training to transcribe the participants' productions from the DEAP WIA evaluation. These students had previous experience using the International Phonetic Alphabet (IPA) to transcribe the speech of children with and without speech sound disorders. Students were informed that only broad transcription was required, but that they were free to include allophonic details that they perceived as salient or important, for example, to indicate that a child's derhotacized /ɹ/ falls somewhere between /ɹ/ and /w/. For transcriptions in the JC elicitation context, the transcribers received training using the book *Writing Jamaican the Jamaican Way* (Jamaican Language Unit 2009), as well as additional practice guided by the third author, a native speaker of JC and principal investigator of the Jamaican Creole Language Project. In this training practice, the students transcribed an adult native speaker of JC producing the items from the DEAP WIA evaluation. After transcribing all tokens, the students received feedback on their transcriptions from the second and third authors.

The consensus procedure was carried out using the blind transcription feature in Phon. This allowed two students to independently transcribe each session without seeing each other's transcriptions. A consensus transcriber then viewed both original transcriptions and could either endorse one of the two options or make additional modifications. The two consensus transcribers, the second and third authors, have extensive experience transcribing the speech of children with and without speech sound disorders. Both consensus transcribers are native speakers of American English; the third author only, is a native speaker of JC and Jamaican English. The transcriptions selected by the consensus transcriber were subsequently used to evaluate the consistency of each speaker's productions across the three repetitions of each word.

Following the standard procedure for scoring the DEAP WIA (which has also been used in previous studies of variability in children's transcribed speech), tokens were coded as consistent or inconsistent (1/0) based on broad transcriptions of each token across the three repetitions. A token was transcribed as inconsistent if there was at least one difference in one segment across the three productions of that token in either language (for example, English: /fɪʃ/-/fɪs/-/fɪʃ/; JC /ɛlifant/-/ɛləfən/-/ɛləfant/). Tokens were coded for consistency and inconsistency independent of whether the child's output featured errors relative to the adult target (that is, three repetitions of /fɪs/ would be coded as consistent). Vowel length distinctions are phonemic in JC but not in English. Therefore, if repetitions differed only in transcribed vowel length, this was coded as consistent in English but inconsistent in JC. We return to this point in the Discussion section.

Analyses

Two statistical models were constructed to address our two main research questions: one for the group analysis assessing whether bilingual children acquiring JC and English are more variable/inconsistent than monolingual children, and the other for the language analysis evaluating whether bilingual children are more variable/inconsistent in the JC context compared to the English context. Logistic mixed-effect models were used for both analyses. Models were fitted using the lme4 package (Bates et al. 2015) in RStudio (RStudio Team 2015).

Group Analysis

The first research question focuses on differences in token-to-token variability between the bilingual and monolingual children in the English language context. To answer the first question, a logistic mixed-effects model was used to evaluate variability in transcribed repeated productions in English by these two groups of children. The binary classification of consistency (1 = consistent, 0 = inconsistent) served as the dependent variable in the model. The independent variable of primary interest was language group (monolingual versus bilingual). However, as noted above, the two groups also differed in mean age even after selecting the older subset of the children from Macrae and Sosa (2015). Therefore, age in months was included as a control variable, along with the interaction between age and language group. Random intercepts were included to reflect the fact that observations were nested within speakers and words.

Language Analysis

The second research question aims to examine differences in token-to-token variability between the JC and English language contexts in the bilingual group only. For this question, a logistic mixed-effects model was used to evaluate variability in bilingual children's transcribed repeated productions across these two language contexts. As in the model described above, consistency across three repetitions of a word (coded as 1 or 0) served as the dependent variable. The fixed effects included language context (JC versus English), age in months, and the interaction between age and language context. Random intercepts for speaker and word were included as described above.

Results

For the first experimental question, participants in the bilingual group were significantly more consistent than participants in the monolingual group ($\beta = 1.30$, $SE = 0.64$, $p = 0.04$). Age was not a significant predictor of consistency ($\beta = $ -1.10, $SE = 1.42$, $p = 0.44$), nor was there a significant interaction between age and language condition ($\beta = 1.49$, $SE = 1.44$,

p = 0.30). Summary results from the model are presented in Table 4.2. The results from this model suggest that, contrary to our hypothesis, bilingual children in our pilot sample were less variable, or more consistent, than monolingual children in the companion sample (Figure 4.1). The results further suggest that this finding cannot be dismissed as an artefact of the difference in age between groups, since there was no significant effect of age in the model.

In the second model comparing variability across languages in the bilingual group, the English elicitation context was associated with significantly greater consistency than the JC context (β = 1.03, SE = 0.48, p = 0.03). Age was not a significant predictor of consistency (β = 0.62, SE = 0.34, p = 0.07), nor was there a significant interaction between age and

Table 4.2. Full Output of the First Model, Including Coefficients, Standard Errors (SE), z-values, and p-values for all Fixed Effects and Variance for all Random Effects

Fixed effect	Coefficient	SE	z-value	p-value
intercept	-1.00	0.61	-1.63	0.10
group	1.30	0.64	2.03	0.04
age	-1.10	1.42	-0.77	0.44
age:group	1.49	1.44	1.04	0.30
Variance of Random Effects: Subject 0.3492, Word 0.7481				

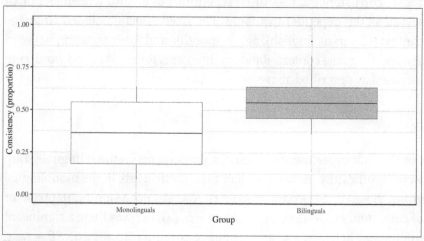

Figure 4.1. Consistency by Group

Table 4.3. Full Output of the Second Model, Including Coefficients, Standard Errors (SE), z-values, and p-values for all Fixed Effects and Variance for all Random Effects

Fixed effect	Coefficient	SE	z-value	p-value
intercept	-0.49	0.51	-0.96	0.34
language	1.03	0.48	2.16	0.03
age	1.62	0.34	1.84	0.07
age:language	-0.01	0.47	-0.02	0.98
Variance of Random Effects: Subject 0.4522, Word 1.6285				

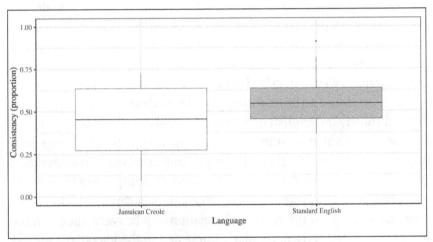

Figure 4.2. Consistency by Language

language (β = -0.01, SE = 0.47, p = 0.98). Summary model results are presented in table 4.3. The results from the second analysis suggest that, consistent with our hypothesis, the bilingual children in our sample were less variable when producing words in English compared to JC (figure 4.2).

Discussion

This pilot study investigated variability in repeated productions of words across two groups: bilingual children speaking JC and English and monolingual children speaking English. Diagnosing speech sound disorders in bilingual populations has been a challenge for SLPs, mostly due to the lack of diagnostic tools available to clinicians to assess these populations

(Skahan et al. 2007). Previous studies have used different types of diagnostic markers when assessing phonological development in bilinguals. One proposed diagnostic marker of speech sound disorder in bilingual children is token-to-token production variability (Preston and Seki 2011). However, there has been disagreement over whether variability in production is considered a normal characteristic or a sign of disorder in speech development (Holm et al. 2007; Macrae and Sosa 2015). Factors affecting variability in speech range from speaker-specific characteristics such as age (Macrae 2013) and expressive vocabulary size (Macrae 2013; Sosa and Stoel-Gammon 2012), stimulus-specific properties such as word frequency and density (Sosa and Stoel-Gammon 2012), and variability and degree of acoustic overlap in the input (Bosch and Ramon-Casas 2011; Sundara and Scutellaro 2011). Here, we are particularly interested in variability in token-to-token productions between bilinguals and monolinguals that could possibly be explained by differences in the variability of their input.

While studies examining bilingual development in children have focused mostly on English and Spanish speakers (Fabiano-Smith and Barlow 2010; Fabiano-Smith and Goldstein 2010), other language pairings such as JC and English have been understudied in the literature (Washington 2012; Washington et al.,2017). It is important to examine a wide range of language pairings, since languages may interact differently, depending on the typological relationship between them. In the present study, we were particularly interested in the idea that a greater degree of lexical-phonological overlap between two input languages may lend itself to greater variability in production (Bosch and Ramon-Casas 2011). For this reason, the main goal of this paper is to take a step towards understanding the nature of output patterns in children exposed to two languages that overlap phonologically and lexically.

The current study addressed two main questions: 1) whether there are differences in token-to-token variability between bilingual children acquiring JC and English and monolingual children acquiring English, and 2) whether bilingual children are more variable across repeated productions in JC compared to English.

Summary of the Major Findings

The second research question tested for differences in token-to-token variability in Jamaican Creole compared to English for the bilingual group. We found a significant effect of language on variability, such that tokens produced in the English context were more consistent than the tokens produced in the JC context. This is consistent with the hypothesis that Creole languages, which exist on a continuum of speaking variants in a multilingual or diglossic society (Kouwenberg and Singler 2008), may be more tolerant of variability than languages that are associated with primarily monolingual, monodialectal communities.

Limitations

We have identified four major limitations to be addressed in future follow-up research. The first limitation was the small sample size of the present study, with only nine children representing the bilingual group and eleven in the monolingual sample. Such small samples may yield results that are not representative in the broader population, limiting the external validity of our results. Indeed, sampling error is apparent in the case of gender in the JC-speaking sample: although no efforts were made to recruit one gender over another, the convenience sample we obtained consisted of eight females and only one male. This gender imbalance represents another potential confound, because unlike the bilingual sample, the monolingual sample was balanced in gender (five males). Effects of gender have been found in studies investigating vocabulary size and speech development, with girls typically showing better language skills than boys (Bornstein et al. 1999; Eriksson et al. 2012). Thus, the lower overall variability observed in the Jamaican Creole group could potentially have been influenced by the higher percentage of females in that sample.

Age differences between the two groups may also have influenced token-to-token variability in production. The bilingual group was older (M=4;4, SD=1.2) than the monolingual group (M=3;6, SD=0.3), even after hand-selecting the oldest individuals from the monolingual sample. Thus, it is possible that the lower variability observed in the bilingual group was in part attributable to their higher mean age. However, age was included as a controlled covariate in both group (bilingual versus monolingual) and language (Jamaican Creole versus English) analyses, and it did not emerge as a significant predictor of token-to-token variability in either model, nor did it engage in significant interactions. This finding makes it less probable that age played a role in the unexpected results found for the group analysis in the present study. Nevertheless, future studies comparing two populations with regard to speech variability should certainly aim to achieve better age matching across groups.

That said, studies examining the effects of age on production variability have yielded inconsistent results. While some have argued that age plays an important role in determining variability (Holm et al. 2007), other studies have disputed this account (Macrae and Sosa 2015; Sosa and Stoel-Gammon 2012). For example, Macrae and Sosa (2015) found that the effect of age disappears when controlling for expressive vocabulary skills. The general idea is that children with small vocabularies tend to have incomplete or poorly specified representations of words (Metsala and Walley 1998), which then results in greater variability in the output. Thus, future research should not only balance or control for a possible effect of age, but also measure and control for expressive vocabulary. This may be especially important in the context of bilingual development, since vocabulary development may appear slower when divided across two languages; a bilingual speaker's variability in a given language should be considered in relation to their measured expressive vocabulary in that language.

A third limitation of the present study is the fact that different coding schemes for transcription across different languages of elicitation may have had an effect on the results. Any alternation in vowel duration (long-short) was coded as inconsistent in the JC context but as consistent in the English context. There was a linguistic rationale for this difference in coding scheme: transcription-based coding of variability in previous literature has consistently used broad (phonemic) rather than narrow transcription, and long-short vowel alternations are phonemic in JC but not in English. However, transcribers in the present study were not speakers of Jamaican Creole, which may have affected their choices in coding the phonemic length contrast in JC. Transcribers' lesser degree of familiarity in transcribing JC may also have played a role in our second finding, that variability was greater in JC than in English. It is possible that listeners are more attentive to fine phonetic detail when transcribing speech in an unfamiliar language versus their native language, and this could have contributed to increased variability in their transcription choices for the JC context. To evaluate this possibility, we conducted a post hoc analysis evaluating reliability across raters in coding a given set of three tokens as consistent versus inconsistent. The results from this analysis, revealed pairwise agreement of 69 per cent, which falls below ideal expectations. We return to this point below with a discussion of strategies that might be adopted to ensure that transcribers are similarly able to judge variability across languages. Importantly, however, inter-rater agreement was identical across the JC and English transcription contexts. This suggests that the difference in variability across language contexts is not wholly attributable to differences in rater familiarity and corresponding differences in the stability of ratings. Of course, further investigation will be necessary to make this claim with confidence.

Lastly, differences in the elicitation procedure across the bilingual and monolingual samples are likely to have played an important role in shaping the results of the group analysis. The standard elicitation procedure for the DEAP WIA is to elicit the complete word list in three repetitions, separated by other activities. The standard elicitation procedure was followed in the monolingual group from Macrae and Sosa (2015). In the bilingual group in the present study, however, elicitation in both JC and English involved three consecutive repetitions of each word. Because speakers may tend to retrieve and reuse the same phonological and/or motor plan when producing the same word multiple times in close proximity, the method used here may tend to underestimate variability in our sample. Future data collection will adhere to the standard protocol to avoid this confound.

Given the limitations of this pilot study, the present results cannot be seen as providing robust evidence either for or against our initial hypotheses. Data collection from a larger sample is ongoing in a National Institutes of Health funded research project (PI Washington). With a larger sample size, groups that are well-balanced in age as well as gender, and elicitation that adheres to the standard protocol, we will be able to better evaluate our hypotheses.

Future Directions

This pilot study was a first step in investigating production variability in children acquiring JC and English, an understudied language pairing characterized by similar phonologies and extensive cognate overlap between the languages. Contrary to our hypothesis, the results revealed greater variability in transcribed token-to-token productions in a previously collected monolingual sample compared to the present sample of bilingual children. Given the aforementioned limitations in the procedure and the presence of confounding differences in age and gender, we do not interpret these results as conclusive. Instead, we plan to address the limitations of this study and then revisit our research questions. In follow-up data collection that is currently ongoing, we have adjusted our elicitation procedure such that it matches the standard approach used with the monolingual comparison group. We will also collect a larger sample that is better matched to the monolingual sample with respect to age and gender.

Finally, to control for possible differences in coding practices used by research assistants when transcribing JC and English, we are in the process of developing a more extensive procedure for training and consensus transcription, for example, expanded training materials and more opportunities to discuss transcription decisions with the authors. Once these issues have been addressed, we hope this work will provide new insight on the effects of bilingual versus monolingual input on children's variability across repeated speech productions. The long-term goal is to arrive at a better understanding of bilingual language development, which may then allow for improved recommendations for diagnosis and treatment of speech disorders in this growing but underserved population.

REFERENCES

American Speech-Language-Hearing Association. (2023). Profile of ASHA Multilingual Service Providers, Year-End 2022. [online]. Retrieved from: https://www.asha.org/siteassets/surveys/2022-profile-of-multilingual-service-providers.pdf

Bates, Douglas, Martin Maechler, Benjamin Bolker, and Stephen Walker. (2015). *lme4: Linear mixed-effects models using Eigen and S4. R package version 1.1–7. 2014.*

Bornstein, Marc H., Ann M.Selmi, O. M. Haynes, Kathleen M.Painter, and Eric S. Marx. 1999. "Representational Abilities and the Hearing Status of Child/Mother Dyads".*Child Development* 70 (4): 833–52.

Bosch, Laura, and Marta Ramon-Casas. 2011. "Variability in Vowel Production by Bilingual Speakers: Can Input Properties Hinder the Early Stabilization of Contrastive Categories?" *Journal of Phonetics*39 (4): 514–26.

Bradford, Amanda, and Barbara Dodd. 1996. "Do all speech-disordered children have motor deficits?" *Clinical Linguistics and Phonetics* 10 (2): 77–101.

Byers-Heinlein, Krista, and Christopher T. Fennell. 2014. "Perceptual Narrowing in the Context of Increased Variation: Insights From Bilingual Infants". *Developmental Psychobiology*56 (2),:274–91.

Devonish, Hubert, and Otelemate Harry. 2008. "Jamaican Creole and Jamaican English: Phonology". In *Varieties of English, 2, The Americas and the Caribbean*, edited by Bernt Kortmann and Edgar Schneider, 256–89. Berlin, New York: De Gruyer Mouton.

Dodd, Barbara, and Paul McCormack. 1995. "A Model of Speech Processing for Differential Diagnosis of Phonological Disorders". In *Differential Diagnosis and Treatment of Children with Speech Disorder*, edited by Barbara Dodd, 65–89. London, Philadelphia:Whurr Publishers.

Dodd, Barbara, Zhu Hua, Sharon Crosbie, Alison Holm, and AnneOzanne. 2009. *Diagnostic Evaluation of Articulation and Phonology US Edition (DEAP).* San Antonio, TX: Pearson.

Dunn, Lloyd M., and Douglas M. Dunn. 2007. *Peabody picture vocabulary test, fourthedition,* (PPVT-4). Circle Pines, MN: American Guidance Services.

Ehrler, David J., and Ronnie L. McGhee. 2008. *The Primary Test of Nonverbal Intelligence (PTONI)* Austin, TX: Pro-Ed Eriksson, Marten, Peter Marschik, Tiia Tulviste, Margaretta Almgren, Miguel Pérez Pereira, Sonja Wehberg, Ljubica Marjanovic-Umek, Frederique Gayraud, Melita Kovacevic and,Carlos Gallegofei. 2012. "Differences Between Girls and Boys in Emerging Language Skills: Evidence from 10 Language Communities". *British Journal of Developmental Psychology* 30 (2): 326–43.

Fabiano-Smith, Leah, and Jessica A. Barlow. 2010. "Interaction in Bilingual Phonological Acquisition: Evidence from Phonetic Inventories". *International Journal of Bilingual Education and Bilingualism* 13 (1): 81–97.

Fabiano-Smith, Leah, and Brian Goldstein. 2010. "Phonological Acquisition in Bilingual Spanish–English speaking Children". *Journal of Speech, Language, and Hearing Research* 50 (1): 160–78.

Fabiano-Smith, Leah., and Katherine Hoffman. 2018. "Diagnostic Accuracy of Traditional Measures of Phonological Ability for Bilingual Preschoolers and Kindergarteners". *Language, Speech & Hearing Services in Schools*, 49 (1): 121–34.

Felsenfeld, S., P.A. Broen, and M. McGue. (1994). "A 28-year Follow-up of Adults With a History of Moderate Phonological Disorder: Educational and Occupational Results". *Journal of Speech, Language, and Hearing Research* 37 (6): 1341–53.

Goffman, Lisa, LouAnn Gerken, and Julie Lucchesi. 2007. "Relations Between Segmental and Motor Variability in Prosodically Complex Nonword Sequences". *Journal of Speech, Language, and Hearing Research* 50 (2): 444–58.

Goldman, R., and M Fristoe. (2000. "Test of Articulation-2" 2nd edition. Circle Pines, MN: American Guidance Service. Harry, Otelamate G. 2006. "Jamaican Creole". *Journal of the International Phonetic Association* 36 (1): 125–31.

Hitchcock, Elaine R., Daphne Harel, and Tara McAllister Byun. 2015. "Social, Emotional, and Academic Impact of Residual Speech Errors in School-Aged Children: A Survey Study". *Seminars in Speech and Language* 36 (4): 283–94. Holm, Alison, Sharon Crosbie, and Barbara Dodd. (2007. "Differentiating Normal Variability from Inconsistency in Children's Speech: Normative Data". *International Journal of Language andCommunication Disorders* 42 (4): 467–86.

Holm, Alson, Barbara Dodd, Carol Stow, and Sean Pert.1999. "Identification and Differential Diagnosis of Phonological Disorder in Bilingual Children". *Language Testing* 16(3): 271–92.

Jamaican Language Unit. 2009. *Writing Jamaican the Jamaican Way*. Kingston, Jamaica: Arawak Publications.

Kouwenberg, Silvia, and John VictorSingler, eds. 2008. *The Handbook of Pidgin and Creole Studies* (Vol. 38). Malden, MA: Wiley-Blackwell.

Macrae,Toby. 2013. "Lexical and Child-related Factors in Word Variability and Accuracy in Infants". *Clinical Linguistics and Phonetics* 27 (6–7): 497–507.

Macrae, Toby, and A.V. Sosa. 2015. "Predictors of Token-to-token Inconsistency in Preschool Children with Typical Speech-language Development". *Clinical Linguistics and Phonetics* 29 (12): 922–37.

Metsala, Jamie L., and Amanda C. Walley. 1998. "Spoken Vocabulary Growth and the Segmental Restructuring of Lexical Representations: Precursors to Phonemic Awareness and Early Reading Ability". In *Word recognition in beginning literacy*, edited by Jamie L. Metsala and Linnea C. Ehri, 89–120. Mahwah, NJ,: Lawrence Erlbaum Associates Publishers.

Pearson, Barbara Zurer, Sylvia C. Fernandez, Vanessa Lewedeg, and D. Kimbrough Oller,1997. "The Relation of Input Factors to Lexical Learning by Bilingual Infants". *Applied Psycholinguistics* 18 (1): 41–58.

Preston, Jonathan L., and Ayumi Seki. 2011. "Identifying Residual Speech Sound Disorders in Bilingual Children: A Japanese-English Case Study". *American Journal of Speech-Language Pathology*20 (2): 73–85.

Rose, Yvan, and Gregory Hedlund. 2016. *Phon 2.1 [Computer software]*.

RStudio Team. 2015. RStudio: Integrated development for R. *RStudio, Inc., Boston, MA URL Http://Www. Rstudio. Com, 42, 14*.

Shriberg, LawrenceD., Diane Austin, Barbara A. Lewis, Jane L. McSweeny, and David L. Wilson. 1997. "The Speech Disorders Classification System (SDCS): Extensions and Lifespan Reference Data". *Journal of Speech, Language, and Hearing Research* 40 (4): 723–40.

Skahan, Sarah, Maggie Watson, and Gregory L. Lof. 2007. "Speech-language Pathologists' Assessment Practices for Children with Suspected Speech Sound Disorders: Results of a National Survey". *American Journal of Speech-Language Pathology* 16 (3): 246–59

Sosa, Anna Vogel. Vogel. 2015. "Intraword Variability in Typical Speech Development". *American Journal of Speech-Language Pathology*24 (1): 24–35.

_____. and Carol Stoel-Gammon. 2006. "Patterns of Intra-word Phonological Variability During the Second Year of Life". *Journal of Child Language*33 (1): 31–50.

Sundara, Megha., and Adrienne Scutellaro. 2011. "Rhythmic Distance Between Languages Affects the Development of Speech Perception in Bilingual Infants". *Journal of Phonetics* 39 (4): 505–13.

Washington, Karla N. 2012. "Translation to Practice: Typical Bidialectal Speech Acquisition in Jamaica". In *Multilingual Aspects of Speech Sound Disorders in Children*, edited by S. McLeod and B.A. Goldstein, 101–105. Bristol, UK: Multilingual Matters.

_____, Megan McDonald, Sharynne McLeod, Kathryn Crowe, and Hubert Devonish. 2017. "Validation of the Intelligibility in Context Scale for Jamaican Creole-speaking Pre-schoolers". *American Journal of Speech-Language-Pathology* 26 (3): 750–61.

Williams, Kathleen T. 2007. *Expressive Vocabulary Test,*Second Edition (EVT-2) Coushatta, LA: Pearson Assessments.

CHAPTER 5

Caribbeanizing a Culturally Responsive Approach

Dub and Dancehall Literacy

LISA TOMLINSON

INTRODUCTION

To ensure a safe and welcoming learning environment, instructional spaces[1] must be responsive to learners' cultural needs. Hence, in order to enrich Caribbean learners' cultural and linguistic identity, literacy programmes must take into full account Caribbean cultural materials.[2] Bearing in mind that learners come into learning spaces with individual and defined social experiences that help to shape who they are (Apple 1995; Beegle 2000). As such, a culturally responsive pedagogy can be used to achieve teaching success. Gloria Ladson-Billings introduced the term "Culturally Relevant Teaching" (CRT) to describe teaching as "a pedagogy that empowers students intellectually, socially, emotionally, and politically by using cultural referents to impart knowledge, skills, and attitudes."[3] In this way, CRT "integrates a student's [learner's] background knowledge and prior home and community experiences into the curriculum and the teaching and learning experiences that take place in the classroom [instructional spaces]."

Other theorists, such as Gay (2000) and Villegas and Lucas (2000), use the terms "Culturally Responsive Teaching" or "Culturally Responsive Pedagogy" (CRP) interchangeably to describe teaching that takes into account the diverse ways learners acquire knowledge and that these differences may be tied to a number of variables like background, community, family structure, language, and social or cultural identity. Theorists and practitioners of culturally responsive pedagogy go beyond simply acknowledging the "cultural uniqueness" of each learner nor does it mirror the face of traditional multiculturalism; instead they purposely cultivate cultural diversity in the classroom in order to build and facilitate effective conditions for learning. As such, Gay points out that the users of this practice should competently draw on the learner's cultural knowledge, prior experiences, and performance styles to make learning more appropriate and effective, further emphasising that this pedagogy "teaches to and through the strengths of these students. It is culturally validating and affirming".

Given the multicultural nature of some societies, this learning approach has been adapted in places such as Ontario, Canada to address the diverse needs of learner population. Uniquely, this approach has also been applied in correctional institutions to facilitate music instruction to incarcerated African American youths. In this way, incarcerated African American youths were able to connect to their vernacular culture, among other culturally relevant themes expressed in hip hop lyrics, to achieve musical success while also developing critical consciousness. The use of this non-conventional approach to teaching, attempts to do more than just celebrate African American music forms, but rather acknowledges that the process of learning can be multifaceted as well as validating the learners' home language and culture.

In addition, culturally responsive pedagogy consists of three dimensions in its delivery: (i) institutional, (ii) personal, and (iii) instructional. While theorists cite that all three dimensions are foundational to the establishment of an inclusive school learning culture, the final section of this paper will take up only the use of the instructional and personal dimension in the facilitation of literacy instruction and language learning in the Caribbean. As the aim of this section is to build on the transformative approach to acquiring different forms of literacy, I will highlight the ways in which the use of the two dimensions (instructional and personal), departing from the traditional teacher-centred approach, can help in the process of consciousness raising and the facilitation of language instruction. Given that the multiple forms of oral literacy such as music, have been previously examined elsewhere, by means of critical literacy paradigm, I will look at acquiring literacy through "oral texts" with an emphasis on the use of other oral literature such as Jamaican dub poetry, dancehall lyrics, and Caribbean proverbs. First, I will begin the section with a brief description of the author's initial use of this teaching pedagogy in a community-based setting of adult learners. Then, I will contextualize the culturally responsive framework within a Jamaican literacy instructional space. Significantly, this proposal also has strong implications for school districts in North America and the United Kingdom – regions with robust Caribbean diasporas, yet not enough representation in the teaching profession.

Adult Literacy and a Cultural Response Teaching

Instructional dimension includes having good knowledge of your learners and considering the practices of the learning environment that results in a culturally responsive instructional setting. The personal dimension incorporates the thoughts of culturally responsive educators and the practices they take on to support the development of all learners. Culturally responsive educators are not only self-aware, but they also possess an in-depth understanding of their learners and how they can best learn. Hence, the idea of applying culturally responsive pedagogy to teach adult literacy came out of the author's teaching experience in Toronto, Canada. In the early 2000s, she taught a beginner to intermediate adult literacy group. The literacy programme was operated in a local community health centre. The programme was funded by UNICEF – the United Nations Children's Fund – and the Ontario provincial government. The learning objectives were based on individual goals. For instance, some of the learners wanted to improve their literacy skills to fill out forms, read the daily newspaper, or to assist with their children's homework. The programme was based on an ongoing intake and the learners attended the programme three times per week. The class consisted of adult men and women ranging in age from 25 to 55 years-old who came mainly from the Caribbean (Jamaica, St Vincent and Grenada respectively). There were two students who came from English-speaking African countries and one student was a Canadian-born white person.

Given the fact that a large percentage of the students came from the Caribbean, it provided the ideal opportunity to include culturally appropriate material originating primarily from that region. Therefore, a culturally responsive approach was applied wherein the students were encouraged to draw upon personal experiences, cultural history as well as prior knowledge of their learning experiences. Anansi stories, Creole-based proverbs and later the author shared dub poetry along with other genres of Caribbean poetry (short in length and easy-to-read) written in Standard English (SE) and the nation languages of the different countries. The use of storytelling and proverbs as instructional tools were also relatable to the West African students who came from cultural backgrounds where orality is valued as a transmitter of knowledge and folk wisdom. The West African learners were also encouraged to draw on proverbs that were non-English and that were written in their respective languages. The following sections will expound on the use of proverbs and dub poetry as two of the many instructional resources that were used in the literacy programme.

Literacy and the Socio-cultural Conscious Educator

Villegas and Lucas identify several characteristics of culturally responsive educators. Here, I draw on socio-cultural consciousness and the constructivist approach because both styles encourage active learning as well as force learners to reflect critically on what is being taught. The former approach is also aimed at the educators' skill to inculcate knowledge through a socially conscious lens. For instance, in drawing on the learners' prior knowledge of Creole proverbs, I began with a general discussion that involved soliciting questions from learners which allowed them to reflect on the different struggles they have faced, major crises in their lives, and decisions they have had to make, all tying back to the proverbs with which they were familiar. I also posed specific questions such as whether their own experiences correlated with proverbs and whether these popular sayings helped them to better understand their day-to-day realities. The use of this actual cultural text (proverbs) to instruct literacy supported a culturally responsive pedagogy because it took into consideration the learners' prior learning experiences and their linguistic background. The proverbs were taken from both the students' memory as well as popular songs and they represented a broad spectrum of the Caribbean. Most students recognized the proverbs and were able to come up with proverbs of their own that carried specific cultural meaning in their environment as well as how these various proverbs served as guidance throughout their lives. More considerably, the students got the chance to use the nation languages without shame or trepidation as they related the proverbs to the group. For example, a Jamaican student excitedly recalled and blurted out the proverb "fiyah deh a muss muss tail him tink a cool breeze" in which she explained to the students that her grand-aunt regularly uttered the proverbial expression as a warning to be aware of danger and not to be naïve. From this exercise, students were also able to make linguistic comparisons with how the proverbs are said in their own nation language.

In general, the learners recognized that the proverbs were better understood in their early adult years and they still found themselves passing down these cautionary sayings to their children (especially the women). Proverbs, for much of the learners' lives, essentially served as a source of worldview and for the first time, all the learners admitted that the use of their nation language can be meaningful and can be drawn on to express important thoughts such as expert advice. One student openly confessed that, for him, Caribbean proverbs had very little value because the Creole somehow distorted or interfered with the intended meaning(s). The learner's response to what he believed to be the inability of Creole to convey important messages, took me back to Louise Bennett's popular poem "Jamaica Philosophy". When Aunty Roachy describes Jamaican proverb as philosophy, the antagonist Muches is flabbergasted that the "deestant" word such as philosophy can be used to describe "de ole jamma bad talkin proverbs-dem". Bennett's legitimizing proverbs (*in spite of them being expressed in Jamaican*) reveal how African Caribbean people "have consciously used and understood proverbs as central in their lives and pointedly, avoid obeisance to European prescriptions".

According to Paulo Freire, the working-class poor, despite their continued oppression, marginalization and disparagement at the hands of the elite and dominant culture, nonetheless have access to forms of wisdom and knowledge that arise through day-to-to experience via proverbs. In the preface to his book *Jamaican Sayings,* Watson concurs with Freire as he highlights proverbs as "an ongoing process of cultural and historical reappraisal and synthesis taking place in the lives of Caribbean people". Therefore, an instructor using a CRP approach that includes proverbs, should not only have knowledge of proverbs, but also, he or she must see them as culturally relevant to learners' lived realities as advocated by Freire and Watson as well, instructors ought to see its use as a valuable learning tool.

As expected, several learners were unfamiliar with the written version of the Anansi stories and there were some challenges. For instance, the spelling of the word "Anansi" and the overall spelling of the Creole words were new to many of the learners even though there is an existing orthography for Jamaican Creole (JC). However, not many people know about this writing system found in the Cassidy and LePage *Dictionary of Jamaican English,* nor are they aware of the codified version of JC which was prepared by linguists at the Jamaica Language Unit of the University of the West Indies, Mona Campus. Also, take into consideration, the nation languages are simply not used as a model of formal language instruction in the Caribbean classrooms.

The introduction of dub poetry as a learning resource was also a new instructional approach for students because the literary genre had never been taught to them while in school. Some of the students, however, were acquainted with dub or the aesthetics of oral performance and knew of a few dub poets from the region. The thematic elements of the poems were especially germane to learners because one of the poets included in the lesson, highlighted social issues facing their respective countries. Mutaburuka's poem, *Nursery Rhyme Lament* for instance, got the attention of the learners because it discussed the harsh reality of poverty and the struggles of the working-class in urban Jamaica:

Fus time, jack an' jill
Use fi run up de hill every day
Now dem get pipe, wata rate increase
Every day dem woulda reincarnate humpty dumpty
Fi fall of de wall, likkle bway blue
Who love to blow him horn to de sheep in the meadow
Likkle bway blue grow up now

An' de sheep dem get curried
Ina likkle cold suppa shap dang de street

Yuh rememba wen man dida panda fi guh moon
Yet dem did 'ave de cat a play fiddle
Suh de cow coulda jump ova it every full moon
An' . . . lite bill increase
. . . Den there was de old ooman
Who neva huh nuh family plannin clinic
She use fi live somewhey dung a back-o-wall
Ina a lef' foot shoe
Back-o-wall tun Tivoli Gardens now
Suh she move

Kack sprat . . . yes jack sprat
Who could'nt stan' fat
Him start eat it now
But him son turn vegetarian
'Cause meat scarce.

The theme of poverty expressed in the poem also resonated with the learner's current situation in Toronto. As we discussed the poem's subject matter, they took advantage of this opportunity to voice the difficulty to meet their daily domestic commitments (that is, cost of food, paying bills, and so on.). Issues of chronic unemployment and accessing adequate housing were also of concern for many of the learners. Once again, the students were captivated that a meaningful critique could be taken from the language itself or rather, that the language can be expressed so effectively in poetry form. I took this observation as the students' way of unconsciously or consciously discerning that the "broken" and or "bad" language they were often taught to accept, can perchance be anything near literature. For instance, a male student remarked that for him, growing up in a colonial educational system in St Vincent, poetry meant William Shakespeare or Samuel Coleridge. The students from Nigeria also shared this sentiment and went as far as to remind the group that to be a good poet meant to be "well-read" in SE as well as to demonstrate superior writing skills, again in SE. Another student added that Creole was mainly reserved for the home or for popular culture such as music, but certainly not for formal settings such as, a language classroom. Finally, some of the students were surprised that they were even able to sound out the Creole words on their own considering that they had never learned the structures of the local language in school.

In a similar way, I used historian Afua Cooper's poem *Oh Canada,* which pointed to the immigrant experience of Black Caribbean domestic workers and the exploitation of their labour. This poem especially resounded with the female learners as many of them worked as domestic helpers or held similar low paying jobs as office cleaners. In the poem the speaker recounts:

VII
the missis told her that her duties were
light housekeeping
but she was up from six o'clock to
whenever the family went to bed
which was usually by midnight

VII
cooking
cleaning
washing
ironing
her weekend began saturday night and ended
sunday evening
at five, and this was every other weekend. spring.
time for spring cleaning
her missis told her to climb on the ladder
so she could reach the top windows.

Cooper's poem of the struggle one encounters in the host country, also generated discussion around the theme of poverty. The women learners, however, were more aware of and sensitive to the gender issues that affected their everyday lives. The conversation centred primarily around a gender analysis of the poem. One of the learners pointed out that women with limited literacy skills, like herself, were frequently subjected to a minimal income similar to the worker mentioned in the poem. The learners also voiced their disappointment in having to leave their native countries and still having to struggle to obtain an improved quality of life for both them and their children. In effect, a culturally relevant pedagogy not only takes into account the "individual characteristics of academic achievement and cultural competence" but it also inspires learners (as with the use of critical literacy) to "develop a broader sociopolitical consciousness that allows them to critique the cultural norms, values, mores, and institutions that maintain and produce social inequalities". Therefore, the students were given the opportunity to write about the inequality and discrimination they encountered in Canada using their home language (which some of them proudly shared to the group).

I intentionally selected one of Cooper's poems written in SE to illustrate the poet's capability to traverse between the two languages, Jamaican and Standard English. Consequently, dispelling the view that the usage of Creole can interfere with acquiring SE. Two of the learners, however, still chose not to write their poem in their Creole. These students embraced the belief that, the use of the nation language(s) can interfere with their literacy learning and hinder them from acquiring the requisite knowledge and skills in SE. Contrary to their perception of the use of the local language in a formal learning environment, research studies have shown that the inclusion of students' home language into the classroom resulted in their ability to efficaciously code switch from SE to their local dialect (African American English) as well as gaining better academic success in science and math. Although the research itself did not apply a CRP framework, it evidently speaks to its pedagogical principles that recognize the value in including the learners' home language(s) into their learning experience.

Seemingly, culturally relevant materials such as the Creole proverbs, and dub poetry taken from the indigenous knowledge forms in Caribbean culture, deepened the learning experience and resonated with the culturally responsive needs of the learners, despite the fact that none of the learners were ever instructed in the nation languages. At the same time, the pedagogy allowed for the instructor to see the learners' diversity in terms of strengths rather than as challenges and or deficiencies of the learners or particular communities, which has been the case in learning environments that are inclined to privileging the values of the dominant culture over the home culture. The use of Ebonics in the classroom by African American children, for example, has been described in the educational literature as "verbally deprived", "language impoverished" or "linguistically retarded".

Contrary to linguistic ideologies that position non-standard English varieties in similar terms as Ebonics, many of the learners in the literacy programme demonstrated their creativity in writing poems in Creole, while others exhibited their strength in the performance of the poems itself. Although learners shared similar cultural and linguistic backgrounds, gender analysis in some cases were central in discussing the poems. Sometimes, the close examination of gender or women's experiences made the male learners detach themselves from the discussion although a few made the attempt to participate.

With such an accessible and broad range of oral culture, one can only imagine the nature of learning and the rich synergy that can emerge in a learning environment that incorporates culturally responsiveness to facilitate literacy in Jamaica, the wider Caribbean region or even its diaspora. By engaging popular music, for example, and then engaging in discussion about the lyrics, analysing the use of language, and going further to do research to corroborate related themes expressed in these songs, educators are bound to see constructivist learning in action as learners are empowering their own learning as a result of the catalytic role of popular and culturally relevant materials taken from personal experiences. In accordance with Carolyn Cooper, the music, as in the case of the proverbs, acts as a pedagogical musical source that is both entertaining and instructional. Accordingly, the last section of the paper contextualises the use of culturally responsive pedagogy within a Jamaican learning setting applying dub poetry and dancehall lyrics, with a focus on the Jamaican language.

The Jamaican Experience and Cultural Responsiveness: Dub and Dancehall Literacy

In developing critical thinking and literacy skills, educators are encouraged to assign learners activities that facilitate a comparative analysis of songs alongside other forms of oral literature that already make up their social experiences. As such, dub poetry can be juxtaposed with similar culturally relevant pieces such as dancehall lyrics to heighten students' awareness of Caribbean experiences in and even outside the region. Also, both popular art forms (music and dub poetry) transcend themes of class, gender, race, neo-colonialism and imperialism in the Americas and globally, so the lyrics work well in providing avenues for critical reading. By including culturally specific materials such as lyrics from popular music and other oral art forms of literature such as dub poetry, learners can gain a broader understanding of their cultural sur-roundings and are able to even gain knowledge of social issues impacting their society. Similarly, learners gain insight into cultural and political movements that have helped to shape Caribbean national identity and serve as excellent reference points to Caribbean history.

This inclusion of Caribbean oral traditions complemented with popular music is a more pragmatic way of reshaping the pedagogical realities of Caribbean students while simultaneously improving literacy and language skills. Using dub poetry from other parts of the Caribbean diaspora is another way of exposing students to a wider social and political spectrum, thus helping to shape Caribbean regional identities or simply sharing Caribbean diasporic experiences.

Outside of Jamaica, Canada has one of the largest and thriving dub poetry communities. Interestingly, several dub poets, such as Clifton Joseph from Antigua, Adri Zhina Mandiela from Jamaica and Ishaka from St Vincent, just to name a few, migrated from the Caribbean to Canada, and have subsequently enriched the quality of dub poetry in Canada in terms of subject matter, artistic performances and linguistic variations. These dub poets, originally from the Caribbean, who have settled in Canada, have expanded the repertoire of dub aesthetics. There has been the infusion of jazz and blues rhythms and African cadences, which is very much congruent with what Barbadian historian and poet Kamau Brathwaite has done to written poetry.

Some dub performers also draw on Rastafarian linguistic patterns and cultural aesthetics, while others articulate their personal, political, and social experiences of living in and between the Caribbean and Canada. The presence of Rastafarian unique linguistic patterns add to a CRP in the way that it opens opportunities to closely examine language. Velma Pollard summarizes the various methods that are used by Rastas to decol-onize SE, one of the categories being a morphological implication; for example, making a change to the word oppress to "downpress". This type of linguistic discourse can help a student to become more aware of language change as well as structure.

Returning to my discussion on the use of dub poetry outside of Jamaica, Jamaican-Canadian dub poet, Lillian Allen, for example, critiques police racial profiling in Canada and uses her poems to underscore the Black Caribbean migrant presence. In her poem, *Rub a Dub Style Inna Regent Park,* the focus is on Caribbean migrant experiences in low-income communities in Canada, and teachers can possibly encourage learners to engage in discussions and deep thinking around issues of the socio-economic marginalization of Caribbean immigrants in North America. Allen narrates:

> Monday morning broke
> news of a robbery
> Pam mind went
> couldn't hold the load
> dem took her to the station
> in a paddy wagon
> screaming
> her Johnny got a gun
> from an ex-policeman
> Oh Lawd, Oh Lawd Oh Lawd eh ya
>
> —
>
> forget yu bills them
> an irie up yuself
> forget yu dreams gathering dust
> on the shelves

The major theme in the poem can open dialogue around police violence in Jamaica as well as encouraging learners to link their localized realities of police social containment and harassment within disenfranchised communities in the diaspora. Like the critical literacy approach to Jamaican popular music, cultural responsiveness, permits learners to "develop a critical consciousness through which they challenge the status quo of the current order" and become social activists within their community.

The accessibility of these different types of cultural expressions can also add to a language learning experience for Jamaican learners. The exercises involving critical thinking can extend to language learning by simply getting students to become aware of how linguistic change (as demonstrated with Rastafarian linguistic pattern) can also be influenced by linguistic trends in popular culture. Dancehall artistes, for example, are known to contribute widely to the Jamaican lexicon. A good illustration of such a reconceptualization is offered in the several publications of dancehall dictionaries such as Chester Francis Jackson's *The Official Dancehall Dictionary* (1995) and the more recent, *Dancehall Dictionary: Learning to Speak like a Jamaican* (2014) by Joan Williams and Shawn Grant.

Through their creativity, DJs are constantly adding new vocabulary and expressions to the Jamaican language. For example, words such as "selecta" and "massive" are vocabulary associated with dancehall that has evolved through the culture. Although selector and massive have their specific functional meaning in SE, they have been semantically broadened and given distinctly new meaning, not only to the dancehall culture, but also to the Jamaican language.

Indeed, Caribbean nation languages foster a rich cultural heritage in song, poetry, theatre, folktales, proverbs, riddles, and varied performances, among other cultural expressions. A part of culturally responsive learning pedagogy can be beneficial in encouraging learners to listen to dub lyrics (written in Creole) and then charged with writing down words in their native language. Learners are then instructed to identify unfamiliar words that they do not understand and to discuss them in order to perform contrastive analysis of Jamaican and SE. Furthermore, the lyrics of dancehall music rely on Jamaican as their primary vehicle of expression.

Like the nation languages, dancehall music has been historically treated as an inferior genre. And like the language system, dancehall is not accepted as an appropriate medium for communicating serious thoughts, learning tools, or for carrying socio-political analysis for that matter. However, by using dancehall lyrical content to develop critical thinking skills, learners can also recognize how Creole and the content of this music form can speak to social and political issues, which has been demonstrated throughout this paper with the use of proverbs and dub poetry. Undeniably, the adult learners in the literacy programme garnered a greater appreciation of their nation language once they were able to see its ability to articulate their worldview, function as a literary expression, and possess linguistic properties as SE.

In his thesis, *Jamaican Dancehall: Misconceptions and Pedagogical Advantages*, Owen Joseph maintains that analysing the various facets of dancehall music can assist in the development of critical thinking skills, an element he concludes "is essential to an adolescent's intellectual development" Like the dub poets, many of the dancehall artists use the nation language to critically comment and challenge concerns of the disenfranchised and attack government officials for their neglect of working class communities. Damion Marley's song "Welcome to Jamaica" for example, disrupts the tourist gaze by exposing the daily political violence and struggles of the poor working class:

> Out in the streets, they call it murder
> Welcome to Jamrock, camp where the thugs dem camp at
> Two pound ah weed inna van back
> It inna you hand bag, you knapsack, it inna you backpack
> The smell ah give your girlfriend contact
>
> Some boy nuh know dis, dem only come around like tourist
> On the beach with a few club sodas
> Bedtime stories, and pose like dem name Chuck Norris
> And don't know the real hardcore
>
> Cause Sandals ah nuh Back-To
> The thugs dem will do whe dem got to
> And won't think twice to shot you
> Don't make dem spot you, unless you carry guns a lot too
> A bare tuff tings come at you
>
> When Trench Town man stop laugh and block off traffic
> Then dem wheel and pop off and dem start clap it
> With the pin file dung an it ah beat rapid
> Police come inna jeep and dem can't stop it

Just as Mutaburka's poem *Nursery Rhyme*, learners can engage in an analysis of the lyrics of "Welcome to Jamaica" to examine social concerns affecting the country. Learners can also identify the inventive ways that the DJ adds to the Jamaican lexicon pointing to expressions such as "clap it" which, in this context, imbues an entirely new meaning to refer to the firing of gun shots.

In addition, oral literary forms such as proverbs can certainly be extracted from this exercise with younger learners as both dub and the lyrics of Jamaican popular music such as dancehall incorporate wise sayings. Anand Prahlad's book, *Reggae Wisdom: Proverbs in Jamaican Music*, is quite a useful cultural resource in a discussion of proverbs as the book looks at the use of proverbs and its grounding in a personal and social understanding of reggae discourses. However, from a culturally responsive lens, his book provides a teachable way of familiarizing students with the critical study as a cultural and socio-political expression and serves as a resourceful guide for learners and educators of literacy as well as language education. It is also transformative in a learning space that values oral culture much like how hip-hop has been embraced in many fields of humanities and education, including literacy. *Rhymes with Reason* for example is an interactive online series developed by Austin Martin that teaches college-level vocabulary and American history concepts using hip-hop lyrics rooted in AAVE (African American Vernacular English) or "Ebonics". Closer to home, the University of the West Indies currently offers an undergraduate course entitled *Reggae Poetry* that takes a literary slant as well as a socio-historical look at reggae and dancehall lyrics.

CONCLUSION

Significantly, the use of CRP should not be idealized in its delivery of culturally relevant education and in garnering recognition of learner diversity. The limitation of the CRP must be fully acknowledged and addressed before applying it. While having shared cultural background as learners, educators can still be detached from their social realities which can create personal and professional tension. For example, an educator who harbours negative attitude towards the use of nation language as a tool of instruction or expression in a learning environment, would be unsuccessful in applying culturally relevant material that draws on the home language of the learners. Therefore, the educator must be prepared to develop the knowledge, skills, and characteristics needed to be an effective, culturally responsive instructor. In this way, educators must reaffirm a student's linguistic culture in the classroom as well as the competence of students' experiences and communities in a meaningful way.

As Villegas and Lucas observe about culturally responsive educators, "they use what they know about their students to give them access to their learning". Therefore, coupled with the change in cultural attitude towards the native language, is educators' knowledge of the structures of the language of literacy which in this case is English and Jamaican. Professor Emeritus Beverly Bryan maintains the importance of instructors having a solid knowledge of both English and Jamaican. Bryan stresses that educators today must know the structures which include the mechanics, grammar and spelling systems of the learners' language(s) used in and outside of the classroom. This knowledge will develop the educators' capacity to better assist learners with their awareness of the two languages through risk-taking and "spirit inquiry".

I add that a culturally responsive approach like this will allow students to foster mutual respect for both languages, thus gaining greater appreciation for Jamaican orature as legitimate means of communication and as a sound literary body, and challenge linguistic ideologies that perceive Creole as sub-standard and inferior languages. Addressing practitioners, learners, and researchers of critical literacy approach, Morrell maintains that while "[l]iterature should be critiqued using a variety of historical, social, and cultural lenses, oppressed literatures need to be excavated and promoted with a sense of pride and purpose as well".

Ultimately, pulling from the learner's cultural and linguistic backgrounds as a tool for learning is crucial in culturally responsive pedagogies. The Pedagogy is also a radical step in transforming traditional educational spaces because in many ways it disrupts an educational hegemony that for centuries has privileged one cultural learning style and Euro-Western values, scribal versus oral and nation language versus the standard. CRT recognizes and respects the strengths that a learner's lived realities and home culture along with his or her language carries to the learning environment. Learning experiences are intended to be relevant and realistic, allowing learners to imagine themselves in the daily learning of the instructional spaces.

As Elabor-Idemudia poignantly asserts, "oral features such as ritu-
alistic chants, riddles, songs, folktales and parables, articulate not only
a distinct cultural identity, but also give voice to a range of cultural,
social and political, aesthetic and linguistic systems which have now
been muted by the long history of colonialism and cultural imperialism". Certainly, the oral transmission of cultural lessons, anchored in
a culturally responsive frame, echoes to the learner and the community
that learners, parent(s) and the community's knowledge and experiences
are not only valuable, but they are also paramount in the learning process
and in gaining critical language and literacy skills. Therefore, applying
and fostering a culturally responsive teaching that includes a dancehall
dub-literacy programme of instruction can become the catalyst for radical
educational transformation.

NOTES

1. I use the term instructional spaces to include any other spaces where learn-
    ing can take place other than a formal classroom setting, that is, community
    centres, prisons, adult learning centres, etc.
2. Caribbean cultural material in this context refers to the cultural artefacts drawn
    from the individual Caribbean territories and used in their respective locals.
    For instance, material taken from the oral tradition (i.e., proverbs and folklore),
    or popular music that would likely include the use of the nation languages.
3. Ladson-Billings, Gloria. *The Dream keepers: Successful teachers of African American
    Children.* (San Francisco: Josey Bass. 1994) 18.

REFERENCES

Allen, Lillian. 1993. *Women Do This Every Day: Selected Poems of Lillian Allen.*
Toronto: Women's Press.

Blake, Mary E and Meta Van Sickle. 2001. "Helping Linguistically Diverse Students
Share What They Know". *Journal of Adolescent and Adult Literacy* 44 (5): 468–75.

Brown-Jeffry, Shelly, and Jewel Cooper. 2011. "Toward a Conceptual Framework
of Culturally Relevant Pedagogy".*Teacher Education Quarterly* 31(8): 65–84.

Cooper, Afua. 1982. *Memories Have Tongues.* Toronto: Sister Vision.

Devonish, Hubert. 1996. "Kom Groun Jamiekan Daans Haal Liricks: Memba
SE A Plie Wi A Plie: Contextualizing Jamaican "Dance Hall" music: Jamaican

language at play in a speech event". *English World-Wide* 17(2): 213–37. Accessed10 May 2019. https://doi.org/10.1075/eww.17.2.05dev.

Elabor-Idemudia, Patience. 1998. "The Retention of Knowledge of Folkways as a Basis for Resistance". In *Indigenous Knowledges in Global Contexts:Multiple Readings of ourWorld*, edited by George J. Sefa Dei, Budd L. Hall, and Dorothy Goldin-Rosenberg, 102–19. Toronto: University of Toronto Press.

Watson, G. Llewellyn. 1991. *Jamaican Sayings: With Notes on Folklore, Aesthetics, and Social Control.* Tallahassee, Gainesville, FL: Florida A & M University Press.

Gay, Geneva. 2018. *Culturally Responsive Teaching: Theory, Research, and Practice.* 3rd edition. New York, NY: Teachers College Press.

Joseph, Owen. 2015. *Jamaican Dancehall: Misconceptions and Pedagogical Advantages.* Bloomington, IN: Booktango.

Ladson-Billings, Gloria. 1995. "But That's Just Good Teaching! The Case for Culturally Relevant Pedagogy". *Theory Into Practice* 34(3): 159–65. https://doi.org/10.1080/00405849509543675.

Morrell, Ernest. 2008. *Critical Literacy and Urban Yyout : Pedagogies of Access, Dissent, and Liberation.* New York, NY: Routledge.

Mutabruka. 2015. Nursery Rhyme Lament. *www.jah-lyrics.com.* (https://www.jah-lyrics.com/song/mutabaruka-nursery-rhyme-lament.) (Accessed 16 November 2015.)

Pollard, Velma. 2009. *Dread Talk: The Language of Rastafari.* Kingston: Canoe Press, Montreal and Kingston, London Ithaca, NY: McGill-Queen's University Press.

Richards, Heraldo V., Ayanna F.Brown, and Timothy BForde. 2007. "Addressing Diversity in Schools: Culturally Responsive Pedagogy". *TEACHING Exceptional Children* 39(3). 64–68. https://doi.org/10.1177/004005990703900310.

Thompson, Jason D. 2014. "Towards Cultural Responsiveness in Music Instruction with Black Detained Youth: An Analytic Autoethnography". *Music Education Research* 17(4): 421–36. https://doi.org/10.1080/14613808.2014.930117.

Villegas, Ana María and Tamara Lucas. 2002. "Preparing Culturally Responsive Teachers". *Journal of Teacher Education* 53(1): 20–32. https://doi.org/10.1177/0022487102053001003.

Wolfram, Walt. 1999. "Myth 13: Black Children are Verbally Deprived". In *Language Myths*, edited by Laurie Bauer and Peter Trudgill. London: Penguin.

CHAPTER 6

The Slighted Language Skill

Advocating for Best Practice in Listening Instruction in English as a Second Language

JANICE JULES

INTRODUCTION

While the terms hearing and listening are often used synonymously, suggesting similarity in the two concepts, the distinction in the meanings must be clear. The basis for this clarification is that whereas hearing is a physical ability which enables auditory perceptions of sound waves, listening is an acquired skill resulting in the interpretation of the audible sounds (Ahuja, Ahuja and Ahuja 2010). By its very nature, listening is considered an active cognitive ability that assists human beings in understanding the world (Rost 2015). This faculty is a requisite component in successful communication (Pourhosein, Gilakjani and Sabouri 2016). In fact, in many instances, verbal misunderstanding can be traced back to the hearers' lack of effective listening skills. With this awareness, linguists such as Celce-Murcia (2013) and Morley (2013) find difficulty in assessing the reasons for the nearly total neglect of listening skills during instruction. Yet, it is noteworthy that during the early 1960s, proponents of the Direct Method hypothesised that learners should study the common, everyday speech in the target language and be engaged in some conversational activity to use language in real context (Larsen-Freeman 2000). Hence, Richards and Rodgers (2001) claim that one of the basic principles of the Direct Method was the primary focus given to listening and speaking practices. This environment led to the coining of the term "aural-oral" and the formulation of the phrase "audio-lingual" (Richards and Rodgers 2001). Richards and Rodgers perceive that even today, audio-lingual principles are still being widely used. Nonetheless, Celce-Murcia (2013) asserts that in language teaching, the aural-oral aspect was never given the prominence it deserved.

Furthermore, a brief look at language teaching in the 20th century, with distinct focus on the period from the 1940s through to the 1960s, reveals that little or no consideration was given to listening (Littlewood 2010,Wilcox-Peterson 2013). During those earlier periods, the neglect of listening resulted from pedagogical instructional methods associated with procedures such as the British Situational Approach and the American Audio-lingual Method (Richards and Rodgers 2001). The fundamental principles of these early language learning theories disregarded the importance of aural skills. The fact that listening was labelled as passive, further contributed to the notion that meaningful participation in the skill was not paramount (Celce-Murcia 2013; Morley 2013). An additional area of concern is that because listening seldom received any overt attention in the listeners' native language, its importance and complexity had been concealed (Morley 2013). As a result of the earlier erroneous judgements, over the years authorities in language teaching have deemed listening as the most overlooked skill (Geddes 1989; Littlewood 2010; Morley 2013; Wilcox-Peterson 2013). In other words, for decades, listening was the slighted language skill.

Another point to ponder is that along with listening being rebuffed as a language skill, listening instruction is considered an area that often presents the most challenge to language learners (Celce-Murcia 2013; Morley 2013). For this reason, their success in the acquisition of the target language relies on the teaching and learning environment in which pedagogical best practices are applied through effective materials, activities and instructional strategies (Zemelman, Daniels and Hyde 2012). Attention to these areas creates an environment conducive to the learners' enhanced listening proficiency. According to Wilcox-Peterson (2013), in such a favourable teaching-learning setting, the language instructor is more prepared to provide the most beneficial types of listening and communication activities for learners. Therefore, according to Littlewood

(2010), as learners engage actively, interact, discuss and collaborate, they are better equipped to enhance the development of their listening. In addition, instructors' comprehensive knowledge of the intricacies within the listening process is also a crucial component of the application of instructional best practices.

In this regard, informal observation seems to reveal that in some instances, instructors in English as a Second Language (ESL) in an Anglophone Caribbean setting continue to deliver listening instruction with the notion of best practices left wanting. Thus, based on the aforementioned literature on language teaching and learning, this research focuses on listening instruction at the tertiary level in teaching ESL in an Anglophone Caribbean country. Accordingly, based on data analysis, it is deemed reasonable to advocate for the application of best practice principles in this environment. To this end, the overarching question that guides this research is: "What evidence of the application of best practices in listening instruction is revealed from the naturalistic, persistent observation of a purposive sample (n=25) of students studying ESL in an Anglophone Caribbean setting?"

LITERATURE REVIEW

Repositioning Listening Instruction in ESL

Learners' ability to understand the spoken language and the appropriate application of the acquired knowledge have important roles in second language learning (Renukadevi 2014). For this reason, Renukadevi (2014) considers listening to be the very basic language skill which interrelates and interposes constantly with the other language skills such as speaking, reading and writing. Further, Wilcox-Peterson (2013) points out that listening enables language learners to have the most direct connection to meaning in the target language. "Through listening, learners are able to acquire an awareness of how the language systems of the target language work, and interconnect at various levels, as well as establish a foundation for more fluent productive skills" (Wilcox-Peterson 2013, 87). Consequently, when good listeners are engaged in any type of spoken discourse, there are a number of processes which work simultaneously on various levels to enable them to understand the incoming speech and establish communication (Ahuja, Ahuja and Ahuja 2010; Wilcox-Peterson 2013). In addition, whereas (Renukadevi 2014) the other skills such as reading, speaking and writing are essential to develop language proficiency, the development of language expertise is associated with listening. Bano (2017) denotes that listening must be the most practiced skill to communicate. Moreover, (Renukadevi 2014) as learners understand spoken language by listening, it is easier for them to improve the other skills.

Nonetheless, against this background which elevates the importance of listening, Morley (2013) highlights that it has taken many years for language-teaching professionals to realize the importance of the skill. According to Ahuja, Ahuja and Ahuja (2010) and Morley (2013), although listening is used far more often in normal daily life than any other language skill, it was only during the 1970s that the status began to change somewhat. The shift in attention to listening is associated directly with the emergence of Communicative Language Teaching (CLT) in the 1970s and early 1980s. Renukadevi (2014) claims that with the focus on proficiency, listening was highlighted as it forms the concrete foundation for complete language proficiency. Thus, (Morley 2013) learners who are constantly developing and improving their listening skills are better able to improve the quality of their language production. It is noteworthy that (Renukadevi 2014) language learning depends largely on listening because one of the principles of CLT is that listening is the basis for communicative competence as it supplies learners with the aural input which enables them to interact in spoken communication. The importance of listening in ESL is further reinforced as no other type of language input is as easy to process as oral communication which is received through the skill of listening (Ahuja, Ahuja and Ahuja 2010; Wilcox-Peterson 2013).

Therefore, in contrast to earlier perceptions, for approximately the last five decades, it appears that those involved in language instruction have done some transitioning towards a significant realization, that listening plays a pivotal role in the communication process (Littlewood 2010; Morley 2013; Celce-Murcia 2013). Further, "language instructors in this contemporary era seem to be more aware of the importance of effective teaching of listening" (Celce-Murcia 2013, 68). Generally, this paradigm shift in the language learning and teaching process correlates directly with the premise that (Vandergrift 2007) listening as an interactive skill is now considered a process rather than passive, so that as an active process of meaning making rather than a product, listening should be a major focus from the beginning.

Accordingly, although research shows that (Celce-Murcia 2013; Wilcox-Peterson 2013) in ESL classrooms. worldwide there is some effort to give listening the central focus in language learning which it warrants, some concern still exists. The reality is that despite this claim of repositioning in listening instruction, some authorities still need to keep pace with the methodology. To this end, Ahmadi (2016) declares that the skill continues to be ignored in second language learning and research. Furthermore, Renukadevi (2014) states that listening needs to be fully integrated into the curriculum. An additional perspective is that (Wilcox-Peterson 2013) there is consistent apprehension about the level of attention given to the application of best practices during listening instruction. Hence, it appears that the transition of listening instruction in ESL with employment of best practice principles continues to be an issue of concern. Consequently, the proposition is that best practice in listening instruction in ESL in the Anglophone Caribbean setting is not an exception in the worldwide language teaching movement.

ESL Learners' Engagement with Real Listening

Renukadevi (2014) proposes that as listening is associated with learners' acquisition of the highest level of language competence when compared with the other skills speaking, reading and writing, this skill is considered as a language forerunner in effective communication. For that reason, (Vandergrift 2007; Renukadevi 2014) the approach to assist ESL learners in achieving optimum success correlates with the growing focus on teaching listening as a process. Despite this instructional transition, learners frequently relate their challenges in trying to attain proficiency in this skill. Authorities are of the view that their difficulty stems from the fact that (Littlewood 2010; Wilcox-Peterson 2013; Renukadevi 2014) unlike the other language skills, listening comprises interrelated sub-skills such as receiving, understanding, remembering, evaluating and responding. This interrelation contributes to listening being associated with anxiety and stress as learners are required to actively participate in the interpersonal and interpretive modes of communication (Renukadevi 2014). Therefore, for all the positive change in language instruction which can be linked to CLT, comes the reality that listening is not a simple skill, but rather a very complicated and elaborate process which must be taught to facilitate learners' development (Littlewood 2010; Wilcox-Peterson 2013; Morley 2013).

Another area of discord is that in the classroom, instructors often tend to speak at a slow, unnatural rate in an attempt to enhance the clarity of the utterances for learners (Littlewood 2010). The result is a complete contrast when learners encounter language produced at a normal rate outside the classroom environment. The differences with the language produced in the classroom and speakers' output in real situations outside of the formal teaching learning environment are evident. This clear distinction in the language based on the settings contributes to learners' difficulty in listening and understanding the target language. That being the case, learners tend to perform well in formal language teaching situations but are generally unable to transfer their language skills to communicate in the real world outside (Porter and Roberts 1987). Therefore, it is vital for ESL learners to become accustomed to speech which is not perfectly planned but which contains all the false starts and hesitations which characterize most everyday speech (Littlewood 2010). This means that "learners must understand speakers who vary in the tempo of speech, clarity of articulation and regional accents and they must be prepared to extract meaning from whatever language is directed at them" (Littlewood 2010,65). In light of this, Vandergrift and Goh (2012) maintain that learners need to control their listening.

While acknowledging that language learners can demonstrate some inability to function as efficient listeners outside of the classroom, instruction based on the application of best practice in communicative strategies allows for rectification. The related principles ensure that learners are provided with contexts which are conducive to practise their listening skills to become proficient interlocutors in real or authentic communication (Zemelman, Daniels and Hyde 2012). Furthermore, Geddes (1989) believes that the nearer instructors get to simulate the kind of communicative situations that learners will encounter outside the classroom, the environment will be more favourable for developing effective listening skills. With the aforementioned points in mind, it is imperative that instructors are aware that the sound, rhythm, intonation, and stress of the language can only be adapted suitably through listening, and for ESL learners to understand nuances in the English language they must be able to listen (Renukadevi 2014). Thus, to assist in language learners' success, listening tasks should be as realistic as possible so they can relate what they are doing in the formal teaching learning environment to some situation in which they may be required to use the second language in real life (Geddes 1989).

Listening: The Two-way Process

Brown (2006) states that top-down and bottom-up processing produces the understandable input with listening. As a direct result of the complexity associated with listening, those involved in language teaching should be aware that "the externally based bottom-up and the internally based top-down modes operate in a cooperative process" (Wilcox-Peterson 2013, 93). For effective listening, "listeners need to reconstruct the original intention of the speaker by using both processing strategies and draw on what they already know to make use of new knowledge" (Nunan 2000, 211). This means that as language learners listen to speakers' utterances, they are expected to mentally process the spoken language to make it understandable and receive the messages (Fauzi and Angkasawati 2019). The bottom-up mode or "outside the head" processing requires learners to isolate small units such as sounds, words clauses and sentences and analyse them at successive levels to organize the message. With the constructive process of "inside the head" or top-down listening (Fauzi and Angkasawati 2019) as active participants, language learners use prior knowledge and experiences that are similar to the new input to infer and guess to understand what they hear.

Richards (1999) proposes that bottom-up processing alone often provides an insufficient basis for listening. If the listener is unable to make use of top-down processing as well, language learning is lacking an essential component which will retard the process of the acquisition of effective listening skills (Richards 1999). As learners listen to discourse, they try to construct and interpret meaning based on their background knowledge of the target language within the sociolinguistic context. The result is that much of the difficulty they experience is reduced if they are able to apply prior knowledge. This means that like other language learners, those engaged in ESL must have enough relevant background knowledge of the culture and the particular area of focus to enable them to assess the context and appropriateness of what is said (Browne and Yule 1989). As a consequence, ESL learners who do not possess the necessary background information, are often rendered incapable of achieving success at using top-down listening processing to acquire a high level of communicative competence in English.

Current Perspectives on Best Practice in ESL Listening Instruction

The dynamic nature of language is one of the factors which has contributed to the call for a mix of methods in second language teaching (Ellis 2018). Presently, attention is also given to what is termed (Kumaravadivelu 2003) post-method pedagogy which deals with a shift away from the total reliance on the theoretical principles of methods towards a focus on pedagogy with implementation of teacher autonomy. With this conceptualization, as language teachers pay particular attention to the peculiarities of the teaching-learning environment, they make instructional decisions which cater directly to the learners' needs (Kumaravadivelu 2003; Can 2012). It is clear that these current trends further reinforce the need for the high level of efficiency associated with applying instructional best practices. Ideally, the primary objective of every ESL class should be to deliver listening instruction which produces learners with the capacity to use the target language effectively to function in the world. This purposeful attention to instructional best practices sets out to ensure that learners perceive language as functional, meaningful and highly relevant in their daily lives. In addition, with focus on the related best practice principles, "there are increased opportunities for learners to use the target language and to experience a personal sense of relevance and achievement" (Crookes and Chaudron 2013, 8). Furthermore, the attention to best practices in listening instruction "enables learners to become active participants in the learning process" (Savignon 2013, 13).

As language instructors focus on best practices in listening instruction linked to the interactive and communicative features of strategies, learners can experience higher levels of satisfaction. The learners' gratification occurs as a direct result of their active involvement in the sessions. Such learner-centred instruction facilitates greater focus on achieving the learning objectives for each individual learner which can result in enhanced learner fulfilment and enjoyment of the listening instruction. In fact, Crookes and Chaudron (2013) assert that when learners enjoy learning, the entire process becomes more valuable and worthwhile for them and there is longer retention of knowledge.

Theoretical Framework for Observation

In language teaching, the inherent features of best practice are directly related to the theory of language as communication. Consequently, in listening instruction the focus on language as used in real-life correlates with the application of best practice principles. Zemelman, Daniels, and Hyde (2012) assert the interrelatedness of these principles and group them into the three main clusters, "Student-centred", 'Cognitive" and "Social". Specific examination of "Student-centred" reveals the inclusion of the principles "Experiential", "Holistic", "Authentic" and "Challenging". Zemelman, Daniels, and Hyde (2012) with "Experiential", in this teaching-learning environment, learners' active, direct and real participation is considered the most powerful and natural form of learning.

Further (Zemelman, Daniels, and Hyde 2012) learners are empowered with exposure to genuine, rich, complex ideas and materials associated with the "Authentic" best practice principle. It stands to reason, that authenticity should be evident in language instruction from the initial stages. In actuality, (Zemelman, Daniels, and Hyde 2012) the early focus on authenticity results in the development of learners' language skills through task-oriented instruction in which they listen to content in spoken discourse through meaningful interaction. Another consideration is the premise that learners achieve their optimum success when they experience instruction that centers on (Zemelman, Daniels, and Hyde 2012) the "Holistic" principle with materials used in purposeful contexts. It is also paramount that learners are presented with whole concepts and situations as opposed to isolated subsections that make it difficult for them to experience how these ideas and events are utilized or applied in real life (Zemelman, Daniels, and Hyde 2012). Moreover, language learning is further enhanced when learners are encouraged to develop a sense of responsibility for their own learning as they encounter genuine challenges and choices while engaging in tasks and activities Zemelman, Daniels, and Hyde 2012).

With the introduction of their model of best practice, Zemelman, Daniels, and Hyde (2012) set out to assist learners in monitoring their own learning. Based on the fundamental tenets of a theory of learning, learners are also encouraged to develop the ability to apply language knowledge appropriately in the various communicative episodes (Littlewood 2010). As best practice principles become the norm in classroom instruction, the teacher is able to cater to the needs of individual learners as well as motivate them to experiment and apply their creativity with the language (Zemelman, Daniels, and Hyde 2012). In accordance with the underlying principles that cater to the overall development of language learners, the aforementioned theoretical perspective appears to attend to the established areas which equip learners with lifelong skills to achieve success. For these reasons, the "Student-centred" cluster of Zemelman, Daniels, and Hyde (2012) best practice framework was considered most adequate to guide the academic principles of this applied research on ESL listening instruction.

THE CONTEXT OF THE RESEARCH

Brief Overview of ESL Teaching at the University of the West Indies

The official delivery of ESL programmes at the campuses of the University of the West Indies (UWI) began in 2001. At that time, the focus was on the six-week ESL summer programme with university lecturers from campuses of the "Universidad Nacional" (National University) in Colombia. In 2008, there was expansion to a four-month semester programme with larger cohorts of Venezuelans from Petroleos de Venezuela S.A. (PDVSA).

With further extension of the programme from 2015 to 2017, particular campuses delivered ESL to cohorts of adult learners from countries such as Ecuador and Panama with plans in place for the inclusion of other Latin American countries. With this current programme, students live in the Caribbean country in which the campus is located to immerse themselves in the culture as they receive ESL instruction. As participants in the programme, they receive instruction in seven language areas: language structure, writing, phonology, reading, conversation, listening and listening comprehension.

Context for Observation

This researcher's informal observation as an instructor in the ESL at one of the UWI campuses from 2001 to 2008, along with empirical results of unpublished work (Jules 2010) indicates that second language learners required an approach to teaching which facilitated their optimum success in enhancing their listening proficiency. The overall findings from previous research signified that (Jules 2010) participants from study samples in 2005 and 2006 experienced some difficulty with listening to communicate in the target language. In addition, all participants were of the view that their inability to listen and comprehend in the target language was the most necessary skill for them to acquire (Jules 2010).

In 2017, the application of best practices in listening emerged as an area for further examination from graduate research which (Carroll 2017) sought to gather data on students' motivation in ESL classes. Hence, based on the earlier impetus from 2010, it was deemed valuable to use systematic observation of ESL listening instructional sessions to gather information on the application of best practices.

METHODOLOGY

In 2017, as a nonparticipant observer, the graduate researcher visited the cohort of students during the instructional sessions at the UWI campus. Twenty naturalistic persistent observation sessions occurred between 25 April and 16 May 2017, with each lasting from one to two hours. Lincoln and Guba (1985) indicate that this type of observation is carried out to facilitate the isolation of common features in the setting. Qualitative data were gathered from field notes for an overall description of the participants' behaviour. The recordings provided detailed, chronological data on instructors' methodology, application of best practice principles, learners' language behaviours, instructors' teaching style and interactions with learners during the sessions. Reflective notes were the other classification of data which focused on the researcher's thoughts, experiences and personal reactions.

Study Sample

The study was conducted with a purposive sample of a very specific population (n=25) of ESL students at a campus of the UWI. Creswell (2008) proposes that the purposive component ensured the sample was information rich. This sample was considered adequate for the research because each member was an ESL learner and he or she was enrolled in the programme at the UWI. In addition, the participants were accessible and agreed to be studied, so they were willing to facilitate the research. The sample was organized as Group 1 (n=13) and Group 2 (n=12).

RESULTS OF OBSERVATION DATA

The observation data were coded to attend to emerging themes based on (Zemelman, Daniels, and Hyde 2012) best practice principles within the "Student-centred" cluster. Hence, data was categorized according to the five themes: 1. "Student-centre"', 2. "Experiential', 3. "Holistic", 4. "Challenging" and 5. "Authentic". To corroborate the analysis of empirical findings, a member-check was done with four participants who volunteered for the process. This is associated with (Guba and Lincoln 1994) qualitative procedures carried out after the data assessment so participants can approve or disapprove of the findings.

As the examination of any language skill cannot be assessed as a separate entity, listening data linked to the others' language skills were analysed. Data were taken from the areas instructed by the three tutors who agreed to be observed during their sessions. While there were twenty observations overall, data are presented from fifteen observation sessions: 2, 4, 5, 6, 7, 8, 9, 10, 11, 12, 14, 15, 18, 19 and 20. Accordingly, data from the sessions which focused primarily on correction of homework assignments were assessed as lacking in the required rich information and were not analysed. Further, no formal data were gathered during the sessions with guest tutors as these were evaluated to constitute a major change in the research environment. For these reasons, data from five sessions were neither documented formally nor analysed. Based on the timetable allocation, the sessions observed were identified as "Listening", "Language Structure", "Conversation" and "Phonology". The data gathered are categorized as themes and the analyses along with findings are presented.

Observation of Listening

Observation 6

(Group 1)

This was a dictation session and participants were all engaged and listening to the instructor's reading a short extract from a text. The instructor attempted to speak at a normal rate and participants were required to write what they heard. The instructor requested each participant's work and made the corrections. A whole-class pattern was used to discuss the most common errors made. For the conclusion, participants were given a copy of the extract with the correct content.

Observation 12

(Group 2)

Each participant was assigned 45 minutes of independent listening in the Language Laboratory. The session lasted for two hours, from 3:00 to 5:00 p.m. and participants selected the most convenient period. Each participant was assigned a computer which facilitated various listening activities while the instructor monitored them using the control computer. Each participant was required to make a concise written recording of the main details he or she heard during the activity. To conclude, each participant had a conferencing session with the instructor. The interaction focused on discussing the content of the activity and any challenges and successes the participants encountered.

Observation 19

(Group 2)

The instructor placed participants into two groups and asked them to listen to an audio based on a scenario which required them to formulate a solution to a problem. The instructor explained the activity and requested participants to converse about the information. Each group was instructed to select a member to guide the discussion and document the solution. As the participants listened to the audios, they contributed meaningfully to discussion that ensued. There was often much debate among the members of each group as they gave feedback to responses. Participants' variance in opinion was counteracted with negotiation of meaning to arrive at an agreement. The instructor interacted with the participants in each group and asked questions to guide their interpretation of the information which they heard on the audio.

Observation 20

(Group 1)

The main activity for this lesson required participants to write the missing lyrics as they listened to a song via an audio recording. They exhibited no timidity in asking the instructor for help when they needed it. However, the participants demonstrated extreme hesitance when asked to share the lyrics they had written and some spoke Spanish during that period. The class ended with participants watching a tourism-related video on their home country. They were required to discuss whether the information was a true representation of their country. Despite a disturbance with excess noisiness caused by a few participants, overall, the majority were very engaged and alert throughout the lesson.

Themes from Observation of Participants' Listening Sessions:

1. Student-centred
2. Experiential
5   Authentic

Summary

Generally, during listening instruction, the objective is for a student-centred approach which attends to learners participating actively in their own learning (Zemelman et al. 2012). This environment also best facilitates catering to the learners' specific listening needs. Based on the data, a high level of student-engagement was evident during sessions 12, 19 and 20 which supported the application of the student-centred best practice principle. According to Howard, Shaughnessy, Sanger, and Hux (1998) instruction which encourages student engagement facilitates the development of oral language. In particular, the activity in Observation 19 was highly interactive as the instructor utilized "student to student" and "student to group" interaction patterns. On the other hand, in this setting, the activity in observation 6 which was teacher-fronted or teacher-dominated, was counter to the student-centred principle.

In many classrooms (Howard, Shaughnessy, Sanger, and Hux 1998) the teacher dominates and this has a negative influence on the development of learners' oral language. Further, while the instructor opted to use the text as a source, this activity was favourable for authentic material. Zemelman, Daniels, and Hyde (2012) surmise that this medium enhances the meaningfulness of the interaction and makes participants aware that material from within their setting adds value to the learning process. This meant that while the final activity in Observation 20 showed effective use of authenticity with the materials, the "Authentic" principle was not applied in Observation 6.

Moreover, in observations 19 and 20, participants were exposed to the "Experiential" best practice principle. This was assessed as appropriate as learners must be (Zemelman, Daniels, and Hyde 2012) active participants in real-life experiences which are crucial to their normal everyday acquisition of knowledge and mastery. For the activity in Observation 19, participants applied their English proficiency to solve the specific problem. Hence, they utilized several communicative skills including discussing, negotiating meaning and giving and responding to feedback (Larsen-Freeman 2000).

Observation of Language Structure

Observation 9

(Group 2)

For the first half of this lesson, participants engaged in a self-correction session. They responded after being selected by the instructor to answer their homework questions. Participants were alert and engaged for much of the activity and responded to their classmates as they spoke, so that generally, the interaction appeared to be meaningful. At some periods of this session, some participants were distracted and appeared to be engaged with another activity, other than the work assigned by the instructor.

Observation 11

(Group 2)

Most of the session comprised an activity which required the participants to rearrange scrambled sentences to create a dialogue. Following this task, they were required to engage in role-play based on the content and participants appeared to be very alert throughout the session. They were required to listen as each group read the sentences and then dramatize the scenarios which developed from the arrangement. While the activity lasted for more than half of the allotted time – 120 minutes – most students remained completely engaged during this task.

Observation 10

(Group 1)

Before the listening activity commenced, participants were informed that they would be listening to a short extract via a video recording. The instructor ensured that all the verbs in the extract were in the simple present tense. The participants were instructed to write the utterances they heard and then to identify all the verbs by placing a circle around them. They were then required to rewrite the verbs in simple past tense and allowed to view and listen to the video, twice. The participants were asked to interchange their pieces of writing and each was given a word-processed copy of the discourse to carry out the correcting procedure. Following this activity, the instructor read the full extract. After the participants' work was returned at the end of the correction process, each was asked to examine his or her submission. The instructor encouraged participants to identify any areas in which they experienced difficulty.

Themes from Observation of Participants' Language Structure Sessions

3. Holistic
2. Experiential

Summary

Findings from Observations 9 and 10 showed that the holistic nature of language appeared not to be the focus of the instruction because in each instance, the language structure was presented as an isolated aspect. This meant that there was no application of the "Holistic" best practice principle. This type of instruction conflicts with the established theoretical perspectives as (Zemelman, Daniels, and Hyde 2012) language learners acquire more success with instruction which deals with exposure to complete aspects applied in meaningful settings rather than dealing with content as segregated subsections that are false representations of the real use. The results from the two observations also highlighted the instructor's attention to what can be considered as oversimplified content.

In contrast to the findings of Observations 9 and 10, Observation 11 revealed the instructor's attention to Experiential principle with the application of role play. This presented the material in a meaningful context and enabled participants to be exposed to how their knowledge of situations is applied appropriately in their everyday routines (Zemelman, Daniels, and Hyde 2012).

Observation Data of Conversation

Observation 7

(Group 1)

The session was held outside of the classroom, in an open area of the campus. The participants experienced greater difficulty staying focused on the instruction in that setting as compared to the classroom. They appeared to be distracted by the normal outdoor activity such as students passing by. The instructor placed participants in groups of three and their task was to select a topic from a hat and present orally to the group. For most of the session, the participants were alert and engaged with each other. However, their level of alertness was not as sustained as during previous in-class sessions.

Observation 4

(Group 2)

The participants were placed into pairs and were required to converse with each other to complete a game. While one participant was given a work sheet with a list of conversation responses, the other participant had the conversation starters. As one participant read an utterance to begin a conversation, the other examined the work sheet and selected an appropriate response to the utterance. Participants engaged in meaningful conversation to determine the appropriateness of the utterances while the instructor moved among the pairs and listened to the language produced. The participants were encouraged to formulate their own utterances as conversation starters and responses. To conclude the activity, each group was required to orally present to the whole class and share the language that was generated during the interaction.

Observation 15

(Group 2)

At the beginning of the session the instructor gave participants the opportunity to volunteer to talk about the activities they engaged in over the
weekend. Classmates were required to listen to the presentations to
enable them to ask questions. Participants were very hesitant to volunteer and were usually selected by the instructor. During the latter part
of the session, participants became disruptive as more than a third of
them commenced speaking in Spanish while involved in group work. As
participants engaged with the activity, their actions often deviated from
the set instructions they were given.

Observation 8

(Group 1)

Participants were asked to walk around the environs of the campus for
approximately ten minutes and initiate conversation with strangers, by
using appropriate conversation starters. They were required to document
the various responses, especially those which they were not exposed to
within the class session. Each participant was given the opportunity to
report on his or her interactions while classmates asked questions to
gather more information of the communicative episode or for clarification. Some participants related their challenges in using the appropriate
starter during the interactions.

Observation 14

(Groups 1 and 2)

For this session, participants interacted with guest speakers. Initially,
their conversation with the native speakers was limited, but this increased
to more sustained discourse as time progressed. A few participants did
not want to talk as much as their classmates and made no eye contact
with the speakers. Some participants talked in Spanish to their friends
in groups near to them, while others used this language when they were

trying to get classmates to understand their point of view. There were gaps of silence between conversation topics when the participants were not attentive and alert, but for most of the activity, most of them were very engaged with the guests.

Observation 5

(Group 2)

The instructor used an audio recording and allowed participants to listen to utterances which they heard normally during a variety of their daily routines. The participants were arranged in small groups of three or four and the instructor encouraged them to respond appropriately to the utterances. As a result of the small numberof participants engaged in the activity, the instructor motivated those who exhibited a lack of confidence to contribute to the activity.

Themes from Observation of Participants' Conversation Sessions:

2. Experiential
4. Challenging
5. Authentic

Summary

Generally, the results of Observations 4, 5, 7, 8, 14 and 15 reinforced the notion that (Zemelman, Daniels, and Hyde 2012) active, hands-on, concrete experience associated with the "Experiential" best practice principle, is the most formidable and typical form of learning. Instruction, specifically during Observations 8 and 14, revealed the instructor's effort to facilitate participants' exposure to the direct use of oral language for communication, as they listened to the native speakers' discourse. In particular, instruction during these sessions also highlighted application of the "Authentic" principle with use of real language in a meaningful context.

In addition, the results of Observations 8 and 14 demonstrated that real communication is often more challenging for learners than the structured type associated with classroom instruction. Instruction in the sessions indicated that consideration was given to the notion that (Zemelman, Daniels, and Hyde 2012) with attention to the best practice principle of "Challenging" learning is most successful in situations where learners are confronted with real challenges in which they are obligated to be responsible for their own learning.

Observation Data of Phonology

Observation 18

(Group 2)

The participants continued to work on an activity with International Phonetic Alphabet (IPA) transcription of the lyrics of an English song from the previous lesson. They were highly engaged and alert throughout the exercise. In addition, they were quiet and in deep concentration for much of the lesson. At the end of the session, they started to speak in Spanish to each other.

Observation 2

(Groups 1 and 2)

This session was a whole class activity in the Language Laboratory. The instructor gave participants worksheets and they were required to listen to an audio of specific vowel sounds to complete the task in thirty minutes. For the concluding activity, the instructor carried out the correction procedure with the whole group.

Themes from Observation of Participants' Phonology Sessions

   3. Holistic
   1. Student-centred

Summary

The results of Observations 2 and 18 replicated those of Observations 9 and 10 with the absence of application of the "Holistic" best practice principle. Generally, the instruction dealt with the phonological areas presented as isolated aspects of language which failed to enable participants to experience the interrelation of the areas as they exist in real language. Further, in particular, Observation 2 revealed instruction with lack of focus on the Student-centred best practice principle.

CONCLUSIONS

One of the aims of any programme in ESL is to improve learners' listening proficiency. Research has proven convincingly (Lightbown and Spada 2006; Zemelman, Daniels, and Hyde 2012) that the application of best practice principles influences the existing teaching and learning environment to an extent which makes it sufficiently favourable for learners to improve their listening proficiency. As this research sought to examine the application of best practices in listening instruction of a cohort of students studying ESL in the Caribbean, the details which follow are deemed relevant.

LISTENING FOR MEANINGFUL COMMUNICATION

Based on the findings, while learners were exposed to a variety of listening episodes such as musical lyrics and interaction with guest speakers, the call for an increase in the quantity and variety of authentic experiences seems well-founded. According to Omaggio-Hadley (2008) to enhance learners' understanding, they should be provided with several opportunities to listen for a variety of different purposes. Furthermore, (Nunan 2010) the opportunity to engage in communicative listening activities from the initial stages of instruction is useful for learners as they experience instruction with content and materials that are interesting, real and functional. With these aspects in mind, (Browne and Yule 1999) learners need to do a wider variety of things and to be actively involved in reacting appropriately as they listen rather than simply answering questions based on what they hear. The views of authorities (Browne and Yule 1999; Omaggio-Hadley 2008; Nunan 2010) highlight the importance of using language for meaningful communication during the listening activities rather than merely for rote-like practice. In this regard, the findings revealed that in some instances, during instruction, participants lacked exposure to the varied communicative experiences which enabled them to use English effectively in sociocultural situations such as the usual interactions which occurred in the bus terminal, supermarket, market-place and fast-food outlet or restaurant. Thus, an intensified focus on applying the "Authentic" best practice principle was required. Attention to this principle stipulates that learners experience (Zemelman, Daniels & Hyde,201) authentic, rich and intricate episodes of real and functional language in purposeful settings.

Further, an environment conducive to ESL learners' success requires that along with experiencing the interrelation of all the language skills, learners should be able to use a range of communicative skills to convey their messages. As they carry out this action, they demonstrate acquisition of a comprehensive and deep understanding of the language. Moreover, the nature of listening stipulates that (Littlewood 2010) learners should engage in an active process of listening for meaning, so that they can be motivated by a communicative purpose.

REAL LANGUAGE FOR LISTENING

Another point to consider is that it is misleading to suggest that (Geddes 1989) learners can isolate listening from other language skills when dealing with communication. Geddes (1989) claims that while there are times when the only language skill used is listening, when persons eavesdrop on a conversation, listen to the radio, or attend a public lecture, often other language skills will be involved in the communication. To this end, the findings which indicated some attention to presenting listening as a separate area were problematic; this focus did not cater to (Zemelman, Daniels, and Hyde 2012) the "Holistic" best practice principle. In this regard, Littlewood (2010) points out that the prospect of taking part in communicative interaction helps to provide learners with a strong purpose for listening. Through the interactive communicative listening tasks, they focus on using the target language within real situations, as well as the process involved in learning the language. In this way, learners attempt to link their classroom listening experiences with real-life everyday language routines.

As a result of the previous details outlined, listening tasks should be (Geddes 1989) as realistic as possible to help learners relate what they are doing in the formal teaching learning environment to some situation where they may be required to use the language in real life. In addition, the general view is that (Christie, Enz, and Vukelich 2011) teachers provide ideal language environments by engaging students in genuine conversations, conducting stimulating reciprocal discussion, and allowing them to converse with each other. Therefore, the results which revealed ESL listening instruction which followed the current worldwide trend with much attention given to student-engagement were significant.

EMERGING BEST PRACTICE PRINCIPLES

While the primary theoretical framework of the research was best practice principles within the student-centred cluster, the findings revealed that instructors applied some principles within the (Zemelman, Daniels, and Hyde 2012) "Cognitive" cluster. This best practice principle is considered the most powerful learning which occurs when learners can utilise higher-order thinking achieved via self-monitoring to have a comprehensive understanding of the language (Zemelman, Daniels and Hyde 2012). Indeed, language learners must be prepared to extract meaning from whatever language is directed at them (Littlewood 2010). ESL learners' success in this task is dependent directly on their exposure to the effective application of the "Cognitive" best principle during instruction. In addition, as evident in Observation 20, participants experienced the "Reflective" best practice principle which comes within the "Cognitive" cluster. Learners must be provided with opportunities to assess and reflect on their experiences (Zemelman, Daniels, and Hyde 2012). Certainly, the application of the best practice principles from the "Cognitive" cluster is invaluable to the success of ESL learners.

OTHER AREA OF FOCUS

It is also noteworthy that the findings from Observations 8 and 14 high-lighted the importance of attending to participants' cognitive and psychomotor domains as well as to their affective domain. This latter area is associated with the way they deal with things emotionally, inclusive of feelings, values, appreciation, enthusiasms, motivations and attitudes (Hoque 2016). Such affective features manifest in learners' personalities and affect their level of engagement with the content and activities. For this reason, it is beneficial for instructors to observe learners in order to become aware of their individual nature (Cohen, Manion, and Morrison 2017). Such knowledge is worthwhile in understanding learners' language behaviour. Another useful detail is that as participants use the language to express their emotions and feelings, instructors get a true sense of how they are impacted by the language in the related contexts.

ADVOCATING FOR LISTENING IN THE WAY FORWARD

The treatment of listening as the slighted language skill by some individuals in language teaching appears to be retrogressive and dismissive of a crucial point. This is that (Celce-Murcia 2013; Morley 2013; Renukadevi 2014) without listening skills, language learning is impossible. In fact, (Renukadevi 2014) previous challenges towards teaching listening are now better understood because of the new strategies contributing to effective listening. Certainly, within the last five decades the application of best practice principles has emerged as crucial in effective ESL listening instruction. This claim of the worth of these principles reinforces the usefulness of the results from the research which revealed that while application of best practice principles "student-centred" "Challenging" and "Experiential" were evident during listening instruction, there is room for the implementation to be intensified. In addition, the findings showed that more attention should be given to the effective interrelation of the "Authentic" and "Holistic" principles. Based on these results, it stands to reason that to keep pace with the worldwide movement in language teaching, the way forward for ESL listening instruction in an Anglophone Caribbean setting is to advocate for purposeful attention to the intense and effective use of the interrelated best practice principles to assist learners in developing and enhancing their oral communication skills and overall language proficiency.

REFERENCES

Ahmadi, Seyedeh. 2016. "The Importance of Listening Comprehension in Language Learning". *International Journal of Research in English Education* 1(1): 7–10.

Ahuja, Pramila, G.C. Ahuja, and Amita Ahuja. 2010. *Communication Skills: How to Develop Profitable Listening Skills.* New Dehli: Sterling Publishers.

Bano, Farah. 2017. "Towards Understanding Listening Comprehension in EFL Classroom: The Case of the Saudi Learners". *English Language Teaching* 10(6): 21–27.

Browne, Gillian, and George Yule. 1999. *Teaching the Spoken Language: An Approach Based on the Analysis of Conversational English.* Cambridge: Cambridge University Press.

Can, Nilüfer. 2012. "Post-Method Pedagogy: Teacher Growth behind Walls." Proceedings of the 10th *METU ELT Convention.* (http://dbe.metu.edu.tr/convention/proceedingsweb/Pedagogy.pdf.) (Accessed 25 April 2019).

Carroll, Meghann. 2017." Learners' Motivation for ESL Instruction: The Panamanian Experience in the Anglophone Caribbean". MA thesis, University of the West Indies, Cave Hill, Barbados

Celce-Murcia, Marianne. 2013. "Language Teaching Approaches: An Overview". In *Teaching English as a Second or Foreign language,* 4th edn., edited by Marianne Celce-Murcia, 3–10. London: Heinle.

Christie, James F., Billie Jean Enz, and Carol Vukelich. 2011. *Teaching Language and Literacy: PreschoolThrough the Elementary Ggrades,* 4th edn. Boston: Pearson Education.

Cohen, Louis, Lawrence Manion, and Keith Morrison. 2017. *Research Methods in Education,* 8th edn. Oxford: Routledge Publishers.

Creswell, John W. 2008. *Educational Rresearch: Planning, Conducting, and Evaluating Quantitative and Qualitative Rresearch,* 3rd edn. New Jersey: Pearson Education.

Crooks, Graham and Craig Chaudron. 2013. "Guidelines for Language Classroom Instruction". In *Teaching English as a Second or Foreign language,* 4th edn. edited by Marianne Celce-Murcia, 29–42. London: Heinle.

Dörnyei, Zoltán. 2011. *Research Methods in Applied Linguistics: Quantitative, Qualitative, and Mixed Methodologies.* Oxford: Oxford University Press.

Ellis, Rod. 2018. *Reflections on Task-Based Llearning:* Bristol: Multilingual Matters.

Fauzi, Iwan, and Putri Angkasawati. 2019. "Use of Listening Logs Through WhatsApp in Improving Listening Comprehension of EFL Students". *Journal of Applied linguistics and literature* 4(1): 13–26.

Geddes, Marion. 1989. "Listening". In *Communication in the Classroom: Applications and Methods for a Communicative Approach,* edited by Keith Johnson and Keith Morrow, 78–80. London: Longman.

Gilakjani, Abbas Pourhosein, and Narjes Banou Sabouri. 2016. "Learners' Listening Comprehension Difficulties in English Language Learning: A Literature Review". *English Language Teaching* 9(6): 123–33.

Guba, Egon, and Yvonna Lincoln. 1994. "Competing Paradigms in Qualitative Research". In *Handbook of Qualitative Research,* edited by N.K. Denisin & Y.S. Lincoln, 163–94. London: Sage Publications.

Howard, Sandy, Anne Shaughnessy, Dixie Sanger, and Karen A. Hux. 1998. "Let's Talk! Facilitating Language in Early Elementary Classrooms". *Young Cchildren* 53(3): 34–39.

Hoque, Enamul. 2016. "Three Domains of Learning: Cognitive, Affective and Psychomotor". *Journal of EFL Education and Research* 2 (2): 45–52.

Jules, Janice. 2010. "Teaching English as a Second Language: Improving Listening and Speaking Proficiency of Adult Spanish-Speakers using a Communicative Approach".PhD diss., University of the West Indies,Mona.

Kumaravadivelu, Bala. 2003. *Beyond Methods: Macrostrategies for Language Teaching.* New Haven, CT: Yale University Press.

Larsen-Freeman, Dianne. 2000. *Techniques and Principles in Language Teaching.* Oxford: Oxford University Press.

Lightbown, Patsy M., and Nina Spada. 2006. *How Languages are Learned.* 3rd. edn. Oxford,New York: Oxford University Press.

Lincoln, Yvonna., and Egon Guba, 1985. *The Naturalistic Inquiry.* Newbury Park, CA: Sage Publications.

Littlewood, William. 2010. *Communicative Language Teaching.* Cambridge: Cambridge University Press. Morley, Joan. 2013. "Aural Comprehension Instruction: Principles and Practices. In *Teaching English as a Second or Foreign Language,* edited by Marianne Celce-Murcia., 69–84. London: Heinle.

Nunan, David. 2000. *Language Teaching Methodology: A Textbook for Teachers.* Oxford: Oxford University Press.

———. 2010. *Second Language Teaching and Learning.* Boston: Heinle.

Omaggio-Hadley, Alice. 2008. *Teaching Language in Context.* Boston: Heinle.

Porter, Don, and Jon Roberts. 1987. "Authentic Listening Activities". In *Methodology in TESOL: A Book of Readings,* edited by Michael H. Long and Jack Richards. Boston: Heinle.

Renukadevi, Dhandapani. 2014. "The Role of Listening in Language Acquisition; the Challenges and Strategies in Teaching Listening". *International Journal of Education and Information Studies* 4(1): 59–63.

Richards, Jack C. 1999. *The Language Teaching Matrix*. Cambridge: Cambridge University Press.

_____. and Theodore S. Rodgers. 2001. *Approaches and Methods in Language Tteaching: A Description and Analysis*. Cambridge: Cambridge University Press.

Rost, Michael. 2015. *Teaching and Researching Listening: Applied Linguistics in Action*. Oxford: Routledge Publisher.

Savignon, Sandra J. 2013. "Communicative Language Teaching for the 21st Century". In *Teaching English as a Second Language or Foreign Llanguage*, edited by Marianne Celce-Murcia, 13–28. London: Heinle.

Vandergrift, Larry. 2007. Recent developments in second and foreign language listening comprehension research. *Language Teaching*. 40(3). 191–210.

_____. and Christine C. M. Goh. 2012. *Teaching and Learning Second Language Listening: Metacognition in Action*. New York, NY: Routledge.

Wilcox-Peterson, Pat. 2013. "Skills and Strategies for Proficient Listening". In *Teaching English as a Second or Foreign Llanguage*, edited by Marianne Celce-Murcia, 87–100. London: Heinle.

Zemelman, Steven, Harvey Daniels, and Arthur Hyde. 2012. *Best Practice: Bringing Standards to Life in America's Classrooms*. 4th. edn. Portsmouth, NH: Heinemann.

CHAPTER 7

Waa gwaan?

Jamaican Language and Technological Orature in the Creation of
Authentic African Diasporic Identities in the US Hip Hop Generation

RENEE BLAKE AND NICKESHA DAWKINS

INTRODUCTION

In 2015, then US President Barack Obama open his speech at the University of the West Indies in Jamaica with, "Greetings massive! Waa
gwaan Jamaica? Big up UWI". This linguistic crossing into the Jamaican
language is received with joys of laughter, smiles and loud applause from
a largely Jamaican audience indicating that this linguistic act of identity
forms a bond of belonging between Barack Obama, an African American,
and his black Jamaican interlocutors. Devonish (1998b) postulates that
"people like to be with others who they consider to be like themselves.
If people are going to be together without conflict, they have to feel that
they share some kind of common identity" (137). Where people have a
common identity or feel as though they have one, this fosters a collaborative sense of belonging. Moreover, to have a common language in some
sense is to have a cultural bond, and "shared speech is a very important
means of creating common identity" (Devonish 1998b, 137). In this case,
Barack Obama, an outsider, employs language crossing or mimicking
of Jamaican Creole using salient linguistic features and lexical items
as a way to momentarily move across ethnic boundaries (cf., Rampton
1995). What is critical here, we argue, is the fact that Barack Obama uses
a Creole vernacular that Winford (1994, 48) states as "being deeply rooted
in the social life of Caribbean communities as expressions of the social

identity of their speakers, as vehicles of their culture, and as reflections of their personal relationships." And for a place like Jamaica, as part of the Caribbean, the notion of identity, British-Jamaican cultural theorist Stuart Hall (1995) contends, is defined in relation to a cultural past that is enmeshed in the bedlam of colonization and slavery (cf., Blake 1997). According to Hall (1995, 6), "in histories of the migration, forced or free, of peoples who now compose the populations of these societies, whose cultural traces are everywhere intermingled with one another, there is always the stamp of historical violence and rupture." Thus, instead of using English, the linguistic code of the colonial elite, Barack Obama performs a linguistic act of identity by using Jamaican Creole. In doing so, Obama, as a black man, aligns himself with the Jamaican masses of African descent through their local language or what Braithwaite (1984) refers to as "nation language". According to Devonish (2017), "In Jamaica, a cultural struggle has resulted in the largely unwritten Creole becoming the language that expresses an alternative, mass-based sense of national identity, within an official language framework dominated by English. This reverberates globally particularly through music." While an especially notable speech act for a man of stature, Obama's linguistic crossing into the Jamaican language appears to be part of a larger sociolinguistic practice found within contemporary African American orality, particularly in the technological orature of rap and hip hop. In the next section, we analyse the utterances and songs of several contemporary hip hop generation artists including Drake, Nicki Minaj and Rihanna, to highlight their use of the Jamaican language at the level of the lexicon, phonology and/or morphosyntax. In our analysis of hip hop artists in the US context we bring in additional artists, and we draw on Devonish and Jones's (2017) argument for dancehall that new symbols of national and racial iden-tities arise through language. While we argue that hip hop generation artists are utilizing both Jamaican and African American orality as acts of resistance to and liberation from the status quo, we also consider the ways that these languages of resistance fit into a larger discussion in which diasporic or transnational identities are realized in cultural flows through the movement of African diasporic people around the globe (that is, ethnoscapes). Finally, we revisit the origins of the hip hop movement and highlight its historical foundations in and connections to Jamaican ska, rocksteady and reggae, further illuminating recursive historical and diasporic fusions.

Devonish (2017) notes that "history professor Edward Kamau Brathwaite calls it [reggae music] 'the native sound of the cultural revolution that would eventually lead to Bob Marley,'" whose music "hailed a new era of the use of Creole language in music. By the 1980s, a new genre of Jamaican music emerged: Dancehall, with language spoken rather than sung." Through the popular culture of dancehall music and the media, the Jamaican language can be heard in several parts of the world. Along these lines, Dawkins (2008, 2013) highlights dancehall as one of the most popular musical genres in Jamaica today, with its songs "climbing charts" and "making waves" throughout the globe. This music contains popular slangs and words of greetings such as those uttered by Barack Obama. And according to Devonish (1998a, 51), "in the case of Jamaica and its emerging national language, Jamaican, modern electronic technologies have done for speech what print has done for writing, that is, massively increased the potential audience for any given piece of language communication." This means that Barack Obama and hip hop artists alike have access to the orature of Jamaican Creole through electronic mediums such as radio, television, social media (Facebook, WhatsApp, Twitter, YouTube and Instagram), podcast, etc. Devonish (1998b, 50) goes on to say that "orature projects national language and national identity via dancehall music by the performers, the Deejays." However, this projection is not limited to just the Deejays and members of the local Jamaican community as this orature is also fused with or mixed in with utterances made by members of the wider African Diaspora due to accessibility via technology. "The special circumstances of Jamaica and, arguably of people of African origin in the United States via rap, have precipitated the link between traditional technologies of orature and the new electronic mass production and reproduction technologies for sound." (Devonish, 1998b, 51). And it is in this nexus, this fusion, that the African Diaspora meets, negotiates, creates and builds anew.

Jamaican Language and Rhythms in the Hip Hop Nation

Drake is a multi-platinum Canadian rapper and musician, born in 1986 to an African American father and a white Jewish Canadian mother, and raised in Toronto Canada, within a black population predominantly of Jamaican immigrants and their children (c.f., Bascaramurty 2017). Several of Drake's popular recorded songs include Jamaican Creole (JC) phrases such as: *"strength and guidance"* in the song "One Dance", *"wasteman"* (a loser) in the song "Blem", *"big time forward"* (encore) and *"my chargie"* (close/intimate friend) in "My Chargie" featuring Jamaican Dancehall Artist, Popcaan. Moreover, Drake's use of Jamaican terminology is evident in his live performances as well.

Notably, in 2011, Drake appeared during Brit Jam, an annual hip hop and dancehall festival taking place in Jamaica, and appealing to largely African diasporic youth from the United Kingdom, United States, Canada and the Caribbean. Upon being introduced by Jamaican dancehall artist, Mavado, Drake takes the stage and utters the following extemporaneous words using phonology and syntax associated with Jamaican Creole:

Excerpt 1 from Drake:

"Wol aan de wol aan de . . . chruu chruu mi fram farin, bot evri wier mi go daag, mi se Jamieka tu di bloodclaat worl daag! Big op Mavado, big op di general, Alliance, Gully, yu don nuo"

Gloss:

Hold on, hold on, it is true that I am from overseas (a foreigner), but everywhere I go dog (informal reference for friend in rap and dancehall sub-cultures), I say Jamaica to the fucking world dog (I represent for Jamaica). Big up Mavado, Big up to the General, Alliance and Gully" (these are well-known poor working class territories and homes of dancehall music crews in Jamaica).

After this announcement, the crowd erupts with screams of excitement, similar to the reception received by Barack Obama at the University of the West Indies. And to be clear, Drake is not there to perform as a featured artist, but rather to greet the audience and 'big up' the massive. He does this with Creole lexical items like "farin", "daag", "di", "bloodclaat", and "big op", and phonological realizations which include the alternation of the open-mid back rounded vowel /ɔ/ into the open front unrounded vowel [a:] which is lengthened (made tensed) in the words "aan", "daag" and the lax variant [a] in the word "farin". There is also the phonological process of Th-stopping (dental fricative stopping) in the word "di", which represents "the" in English. The data from the excerpt also shows grammatical features which include the absence of consonant clusters ("wol"), generalized case marking ("mi"), and copula absence (mi ø fram farin). Similar to Obama, Drake seemingly evokes a Jamaican ethnic belonging and connection.

One year later in Paris, Drake is introduced to the audience by Mavado, again entering the stage to greet the audience starting with Jamaican Creole.

Excerpt 2 from Drake:

"Paris waa gwaan? . . . Drizzy Drake ina di bloodclaat place. Movado ina di bloodclaat place. Ye man straight! Yow Paris I love you man for real let's go . . . ya'll make some noise for the Gully god Mavado, one time! Ye, Run di tune de!"

Gloss:

Paris what's up? Drizzy Drake is in the fucking place (Drake is here or in the building). Mavado is in the fucking place. Yes, that's right! Hey Paris, I really love you; let's go (let's get this show started). You all make some noise for the Gully god, Movado right now. Yes! Play the tune (start the music)!

Prior to exiting the stage, he commands the sound selector to *run da tune de* ("play that song"). Once again, he uses Jamaican Creole at a Dancehall event, but this time in Europe. Although physically far away from Jamaica and the Caribbean, Drake, as in his introduction at the Brit Jam Stage Show in Jamaica, invokes Jamaica and Jamaicanness with linguistic style – "*bot evri wier mi go daag, mi se Jamieka tu di bloodclaat worl daag!*" (Everywhere I go, I represent *for* Jamaica).

Unlike Drake, international female rapper Nicki Minaj was born in the Caribbean, specifically Trinidad in 1982. As a child, she migrated to New York City with her family. Although heavily identified as Trinidadian, it is Jamaican Creole that she uses when performing (even in the song entitled, "Trini dem girls"). This is evident on the 2011 Sumfest (Summer Festival) stage in 2011 in Jamaica, when she asks the local audience about what part of town they are from:

Excerpt 3 from Nicki Minaj.

"Se yu don nuo, zeen . . . is it Gaza side or Gully side? Which side yu de pan?

Which side yu de pan? Gully? Gaza? . . . Gaza mi se?"

Gloss:

You already know . . . is it Gaza (Portmore community associated with the dancehall artist Vybz Kartel) or Gully (Casava Piece ghetto community associated with dancehall artist Movado) side? Which side are you on? Which side are you on? Gully? Gaza? I say Gaza (I'm on Gaza). These are rival communities with the head of these dancehall crews, Vybz Kartel and Mavado respectively.

Nicki Minaj uses Jamaican Creole syntax in the formation of the question construction "which side yu de pan?"(Gloss: "which side are you on?"), as well as the statement "se yu don nuo" (Gloss: "you already know"). Additionally, she uses the phonological feature of vowel alteration associated with Jamaican Creole; that is, the high mid back rounded vowel [o] realized as a diphthongized high/high-mid back [ʊo] or the low front unrounded vowel [a]. Thus, the word "know" is pronounced as JC [nʊo] and "on" is pronounced as JC "pan". Also, for the word "say", Minaj pronounces the high mid front unrounded vowel [e] as a JC low mid front unrounded vowel [ɛ].

Bell's (1984) notion of audience design is evident in Nicki Minaj's utilization of Jamaican Creole features to communicate her dancehall knowledge to the local community, which is similar to that observed for Drake. Through Jamaican Creole, Minaj communicates she is in tune with current social issues surrounding dancehall music, and uses this knowledge through language to establish solidarity with the audience. Like Barack Obama and Drake, Minaj's linguistic crossing affirms a sense of identity and belonging to Jamaicans and their language. Minaj also collaborates with Jamaican dancehall artists including Beenie Man and Gyptian, and she is known to post short video clips of herself using Jamaican Creole language on social media platforms such as Instagram and YouTube. An excerpt from her 2012 collaboration with Beenie Man in the song "Gun Shot" is in Except 4.

Excerpt 4:

Nicky Minaj's Lyrics in the Chorus of the song "Gun Shot"

"tel dem gyal de, tell yu fren dem . . . a gun shot ina dem bloodclaat."

Gloss:

Tell those girls, tell your friends . . . gunshots will be fired on them (the individuals' bodies are referred to as a Jamaican expletive, 'bloodcloth')

The salient creole features include the morphological formation of the plural, the phonological process of th-stopping also known as dental fricative stopping, and the use of the Jamaican Creole lexicon in the utterance of an expletive. Jamaican Creole has the third person plural pronoun "them" after a noun to form the plural marker in JC "dem", unlike English that does this via affixation by adding the suffix 's' to form the plural of nouns. In the data above, Nicky Minaj demonstrated this morphological construction typical of JC to form the plural for the words 'girl' and 'friend' in the JC: 'gyal + dem' = 'girls and 'fren + dem = 'friends'. Additionally, there is the phonological process of TH-stopping in the word for 'those' represented by 'dem' pronounced in English as 'them. Here, the voiced dental fricative [ð] in English becomes the "voiced alveolar stop" [d] in JC. Lastly, Minaj uses a popular lexical item "bomboclaat", an expletive unique to JC and indexing Jamaicanness.

Jansen and Westphal (2020) provide a multimodal analysis of what they refer to as Minaj's (and Rihanna's) multivocal pop personas. They argue (9) that these Caribbean American artists use Jamaican Creole as a dancehall expression and to give voice to their multiple personal identities and musical genres. And that furthermore, "Minaj expresses her Caribbeanness mainly through JC and a reggae/dancehall register, while Trinidadian Creole is not part of her linguistic repertoire." Their linguistic analysis of three of Minaj's YouTube videos and a Vlog from 2013 to 2015, highlights, in addition to American English and African American English, the abundance of Caribbean English Creole (CEC) features that they say are typical of Jamaican Creole. In the 2013 Mavado performance of his song "Give It All To Me", featuring Nicki Minaj, Jansen and Westphal (2020, 8–9) identify the CEC features in Minaj's performance including:

On a morphosyntactic level, Jamaican features include conjunction *se* (*tell dem se*), pronoun *dem* and *me* in subject position as well as past marker *did* plus aspectual *a* (*everything me did a start dem borrow*), copula absence (*we straight; the flow tight; these bitches my sons*) and the preposition *ina* (*pretty gang ina the place*). For individual tokens Minaj employs a Caribbean pronunciation: she pronounces TH as a stop in *everything*, *the* and *them*. The realization of FACE in *straight* with a down gliding diphthong draft version as /tʃrɪeːt/ is typical of JC. She also uses several lexical items prototypical of Jamaica, dancehall and Rastafari with a Jamaican pronunciation. *Bad gyal*, realized as [bad gjal] with a lowered TRAP and a palatal glide, is Minaj's dancehall catchphrase and *tell dem* (*se*) is a typical dancehall catchphrase. *Lick* (*lick a shot*) is prevalent in JC (Cassidy and Le Page 2002, 273). The term *burn fire*, realized as [bon faɪja], is a Rastafarian "fire bon metaphor" (Cooper 2004, 179–206).

Like Nicki Minaj, hip hop and international pop star Rihanna, was born in the Caribbean, specifically, on the island of Barbados in 1988, and moved to the United States, not as a child like Minaj, but rather as a teenager in 2005 to sign with Jay-Z under the hip hop/pop record label Def Jam Recordings. Her first release, "Pon de Replay" (On the Replay, *Gloss: Replay the Song*) was a pop, rhythm and blues (R&B), and dancehall mix with undertones of her early reggae influence while growing up in the Caribbean. These kinds of musical fusions have continued throughout her career, with marked inclusions of Jamaican orature in songs like "Man Down", "Rude Bwoy" and her most recent hit, "Work", a multicultural and multi-racial musical collaboration with significant nods to Jamaican dancehall, evidenced in an official music video for the song. Lyrics extracted from "Work" can be seen in Excerpt 5.

Excerpt 5: From Rihanna's song, "Work"

"work work work work work work yu si mi afi work work work work work work ... Wen yu ago learn learn learn learn? Yu ago ak laik yu no laik it? Yu know I dealt with you di nicest. No bada touch mi unrighteous. No bada teks mi ina kraisis ... jos get redi fi work work work"

Gloss:

Work work work work work work; You see, I have to work work work work work ... When are you going to learn? You're going to act like you don't like it? You know I deal with you in the nicest way. Don't bother to touch me in an unrighteous manner. Don't bother to text me when you're in a crisis ... Just get ready to work work work work work.

Jansen and Westphal (2017, 9) highlight several CEC grammatical features in the overall song that they attribute to Jamaican Creole specifically as it represents the CEC that has the greatest global reach: the use of *na* as a negator, copula absence (*you na righteous*); the absence of the inflection {–s} on third singular verbs (*he see*); the personal pronouns *me* and *him* in subject position (*me na care if him hurt*); modal auxiliary *hafi* (*me hafi work*); quotative *se* (*he se me hafi work*); and the progressive construction *a go* which indicates prospective future meaning (*when you a go learn*).

While Jansen and Westphal note several general CEC phonological features like monophthongization of the FACE vowel in the words *adoration, patience, decoration,* and *foundation*); word-final (–t, –d) consonant cluster absence for words *dealt, nicest, text,* and *act*); and TH-stopping, i.e. the realization of TH as an alveolar stop in the words *with* and *the*), they argue that these are markedly Jamaican uttered with the distinct Jamaican Creole feature of word-initial H-deletion in words *him* and *hurt*).

Ethnomusicologist Wayne Marshall (2007) argues that,

> . . . we hear how reggae paradoxically disappears into hip-hop's vocabulary by virtue of its very centrality and ubiquity. This is partly KRS-One's fault, for he so successfully infused his influential recordings with reggae borrowings that they almost immediately became more familiar than foreign. But it is no doubt also in part the fault of Biggie and Tupac, whose uses of the melody were likely more widely heard than any others and yet made no overt reference to Jamaica.

Here, Marshall is referring to black hip hop rappers or MCs (emcees), mostly from the New York area who are second generation Caribbean Americans born of Jamaican parentage like KRS-One, and the notorious B.I.G. (Biggie), as well as African American MCs like Mos Def and Queen Latifah in the late 1980s to the early 1990s with songs like "9mm Goes Bang", "Respect", "Definition" (by Mos Def as part of the duo Black Star), and "Princess of the Posse", respectively. A decade after the establishment of hip hop as an art form, young artists like these would sample the sounds or creolized words of Reggae and Dancehall artists or feature the artists themselves (for example, Bob Marley, Yellowman, Sister Nancy, Shabba Ranks, Buju Banton, Beenie Man, Chaka Demus and Pliers, Popcaan), therein contributing to a social and cultural shift in the hip hop soundscape. This continues three decades later as evidenced in the hip hop music of Caribbean descendents in North America, as well

as African Americans including the likes of Kanye West ("Famous"),
Beyoncé ("Hold Up"), and Kendrick Lamar ("The Blacker the Berry").

Diasporic Connections

For Devonish (1997, 76), Jamaican dancehall and rap produced by diasporic African descendents are what he refers to as form of "technological
orature," in which oral expression (spoken and sung) and music are
synchronized to produce new national languages and identities for the
masses, more often the poor, located at the periphery of society that has
entered the "information age." These forms of expressions liberate and
give marginalized black bodies alternative ways of being part of the nation
and beyond through spoken word and altered technologies. Furthermore,
Devonish notes, the kinds of expressive and technological innovations
created in Jamaican and US communities are connected historically
through similar lived experiences and spoken Englishes arising out of
oppressive systems of colonization and enslavement. This fits into Morgan's (2001) argument that rap culture in African American hip hop
communities is comprised of "complex organizational and institutional
structures and activities" in which community members are partaking in
collaborations and co-authorships that "re-construct" what is viewed as
local and regional norms. Morgan (190) refers to these ideological shifts
away from the power structure as processes that "explicitly addresses
racism, sexism, capitalism, and morality in ways that simultaneously
expose, exploit, and critique the practices".

Richardson (2006, 28) goes one step further and argues that despite
varying historical trajectories for African Americans and African Jamaicans, particularly in terms of the differing nature of colonial and post-colonial outcomes in the respective regions, there is an "inextricable kinship"
that, in the case of shared language, represents the various strands of collective histories and experiences connected to a West African background.
And that, furthermore, connected to this shared historical background is
the shared history of slavery, and subsequently "radical movements for
diasporic black liberation, post-industrialization, migration, technological
diffusion of black music around the globe via radio, CDs and, of late, cable
television and internet." For Richardson, dancehall and hip hop share

core aesthetics that are realized through parallel developments in their respective vocabularies. For example, she states (2006, 29), ". . .Dancehall's 'nuff respect' parallels Hiphop's 'props' – both terms acknowledging that first and foremost persons from these backgrounds deserve respect and have something of value to offer . . ." And while African American rappers may use Jamaican words connected to dancehall (for example, Bwoy, gwaan, likkle, tief, vex, a go, inna, pon) partly so as to appear cool, hardcore, urban, African diasporic, or socially, politically or culturally conscious, when placed in a historical context, these acts of identity or performativity can be read as a cross-fertilization that reverberates across geographic boundaries and cultural spaces.

Anthropologist Deborah Thomas (2006, 129) argues that "Black America and black Jamaica exist in *one* transnational sociocultural and political field, a field that is characterized by power relations that are historically contingent yet dynamic." She urges that diaspora should be viewed and understood as a *process* and not a historical event or state of being. When theorizing diaspora at the intersection of music, ethnomusicologist Thomas Solomon (2015) utilizes Appadurai's (1991, 1996) notion of ethnoscapes in which people move around globally and take with them their cultures and identities. Starting in the twentieth century in Jamaica, for black Jamaicans, deterritorialization takes root through transnational migration and technological flow across space, and as a consequence, identity, culture, and language are no longer solely bound by the nation-state. Although black Jamaicanness is rooted in Jamaica, the twentieth century opens up new possibilities for reworking of connections and creating hybridities. Solomon (2015, 205) points out, "Research on music in diasporic communities has demonstrated how music can function as a sort of 'glue' connecting diasporic communities widely dispersed around the globe." Here, we want to be clear that we are making a distinction with sonic diasporas described by Henriques (2008) as being based on feelings, tastes and vibes of sounds, which can be disconnected from people who consider themselves racially, ethnically or culturally connected to its origins. Rather, the *affective* diasporic belonging referred to here is connected to art, music and language practices that "provide frameworks for organizing diasporic experience, including the historical consciousness of having come from somewhere else, and identifying with other people in other places who share this origin" (Solomon 2015, 206). Invoking historian Paul Gilroy (1993, 40), artistic expression, then, for African Americans and black Jamaicans is part of the liberation project "towards both individual self-fashioning and communal liberation" in the African diasporic consciousness.

Origins Revisited

Hip hop folklore has it that this movement started in the early 1970s with Kool DJ Herc, born Clive Campbell, oftentimes referred to as the father of hip hop. The story goes that Herc migrated to the Bronx, New York in 1967 at twelve years old from Kingston, Jamaica with his mother (and other family members) who was coming to the United States for nursing. The Hart–Celler Act, better known as the Immigration and Nationality Act of 1965, "ended an immigration-admissions policy based on race and ethnicity" that privileged Western Europeans over all others for entrance into the United States (MPI 2015). This change in American national law opened the metaphorical floodgates to large migrations from the Anglophone Caribbean. Thus, parallel to Herc, other Caribbean-immigrant children and their African American counterparts were co-creating new musical fusions throughout the urban boroughs of New York City; this included the likes of Grandmaster Flash and Afrika Bambaataa (predated by Grandmaster Flowers and King Charles) (Founding Fathers 2012).

Like many other Caribbean immigrant children at the time, Herc felt awkward and out of place among his peers (Waters 1999). As Herc recalls (Chang 2005, 72) about his public school days in the Bronx, he was decked out in his corduroy coat, flip-up-and-come-over-your-ears snow hat and cowboy boots, and mercilessly teased about his shoes as roach-killers. For Herc, "At that time, being Jamaican wasn't fashionable. Bob Marley didn't come through yet to make it more fashionable, to even give a chance for people to listen to our music." He was warned that "The gangs was throwing Jamaicans in garbage cans!" In recreating himself and his identity and representing an acculturation of sorts, Herc developed and used giant sound systems with loud sonic volume similar to that found on the reggae scene in Jamaica. He also "spoke" (with shout-outs to individuals or rhyming) over the rhythm of a beat, similar to the toaster DJs in Jamaica (cf., Hebdige 1987; Toop 2000). Perhaps most impactful about Herc was his creation of the Merry-Go-Round vibrating loop of instrumental sound breaks with Afro-Latino beats and congas.

Herc attributes his musical knowledge and appreciation to American artists introduced to him by his parents throughout his childhood as well as Jamaican artists whom he listened to growing up. In an informal 2013 Whatzup TV, NY YouTube interview with Herc and the Jamaican reggae, dancehall, and dub artist, U-Roy, in New York City, Herc bows down to U-Roy in acknowledgement of his musical influence on him, and as a consequence on hip hop. U-Roy responds with "Reggae and hip hop is big time family. It a come from the same. Just like when we DJ and we have the singer coming in, and sing and come out. The same way the rappers dem a do now . . . It's family. Very close." U-Roy continues, "Before we start make our own music inna Jamaica. We usta listen to pure American music; people like Ruth Brown, James Brown, Smiley Lewis, Fats Domino, Lewis Prima, and Louie Jordan. . . . So we start listening to de ska until it come to rocksteady until it come over to reggae. It's basically de same thing." However, Toop (2000, 104) pushes back on this idea, arguing, "Tempting as it might be to imagine that hip hop emerged simply through the influence of Jamaican toasters like U Roy and Big Youth, it was, in fact, more subtle than that. Most rappers will tell you that they either disliked reggae or were only vaguely aware of it in the early and middle 1970s." But it is this very subtlety that we think is important in recognizing African diasporic people across the US and the Anglophone Caribbean as connected through language. We argue that in spite of tensions, borders became boundless and boundaries necessarily blurred in the co-construction of authentic African diasporic identities.

CONCLUSION

On 24 March 2020, renowned African American hip hop artists, DJs and producers Timbaland and Swizz Beatz (of Caribbean descent including Jamaica) started the webcast series Verzuz in response to the COVID-19 pandemic. The format of this virtual show is a two hour back and forth "battle" between two iconic hip hop or R&B artists highlighting their musical hits. This impromptu show that generally garners a live viewership of between 200,000 and half million people has seen the likes of T-Pain and Lil Jon, Erykah Badu and Jill Scott, as well as Gladys Knight and Patti LaBelle. The impact of Jamaican dancehall was evident with the inclusion of Bounty Killer and Beeine Man. While in the early 1970s Jamaican artists were still relatively new to the American scene, fifty years later, the influence of dancehall on hip hop, and vice versa is undeniable. Again echoing anthropologist Deborah Thomas, the diaspora is a *process*. On 19 June 2020, marking Juneteenth, the day of liberation for enslaved African peoples in 1865 United States, Verzuz presented a battle between African American artists Alicia Keys (of Caribbean descent including Jamaica) and John Legend. Changing up the individual battle format, they opened with a joint performance of Bob Marley's "Redemption Song". This was followed by Alicia "setting it off" with the dancehall/ ragga single, "Ghetto Story", by Cham and featuring Alicia Keys. John Legend responded with the first song, "The Miseducation of Lauryn Hill", in his recording career on which he played piano. Lauryn Hill is an African American artist with Caribbean music influences.

Richardson (2006, 24) aptly notes that "Nowadays, it is normal to hear Dancehall DJs over Hip Hop Beats and rappers over Dancehall Beats. Collaborations between artists have grown steadily, reflecting and contributing to the crosscultural fertilization of African American and African Jamaican discourse." That is not to say in the process that there are not major tensions or historical concerns, especially regarding the commodification of music. Case in point is the copious sampling of the reggae song "Bam Bam", made popular by dancehall DJ Sister Nancy in the early 1980s. This song can be found (that is, sampled) on "Lost Ones" by Lauryn Hill, "Bomb" by Chris Brown featuring Whiz Khalifa, "Run Run" by Tamar Braxton, "Just Hanging Out "by Main Source, "Compton" by Guerilla Black featuring Beenie Man, "Hip Hop Ya'll" by Da Homlez, "Famous" by Kanye West featuring Rihanna, and most recently, in 2017, on "Bam" by Jay-Z featuring Damian Marley. In a 2018 interview with New Musical Express, Sister Nancy speaks to the years of not being compensated for her musical contribution noting, "Yes, I'm getting the royalties now. I wasn't getting anything for thirty-four years, but in 2014 after they used it in a Reebok commercial I decided to sue them. Now I own 50 per cent of the *One, Two* album. At least I'm getting something now, I never used to get anything."

In a 2018 Rolling Stones article, Sean Paul, Jamaican dancehall artist says, "Dancehall is the son of reggae, but the father of several genres," including hip hop, Afrobeats, reggaeton and grime. And yet anxiety abounds for dancehall artists looking to find their way into the international market distribution system. In terms of the US market, Jamaican dancehall artists face travel restrictions, and some dancehall artists feel their art must evolve further as there is competition from other forms of African diasporic music in addition to pop, dancehall may appeal only to certain demographics, and it may be difficult for artists to find a signing label. And finally, access to advanced technologies and streaming may be hindered by breaks in wireless connections. While ethnomusicologist Wayne Marshall speaks of the disappearance of reggae into hip hop, there is also potential *erasure* that dance hall artists may be weary of, evidenced by the contributions of Sister Nancy. Although Sister Nancy is featured on Jay-Z's sound track "BAM" featuring Damian Marley as well, she is not acknowledged in the credits. Although Jamaican dancehall DJ Agent Sasco is on Kendrick Lamar's "The Blacker the Berry", he too is not credited as a featured artist. So, within a capitalistic orientation, work remains to be done.

Richardson (2006, 22) says "The shifting terrains, experiences, aesthetics and histories that brought about Hip hop and Dancehall go back, back and forth and forth." Jamaican literary scholar, Carolyn Cooper (2004) speaks of the encoded languages of African American Language and Jamaican Creole that like Bob Marley's "Redemption Song" serve as liberation discourses of emancipation. Damien Marley in the "BAM" video says African diaspora peoples are . . . "borrowing from our ancestors, but recreating and re-presenting it. That's who we are. That's where we come from." Jay-Z (of Jamaican parentage) follows with, "We are vessels, right. We're whistles... the wind go through us. We make the noise." Hip hop, with the help of reggae and dancehall, impacted by the predecessors of rap music, is what Carolyn Cooper refers to as the "noise of remembering." Through amplified noise and verbal virtuosity, the historically dispersed African communities use the noise, both separated and fused, for their resistance, their liberation, their freedom, and their power.

REFERENCES

Appadurai, Arjun. 1991. "Global Ethnoscapes: Notes and Queries for a Transnational Anthropology" In Interventions: Anthropologies of the Present, edited by R.G. Fox. Santa Fe, NM: School of American Research, 191–210.

———. 1996. *Modernity at Large: Cultural Dimensions of Globalization*. Minneapolis: University of Minnesota Press.

Bascaramurty, Dakshana. 2017. "Tu di worl": Creole Goes Global. (https://www.dandc.eu/en/article/creole-languages-caribbean-reflect-and-express-peoples-identities.) (Accessed 26 October 2020.)

Blake, Renée. 1997. "Defining the Envelope of Linguistic Variation: The Case of "Don't Count" Forms in the Copula Analysis of African American Vernacular English". *Language Variation and Change* 9 (1): 57–79. https://doi.org/10.1017/s0954394500001794) (Accessed 1 October 2021).

Born, Georgina, and David Hesmondhalgh. 2000. Introduction: On Difference, Representation, and Appropriation in Music. *Western Music and Its Others: Difference, Representation, and Appropriation in Music*, 1–58. Berkeley,CA: University of California Press.

Brathwaite, Kamau. 1984. *History of the Voice: The Development of Nation Language in Anglophone Caribbean Poetry*. London: New Beacon.

Cassidy, Frederic, and Robert Le Page. 2002. *Dictionary of Jamaican English*. Kingston, Jamaica: University of the West Indies Press.

Cham, Baby & Keys, Alicia. 2010. *Ghetto Story Chapter 2*. Youtube. (https://www.youtube.com/watch?v=loPRsrqrDXc&feature=emb_title) (Accessed October 28, 2020.)

Chang, Jeff, and Dj Kool Herc. 2008. *Can't Stop Won't Stop: AHhistory of the Hip-Hop Generation*. New York: Picador.

Chishti, Muzaffar, Faye Hipsman, and Isabel Ball. 2015. "Fifty Years of Immigration and Nationality Act Continues to Reshape the United States". *ILW.COM*. Immigration Daily. (https://www.migrationpolicy.org/article/fifty-years-1965-immigration-and-nationality-act-continues-reshape-united-states) (Accessed 28 October 2020.)

Clifford, James. 1999. *Routes:Ttravel and Translation in the Late Twentieth Century*. Cambridge, MA: Harvard University Press.

Connell, John, and Chris Gibson. 2004. "World Music: Deterritorializing Place and Identity". *Progress in Human Geography* 28(3): 342–61.

Cooper, Carolyn. 2004. *Sound Clash: Jamaican Dancehall Culture at Large*. New York: Palgrave Macmillan.

Dawkins, Nickesha. 2009. "Gender-based Vowel Use in Jamaican Dancehall Lyrics". *Sargasso* 1. 95–114.

_____. 2013. "She Se Dis, Him Se Dat: Examining Gender-based Vowel Use in Jamaican Dancehall". In *International Reggae: Current and Future Trends in Jamaican Popular Music*, 124–66. Kingston: Pelican.

Devonish, Hubert. 1990. "Creole Languages and the Development of a Technological Culture in the Caribbean". *Language Issues* 4(1).

_____. 1996. "Vernacular Languages and Writing Technology Transfer: The Jamaican Case". *Caribbean Language Issues – Old & New*, 101–111. Kingston: University of the West Indies Press.

_____. 1997. "Walking Around the Language Barrier: A Caribbean View of the Ebonics Controversy". *Small Axe: A Journal of Criticism* no. 2: 63–76.

_____. 1998a. "Electronic Orature: The Deejay's Discovery". *Social and Economic Studies* 47(1): 33–53.

_____. 1998b. "On the Existence of Autonomous Language Varieties in 'Creole Continuum Situations". *Studies in Caribbean Linguistics* II. 1–12.

_____. 2007. *Language and Liberation: Creole Language Politics in the Caribbean*. Kingston: Arawak Press.

_____. 2017a. "Tu di worl": Creole Goes Global". *Development and Cooperation*. (https://www.dandc.eu/en/article/creole-languages-caribbean-reflect-and-express-peoples-identities.) (Accessed 15 July 2020.)

_____. 2017b. Jamaica's Nation Language. *Development and Cooperation*. (https://www.dandc.eu/en/article/how-jamaican-creole-became-main-language-artistic-expression.) (Accessed 15 July 2020.)

_____, and Karen Carpenter. 2020. *Language, Race, and the Global Jamaican*. New York: Palgrave Macmillan.

Devonish, Hubert, and Byron Jones. 2017. "A State of Language, Music and Crisis of Nation". *Open Edition* 13(2). (http://journals.openedition.org/volume/5321)

Dwamena, Anakwa. 2016. "How Hip Hop Lost its Accent". *The New Republic*. (https://newrepublic.com/article/136588/hip-hop-lost-accent) (Accessed October 28, 2020.)

Ewoodzie, Joseph. 2017. *Break Beats in the Bronx: Rediscovering Hip-hop's Early Years*. Chapel Hill, NC: University of North Carolina Press.

Founding Fathers. 2014. "Untold Stories of Hip Hop", Narrated by Chuck D. *Youtube*. (https://www.youtube.com/watch?v=1G13bR0B0-8) (Accessed October 28, 2020.)

Gilroy, Paul. 1993. *The Black Atlantic:Modernity and Double Consciousness*. London: Verso.

Hall, Stuart. 1995. Negotiating Caribbean Identities. *New Left Review*. (https://newleftreview.org/issues/i209/articles/stuart-hall-negotiating-caribbean-identities) (Accessed 28 October 2020.)

Hebdiige, Dick. 1987. *Cut "n" Mix: Culture: Identity and Caribbean Music*. London: Methuen.

Henriques, Julian. 2008. "Sonic Diaspora, Vibrations, and Rhythm: Thinking Through the Sounding of the Jamaican Dancehall Session". *African and Black Diaspora: An International Journal* 1(2): 215–36.

Jansen, Lisa, and Michael Westphal. 2017. "Rihanna Works Her Multivocal Pop Persona: A Morpho-yntactic and Accent Analysis of Rihanna's Singing Style. *English Today* 33(2): 46–55.

_____. 2020. *Caribbean Identity in Pop Music: Rihanna's and Nicki Minaj's Multivocal Pop Personas*. Manuscript submitted for publication.

Kalra, Virinder, Raminder Kaur, and John Hutnyk. 2005. *Diaspora and Hybridity*. London: Sage.

Lull, James. 1995. *Media, Communication, Culture: A Global Approach*. New York: Columbia University Press.

Marshall, Wayne. 2007. Follow Me Now: The Zigzagging Zunguzung Meme. *Wayne & Wax*. (http://wayneandwax.com/?p=137) (Accessed October 27, 2020.)

Morgan, Marcyliena. 2001. "Nuthin' but a G Thang": Grammar and Language Ideology in Hip Hop Identity". In *Sociocultural and Historical Contexts of African American English*, edited by Sonja L. Laneheart, 187–209. Amsterdam: John Benjamins.

Negus, Keith. 1996. *Popular Music in Theory: An Introduction*. Middletown,CT: Wesleyan University Press.

Ramton, Ben. 1995. *Crossing: Language and Ethnicity Among Adolescents*. New York: Longman.

Revolt TV. 2020. Alicia Keys and John Legend battle head-to-head on Verzuz. *Revolt Tv*. (https://www.youtube.com/watch?v=7-Q_hwMSY2E) (Accessed October 28, 2020.)

Richardson, Elaine. 2006. *Hiphop Literacies*. Routledge.

Safran, William. 1991. "Diasporas in Modern Societies: Myths of Homeland and Return". *Diaspora: A Journal of Transnational Studies* 1(1): 83–99. https://doi.org/10.1353/dsp.1991.0004

Solomon, Thomas. 2015. "Theorizing Diaspora and Music". *Lide Mesta* 17. 201–19.

Suarez, Gary. 2018. Drake Is Now The RIAA's Top Certified Singles Artist Ever. *Forbes*. (https://www.forbes.com/sites/garysuarez/2018/06/29/drake-riaa/#5d-cc4b8f6c15) (Accessed June 29, 2018.)

The Peopling of New York Final Project: Hip Hop Caribbean Origins. *The Peopling of New Final Project*. (https://eportfolios.macaulay.cuny.edu/luttonprojects15/music-and-art/music/hip-hop/hip-hop-caribbean-origins/) (Accessed 28 October 2020.)

Thomas, Deborah. 2006. "Public Bodies: Virginity Testing, Redemption Songs, and Racial Respect in Jamaica". *Journal of Latin American Anthropology* 11(1): 1–31.

_____. 2007. "Blackness Across Borders: Jamaican Diasporas and New Politics of Citizenship". *Identities: Global Studies in Culture and Power* 14(1–2): 111–33.

Toop, David. 2000. *Rap attack 3: African Rap to Global Hip Hop*. London: Serpent's Tail.

Waters, Mary. 1999. *Black Identities*. Cambridge, MA: Harvard University Press.

Winford, Don. 1994. "Sociolinguistic Approaches to Language use in the Anglophone Caribbean". In *Language and the Social Construction of Identity in Creole Situations*, edited by Marcyliena Morgan, 43–62. Los Angeles: Center for Afro-American Studies, University of California.

XXL Staff. 2017. 20 of the Most Iconic Reggae Samples in Hip-Hop. *XXL Mag*. (https://www.xxlmag.com/iconic-hip-hop-reggae-samples/) (Accessed 27 October 2020.)

CHAPTER 8

Political Cartoons of the 2008 General Elections in Barbados

A Rhetorical Perspective

KORAH BELGRAVE

INTRODUCTION

Barbados is a democracy with a bicameral system of government. General elections for the lower house or parliament are constitutionally due every five years. The electoral system in use, based on the electoral formula used, is a majoritarian one as defined by Norris (1997, 1). This electoral formula requires candidates to win a plurality. This is also known as a "first-past-the-post" system. The country is divided into thirty single-member constituencies. Eligible voters within each constituency cast a single ballot for one candidate; the candidate with the largest share of the vote in each constituency wins the seat in that constituency and is elected to parliamentary office. The party with the overall majority of seats forms the government (Norris 1997, 2).

Over the course of the last few general elections, the Caribbean has seen a significant change in the kind of politics practised. Koetzle and Brunell's (1996, 94) analysis of the changing nature of politics in America seems to hold true for the Caribbean in general and for Barbados in particular. They observe that the dominance of political parties has declined and therefore electoral decisions are made based more on perceptions of candidates and evaluations based on these perceptions than on party policies. This decline has encouraged candidates and voters alike to concentrate more on the charisma and character of individual candidates and less on party image. This position has been further supported by the pull that charismatic leaders have had in the past. During the last twenty-five years, charismatic figures such as Owen Arthur, David Thompson, and Mia Mottley have been able to win over the electorate in Barbados, in spite of the poor showing by some candidates in their respective political parties.

The editorial cartoon has a significant role to play in a democracy. Its role, like that of the editorial, is to address issues of social and political importance in the society, and to persuade readers to agree with their creator's perspective on the issue under discussion. The editorial cartoon is often referred to as a political cartoon; however, Bush (2013, 63) argues that a distinction should be made between the use of these terms. He proposes that though there is a belief that all social issues are political, the social and the political are separate in the cartoon arena. Bush posits that *political cartoon* be used for all cartoons that have a greater political than social purpose, and *editorial cartoon* be reserved for a political cartoon that is drawn contemporary to the issue it examines. This paper uses the term *political cartoon* in the sense proposed by Bush (2013).

A significant role of cartoonists throughout history has been to follow and interpret political campaigns for the public (Press 1981, 50; Buell and Maus 1988, 847). However, that role has taken on an even greater significance in the Information Age. Press (1981, 50) posits that average citizens do not have the time to spare, nor the requisite specialized knowledge to follow and understand what is going on in government. As a result of the lack of time and a general disinterest in politics, the general public is likely to be more amenable to packaged sentiments in the form of cartoons because they are easily accessible in the form of pictures and humorous enough to not appear disruptive to their everyday lives.

The busyness of life is further compounded by this modern generation's enchantment with social media where the medium of communication is quite similar to cartoons – a combination of words and pictures. Besides consuming large amounts of their precious time, social media has made them even more receptive to visual rhetoric. Weseka (2012, 223) believes that the growing influence of visual media in contemporary society is a reason to be alarmed, especially considering what he has called a "paradigm shift from oral argumentation to visual argumentation". Abraham's (2009, 119) suggestion that cartoons transform complex opaque events and social situations into quick, readable depictions that make it easier for the public to understand the nature of these events and situations serves as a plausible explanation for the society's reliance on visual rhetoric. Given this paradigm shift, political cartoons have the potential to act as powerful arguments for particular positions and can affect readers' attitudes as well as beliefs about candidates, events, and issues in elections. This article analyses the political cartoons of the 2008 political campaign in Barbados in terms of their effectiveness in communicating political ideas and attitudes. As Sani et al. (2012, 53) espouse, cartoonists "harness both linguistic and non-linguistic elements ingeniously and persuasively to create effect in a literary or dramatic passion and to evoke a particular response from readers." Further, as they explained, these devices are intended to persuade the public to consider, or make them more receptive to, a different point of view. Cartoons may even provide a rational argument for public opinion that may lead to a positive change in society (53) .

LITERATURE REVIEW

Press (1981, 56) posits that cartoons play a critical role in preserving democracy. According to Press, "democratic governments not only tolerate criticism, but they institutionalize it in such practices as the election, the press conference, the TV talk show or the editorial page with its cartoon. An assumption of democracy is that the government cannot remain democratic without permitting the existence of such critics, independent of the government itself".

Patterson (1980, 5), in analysing the change in the nature of politics in the 1980s, suggested that short-term influences such as election issues and personalities had become more significant in determining voters' choices. This is even more so in the twenty-first century. Therefore, the role of the media in making the public aware of these issues is critical. Patterson contends that "voters' evaluations of the candidates are now based more heavily on what they learn through the media during the campaign"(1980, 5). It is felt that even "such openly biased sources of political information as negative campaign advertising are positively associated with greater issue knowledge among voters" (Koetzle and Brunell 1996, 95).

In keeping with the importance of raising the public's awareness of issues of concern to all, Denton (2005, xii) suggests that political campaigns can be viewed as national conversations since these campaigns consist of talk and human interaction. These national conversations, the essence of which is persuasive, are forms of persuasive discourse designed to cause the electorate to think and act in specific ways based on particular interpretations or meanings gleaned from these public discourses. The political cartoon, as part of this larger discourse, comments critically on events, actions, and personas with the aim of influencing political choice among the electorate. It was recognition of the political cartoon as a powerful means of suasion, and its position in the agenda-setting role of media, that led Medhurst and DeSousa (1981, 198–99) to identify the persuasive techniques used by cartoonists and to attempt a taxonomy for "recognizing and analysing the elements of graphic persuasion as embodied in the political cartoon". They proposed that the canons of rhetoric, with slight modifications, be used as a framework to critique graphic discourse which they see as arguments in which the audience participates. By crafting their arguments as enthymemes, which present a particular pattern of reasoning but omit the conclusions, cartoonists encourage readers to work together with them to create persuasive meaning and arrive at a conclusion.

Other studies have examined how cartoons can be used to influence public opinion. Conners (2005, 479) in examining the use of political cartoons during the 2004 American presidential campaign found that the cartoons were influential in creating the public's perception of Kerry and Bush. She posits that by linking them to natural disasters such as hurricanes and volcanoes, to literary characters and children's fairy tale characters, cartoons helped to reinforce negative perceptions of the candidates. Abraham (2009, 162) in researching the effectiveness of cartoons for orienting social issues concluded, "we may not be certain about the specific effects of cartoons on readers, but there is no doubt about its power to orient social issues and tap the collective consciousness of communities". These studies attest to the significant power of the media to influence voters' perceptions and ultimately their decision-making.

This is especially significant in Barbados where, historically, low voter turnout has favoured the party in power. Parties have therefore gone to great lengths to "educate" the electorate on the issues involved in the campaign and also to influence their perception of candidates.

The Political and Social Context

Barbados is a small island nation of 431 square kilometres with a population of 277, 821 (Barbados Statistical Service 2013, i). In 2008, there were 235, 510 registered voters and thirty seats in the House of Assembly. The members of the House are elected in single-member constituencies. Since Barbados' independence in 1966, two major parties have dominated the political landscape – the Barbados Labour Party (BLP) and the Democratic Labour Party (DLP). In 2008, the DLP and the BLP presented candidates to contest all thirty seats. Of the sixty-nine candidates who contested the general elections, six of them were from minor parties and three were independents. The other parties in the elections were the People's Empowerment Party (PEP) and the People's Democratic Congress (PDC) which presented three candidates each. Opinion polls predicted that the elections would be a fight between the DLP, led by David Thompson, and the BLP, led by incumbent prime minister, Owen Arthur. Mr Arthur had been prime minister since 1994. Historically, a low voter turnout in Barbados has favoured the ruling party (see Appendix A), so the major opposition party makes every effort at election time to encourage voters to turn out in large numbers to vote, and beyond that, to vote for them.

Moreover, the last two general election campaigns in Barbados have seen the steady emergence of a new type of Barbadian voter. These voters in the 18–25 age group have not been exposed to the rhetoric of independence platforms or experienced the buoyancy of independence and sentiments of nationalism that bound their parents to particular parties. They therefore have no clear or strong ties to any political party and are looking to make up their own minds apart from the politics of parents. This group seems to rely more on candidate perception than on parental party ties. Consequently, they look to the media to give them a picture of the candidates. At the same time, political parties have increased their use of Facebook and other social media platforms as campaign tools in an effort to reach this group of voters. This exploits their reliance on media and at the same time encourages that reliance by leading them to believe that the media informs them. Koetzle and Brunell (1996, 95) support the view that weakened partisanship ties has led to the media playing a greater role in deciding electoral outcomes. Recognizing the important role that the media play in politics, politicians in Barbados have spent large sums of money getting their personal message to the public in order to build a good public image.

Barbados has two official print newspapers, the *Barbados Advocate* and the *Nation* newspaper, and one official online e-paper, the *Barbados Today*. There are two other "unofficial" online publications in the form of blogs, the *Barbados Underground* and the *Barbados Free Press*. Both official print newspapers are also available online and the *Nation* has recently launched an e-paper version. The *Nation* is the publication with the largest circulation and the only publication with an editorial cartoonist. The *Barbados Free Press* also publishes political cartoons on an occasional basis as header cartoons. These header cartoons led to the development of a "cartoon" page on the *Barbados Free Press* homepage which consists of archived cartoons with thumbnails to lead to full-page cartoons which are too big to fit on the homepage.

The *Nation* newspaper, as it has done traditionally, launched a special publication during the 2008 general election in Barbados. The 2008 publication was titled *Campaign XPRESS*. This publication, offered on weekdays only for the period 3–14 January, was intended to keep the public abreast of election happenings and also to give them a view of their candidates. The Campaign XPRESS provided daily commentary on and critique of key events, issues and candidates during the approximately fifteen days of campaigning. The editorial cartoons in this publication often reinforced the ideas made in the editorial columns which they accompanied. Coverage of the campaign was also carried in the regular publications – the *Daily Nation*, the *Midweek Nation*, the *Weekend Nation*, the *Saturday Sun* and the *Sunday Sun*.

METHODOLOGY

Medhurst and DeSousa (1981, 199–200) see similar forces at work for the cartoonist as for the orator and argue that "the neo-classical canons of invention, disposition, style, memory, and delivery help to structure the graphic artist's persuasive efforts in much the same manner as they have structured the persuasive efforts of oral persuaders for two millennia". As they explain, "the cartoonist must discover or invent content, arrange that content for specific effect, and stylize the presentation by conscious application of the artistic principles inherent in the medium".

DeSousa and Medhurst (1982, 88) posit further that cartoons serve an agenda-setting function and a framing function, among others. Political cartoons contribute to agenda-setting by providing readers with a sense of the significant issues, events, or topics. The fact that topics appear in cartoons may result in them being discussed by the public and therefore increase their significance in the national conversation. In this way cartoons serve to bring issues to the attention of the public and to introduce them as a topic of conversation. Coombs and Shaw's (1972) theory on the agenda-setting role of the mass media, posits that the kinds of issues people discuss, think about, and even worry about are shaped and directed by what the news media chooses to publish.

Framing is a subtle process of organizing information, in the case of cartoons, through the choice of images, words, contrasts, that influences the audience's understanding of the information. Entman (1993, 52) explains that "to frame is to select some aspects of a perceived reality and make them more salient in a communicating text, in such a way as to promote a particular problem definition, causal interpretation, moral evaluation, and or treatment recommendation for the item described". DeSousa and Medhurst (1982) propose that cartoons, because of their inherent condensed form, function as subtle, yet powerful frames with which to characterize the political process and its players. By reducing a complex issue or event to a simple metaphorical form, they act as a point of reference for deeper discussions (95). The traditional canons of rhetoric from which Medhurst and DeSousa draw to analyse the cartoons also form a source from which critical discourse analysis draws as it attempts to expose the linguistic means by which power is established and/or maintained in societies.

Richardson (2007, 28) proposes critical discourse analysis (CDA) as a tool for analysing newspapers. He defines CDA as an attempt to link linguistic analysis to social analysis. In examining the principles of CDA, he notes that CDA is concerned with the "linguistic character of social and cultural processes and structures", and with the study of power relations. He sees society and culture as dialectically related to discourse, shaping and at the same time being shaped by discourse. Thus "every single instance of language use reproduces or transforms society and culture, including power relations". This makes CDA an important tool for analysing cartoons as well.

Medhurst and DeSousa's rhetorical analysis and Richardson's CDA together provide a means of exploring cartoons as communication tools and examining their possible role in maintaining or reinforcing power relations in a society. Using rhetorical analysis and CDA, this paper sought to analyse the editorial cartoons of the 2008 election campaign in Barbados as political communication and to consider how they worked to set agenda and influence voter perception and attitude.

Data

The political cartoons published in the *Nation* were also published elsewhere. However, the *Nation* was chosen as the source of the cartoons for this analysis since it was the publication in which both political parties advertised. The *Nation*, therefore, provided a comprehensive view of the election campaign in cartoon form. It must be noted that the cartoons published in the *Nation* were also broadcast on TV screens before each political mass meeting held by the opposition DLP and therefore formed a significant part of their strategy. This also meant that the audience for these particular cartoons was extended beyond newspaper readers to the large gatherings who attended the political rallies.

Twenty-seven editorial cartoons appeared in the *Nation* newspapers during the election period. Election Day was set for 15 January 2008. The election date was announced on 20 December 2007, eight months before elections were constitutionally due. The length of the campaign was short and was further shortened by the intervening Christmas celebrations. Campaigning began in earnest on Tuesday, 2 January 2008. The cartoons analysed were all published during the period 3–19 January 2008.

The twenty-seven cartoons for the period were classified as political cartoons based on Bush's categories. They were divided into two categories: cartoons by the editorial cartoonist for the *Nation,* and cartoons which were paid advertisements by political parties. Of the cartoons analysed, seven were published in the *Campaign XPRESS.* These were published in the period 3–14 January. They were all located in the top half of the editorial page and had an average size of 36 square inches. The cartoonist in this instance was Guy O'Neal (Guy-O). Seven other political cartoons ran on the editorial pages of the *Daily Nation,* the *Midweek Nation* and the *Weekend Nation* during the period 1–19 January 2008. These were also created by Guy-O. These fourteen cartoons were classified as political cartoons.

Eight other cartoons ran as paid advertisements by the DLP in the *Nation*'s publications: the *Daily Nation, Weekend Nation,* the *Saturday Sun,* and the *Sunday Sun.* These were labelled "Electoons." They occupied the lower half of the page in the main section of the papers. In addition to these, there were five full-page advertisements which were made up of cartoons and regular advertising copy. One of these seems to be a collection of three previous "electoons", along with two others which seem to present a conclusion to the story told in previous sections. The cartoonist is unknown. There were no cartoons as paid advertisements by the BLP.

ANALYSIS

Three of the twenty-seven, or approximately 11 per cent of the cartoons, dealt with issues of policy. This is in keeping with findings by Koetzle and Brunell (1996,97) that cartoon reporting seldom focuses on substantive issues. They found that cartoons are more likely to focus on candidate traits as well as other "horse race" concerns like candidate standings and strategy . . .; coverage of substantive policy issues is generally confined to broad hot-button issues like the economy, war and peace, and corruption because these substantive issues resonate with the public at large. The other twenty-four cartoons focused on campaign occurrences, candidate character and other electoral issues.

Figure 8.1. High Cost of Living

The cartoon in figure 8.1 is classified under the broad theme of the economy. Here the cartoonist offers a satirical comment on the high cost of living in Barbados and the subsequent hopelessness that pervades the society. The cartoon depicts citizens forced to turn to a life of crime, and also introduces the issue of rising crime and violence as a social problem. The consumer is depicted here as the victim of a robbery, but ironically, even the would-be-robber is affected because the victim has nothing left to steal. It has taken all he earned to buy food. The gloom and darkness of the night is also suggestive of the gloom and hopelessness that has enveloped the society. This draws from and encourages discussion on the cost of living, and also on rising crime in society. It places these on the social agenda and since discussion on the radio call-in programmes often followed themes set by the local newspapers, these would then become the topic(s) for the day.

Figure 8.2. High Cost of Living II

The cartoon in figure 8.2 continued this theme, suggesting that the cost of living had skyrocketed to the point that ordinary citizens needed financing in order to buy food. In this cartoon, the supermarket offers financing options. The couple in the cartoon is representative of the average middle-class couple (suggested by their dress), seen apparently contemplating the loan facility extended by the supermarket. The supermarket offering financing is a satirical comment on the living condition of ordinary citizens, who cannot even afford to buy food, but also a comment on the supermarket franchises as a whole which, like banking institutions, are also exploiting the citizens.

The cartoon in figure 8.3 introduces the issue of campaign financing which was often a discussion topic on radio call-in programmes during the election campaign. David Comissiong, the leader of the third party in the elections often raised this on the campaign trail and the cartoonist, in this instance, depicts a caricature of Comissiong querying the source of the funding. His quizzical expressions as well as his question,

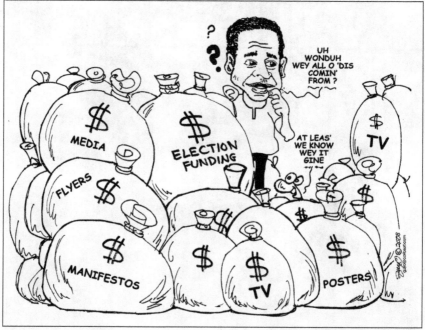

Figure 8.3. Campaign Funds

"Uh wonduh wey all o' dis comin from?" ("I wonder where all of this is coming from") is met by Willi Worm's placatory response, "At least we know wey it gine!" ("At least we know where it is going"). As suggested by the labels on the money bags, there is funding to print manifestos and flyers, pay for television appearances, and so on. This cartoon critiques the existing situation in Barbados in which no party is legally required to declare the source of its campaign funding. There was much discussion about the need for transparency in campaign funding and for politicians to declare their assets once they entered the political race in order to combat political corruption.

The cartoon prompts readers to question not only the source of funds, but also the abundance of funds available for election spending. This is especially cogent given that the BLP also accused the Taiwanese government of funding the DLP's election campaign, which the DLP vehemently denied. The cartoonist uses Comissiong, the leader of a minority party, to question the sources of funding of the two major parties, particularly because his party was not funded to the same extent.

In examining the sources from which cartoonists drew material for their daily messages, the same major topics were found to occur as were reported by Medhurst and DeSousa (1981). They found that cartoonists drew inspiration from four major sources: political commonplaces, literary/cultural allusions, personal character traits, and situational themes. A common topic of political cartoons is the cartoonists' view of the voter. In figure 8.4 below, the voter is represented as undecided until the very end, even in the polling booth.

In the election polls conducted during the 2008 election campaign, a large number of voters represented themselves as "undecided" and much significance was given to the "undecided" voter by managers of the campaigns of both major political parties with strategies designed to persuade the "undecided". This cartoon frames the campaign as a double bind or non-choice for voters. What seems at first glance as a criticism of the lack of seriousness on the part of the voter is really a criticism of the candidates from which voters have to choose. The popular belief among Barbadians that the two major political parties are the same in terms of their ideologies is often cited by voters as a reason for not voting. In essence, the cartoonist seems to be suggesting that "eenie, meenie, mynie, moe" is as good a method as any to select a candidate to vote for, given that there is no real choice.

Figure 8.4. The Undecided Voter

Figure 8.5. Canvassing Cousins

Events which occur unexpectedly during the campaign provide yet another source of content for journalists. These events though they may have considerable impact at the time, have very little meaning outside of the context of the idiosyncrasies of the particular campaign. For example, in the cartoon in figure 8.5, a reader would need to know that Derek Alleyne had previously been campaign manager for his cousin Clyde Mascoll, who was a member of the DLP, before Mascoll crossed the floor of parliament to join the BLP government led by Owen Arthur. Subsequently, Derek Alleyne chose to manage the campaign for the candidate who replaced his cousin Mascoll as the Opposition DLP's candidate for the same constituency. The result was two cousins campaigning on opposite sides of the political fence in the community where they both grew up. The cartoonist brings this to the public's attention, perhaps to comment on the irony of the circumstances. His image of a fence dividing the two people who are striding in opposite directions sets up the context. Both characters are identified with the party they support –one is wearing a T-shirt with the words "Cousin Clyde BLP", and the other's T-shirt reads "Cousin Derek". He also wears a cap with DLP emblazoned on it. They express their displeasure as they pass without exchanging glances, employing what Lawrence Fisher (1976, 227) calls a primary strategy of Barbadian indirect discourse known as "dropping remarks". As Fisher explains, remark dropping is ritualized and identifiable by Barbadians as an aggressive act, and it should be thought of as a form of unambiguously direct confrontation that employs an indirect discourse style (235). It is usually used to goad an opponent during an intermediate stage of a dispute (227). They both "Humnph!" as they pass each other, This interjection is used by Barbadians to express a range of sentiments, from disapproval to aggression. Willi Worm's question mark expresses the bewilderment of the voters at the situation. This cartoon is another example of the "personal" nature of contemporary politics – the focus is more on the cousins and their relationship issues and less on their party's position on the issues.

Medhurst and DeSousa (1981, 202) propose that cartoonists take their inspiration from the popular perception of the politicians' personal character. They point out that these traits cannot be totally manufactured by the cartoonist; they must exist to some extent in popular consciousness or graphic tradition. The cartoon in figure 8.6 is an

Figure 8.6. Obsessed with Power?

example of use of the popular perception of a politician's character trait. Here, the cartoonist combines text and image to speak to the issue of Owen Arthur's alleged obsession with power. This idea formed a part of the popular consciousness of the electorate as it was often the subject of radio call-in programmes.

Situational themes also provide much fodder for cartoonists. Rumours of infighting in the BLP camp were the source for a series of cartoons produced during the campaign. Readers who were aware of rumours of actual physical fights occurring at the BLP headquarters could readily acquire meaning from the cartoons in figures 8.7 and 8.8. Cartoons such as these kept at the forefront of the electorate's collective mind the concerns of struggle for power and lack of clear leadership in the BLP. There was much discussion of a power struggle between the leader of the party and prime minister Owen Arthur and Mia Mottley, who had been deputy prime minister at one point during the government's tenure and had been removed, but not replaced.

Comparing the BLP alleged power struggle to the popular World Wrestling Entertainment Summer Slam event, the cartoonist builds on the wrestling metaphor to present this issue to audiences. The cartoon in figure 8.7 depicts the BLP party headquarters as the "Roebuck Street Slam",

Figure 8.7. Infighting in the BLP

with a wrestling ring as the centre of the cartoon; this is reinforced by the parody of the World Wrestling Entertainment logo in the corners as "BLP WE". Roebuck Street is the street address of the BLP headquarters. This cartoon depicts a tag team match with the principal fighters already in the ring. The character representing Owen Arthur is on the ropes, locked in a "sleeper" hold by the character depicting Mia Mottley and calling for help. There are two other members of the tag team outside of the ring who represent Clyde Mascoll and Reginald Farley, both members of the ruling party. These three, Mottley, Mascoll and Farley were reportedly locked in a battle for the second-in-command position of deputy prime minister. Mascoll calls to Arthur, "Tag me! tag me!" and Reginald Farley, wearing a shirt labelled "Reggie", looks on in consternation.

This cartoon was particularly powerful in its message that all was not well in the BLP camp. The older generation of voters would have been familiar with WWF wrestling events, which often came to the national stadium in Barbados during the 1980s and 1990s. The analogy is also clear to the younger voters who would be more familiar with the WWE pay-per-view events on television. These cartoons kept the idea that there was a struggle for leadership within the BLP a clear campaign issue and clearly undermined the party's attempt to portray a united front publicly. The cartoonist portrays Mia Mottley as much bigger than the other three party members, which alludes to the popular belief that she was much stronger politically and was rumoured to be the next leader of the party.

The cartoon in figure 8.8 was also labelled "Roebuck Street Slam" and continues the narrative started by the cartoon in figure 8.7. It is made up of two panels, like a political comic strip, which form a narrative. In the first panel there are two people in the ring, the caricature of Owen Arthur has managed to tag Clyde Mascoll. This suggests that Mascoll has won out over Farley since Mascoll has the label "2nd Man" on his trousers. The caricature of Mia Mottley is poised to leap from the turnbuckle, as she shouts, "If you think I goin' lose my title to that "rascal", think again!" The word *rascal* rhymes with "Mascoll" and leaves no doubt about the person who is trying to steal her position of second-in-command. In the second panel, Mia executes a diving crossbody to pin both Mascoll and Arthur. The idea that there was a struggle for leadership of the BLP

Figure 8.8. Roebuck Street Slam II

was an ongoing topic on DLP platforms throughout the campaign and these cartoons were often broadcast at the beginning of political meetings. Prime Minister Arthur had often spoken of his policy of inclusion in which he proposed to select people to management positions in the party and the wider society regardless of their political affiliation. This was known to have caused disquiet among members of his own party. The cartoonist emphasises this point with the exclamation at the bottom of the cartoon: "Politics of inclusion . . . causing confusion!!" This is not something the electorate is likely to forget. The shout of caution from Reggie to MIA, "Beat, but don't bite them!" alludes to the widespread rumour of a violent confrontation with another person in which she is alleged to have caused physical harm to her opponent by biting. This is a subtle yet effective attack on her personal image and reminds the public that she is capable of causing harm to others.

In the cartoon in figure 8.9, the audience is invited to supply the missing conclusion to the argument. The newspaper in the cartoon frame carries the story headlined, "Cry of Sabotage at DLP Meeting". This alludes to the claim made by the DLP that their sound system had been sabotaged when it failed to work at an open-air political meeting. The

Figure 8.9. Crossed Wires

audience is left to draw its own conclusion here, assisted by Willi Worm's comment, "No signs o' foul play . . . maybe som'body got dey wires cross (someone got their wires crossed)," as he checks the wires to the speaker for damage. "Som'body got dey wires cross" is a phrase often used to describe someone who got confused or made a mistake. This is one of the few cartoons that criticized the Opposition DLP.

The DLP had suggested that the BLP had paid someone to sabotage their sound system so that the meeting would not be held. However, investigators did not find any signs of sabotage. The audience is left to conclude that the DLP had falsely accused the BLP in order to gain the sympathy of the electorate. The "cry of sabotage" alludes to the idiom "cry wolf" as in the "boy who cried wolf".

According to Medhurst and DeSousa (1981, 206), the basic form of rhetorical disposition, or arrangement, used by cartoonists is contrast. This is largely because of the constraints imposed by having to present their ideas within a single frame as well as the limitations of space allocated to the cartoonist on the editorial page. One or more basic contrasts or tensions are usually built into the frame. These contrasts may be between visual forms, between images and text, between two or more verbal texts, as in figure 8.9 with Willi Worm's text and the text of the newspaper headline, or between popular conception and the visual forms. For example, in figure 8.6, there is tension between visual forms as well as between images and text. There is also tension between the reader's expectation (popular conception) and the artist's rendition of those conceptions. In this cartoon Prime Minister Owen Arthur is portrayed as a toddler who enjoys playing in his "seat of power". The electorate is the nanny, who tells him, "Play time is over buddy . . . time for a change!" Like a recalcitrant child, the baby cries as he expresses his reluctance to give up his toy. The cartoonist employs the figure of synecdoche in which the hands represent the whole – the electorate, and the baby – the BLP party. The contrast between the small baby and the large hands makes it clear that the electorate are the ones with the real power at this time. These contrasts invite the audience to come to the same conclusion as the cartoonist: it is time for a change because the incumbent party has abused its time in office.

Two other forms of disposition also used by a cartoonist, according to Medhurst and DeSousa, are commentary and contradiction. Commentary does not invite debate or question. It is comparable to "pre-digested thought" in argumentation. It presents the reader with a claim without the means of proving its veracity and expects readers to merely recognize the congruity between what exists and what is imaged. As Medhurst and DeSousa clarify, the idea is not to force a clash of ideas, but to imply or reflect a cultural/political truism" (1981, 206–207).

The other minor dispositional form, contradiction, like contrast, also exploits a clash of tensions within the frame; however, its purpose is not to invite attention but condemnation. Contrast as a form of arrangement leads the reader to draw a conclusion; condemnation, however, invites only one conclusion, condemnation of the party, person or idea. The cartoon in figure 8.10 encourages the readers to condemn the BLP's attempt to accuse the DLP of collusion with the government of Taiwan by employing the dispositional form of contradiction.

The large caption, "What will he think of next?" invites the ridicule of the audience echoing the name and closing slogan of the popular television series which ran for some time on the local television station titled, "What will they think of next?". The show discussed futuristic creations of science and technology that were supposed to shape our lives. Many of the pro-

Figure 8.10. Taiwan Red Herring

grammes discussed products that seemed too good to be true, promising good health, long life and a fountain of youth. Each episode of the show ended with the question, "What will they think of next?", suggesting that the ideas were largely imaginings. This cartoon equates the ideas in the cartoon with science fiction and suggests it is merely the product of a fertile imagination and simply an attempt to redirect the public's critical gaze away from his party. Mr Arthur's caricature is pictured struggling under the weight of a gigantic fish labelled "Taiwan Red Herring" which he is dragging along the "BLP Campaign Trail". By labelling the fish a "red herring", the cartoonist invites the public to conclude that Mr Arthur is introducing an unimportant idea to take their attention away from the important ones. This draws on the British custom in hunting of using the smell of smoked dried herring to train dogs to hunt.

Figure 8.11 below employs the principle of contrast in several ways. This cartoon alludes to the King Kong movie to convey the proposition that the BLP is destroying the country as King Kong, the giant gorilla, did to New York City in the movie, *King Kong*. The BLP is portrayed as a colossal gorilla, marching off the edge of a cliff. As the gorilla marches to disaster followed by the economy, unemployment and poor health

Figure 8.11. Better for Barbados

service, as well as crime and cost overruns, he asserts, ironically, "Of course leadership matters most!"

The cartoon satirizes the BLP and the government and invites the reader to contrast the leadership of the BLP with that of the DLP. The DLP is portrayed as an aircraft soaring above the beast and whose leader displays integrity as seen in the scarf around the pilot's neck which is emblazoned with the word "Integrity". Another contrast between visual forms is the large banner flown behind the DLP's plane which reads "ON COURSE."

Another literary allusion used in this cartoon is that of the shepherd leading his sheep. The important sectors of the country are shown as a flock of sheep following the BLP shepherd over the edge of the precipice. This is obviously not a good shepherd. The economy has already fallen off the edge and bleats in shock "Off Course!" The contrast is also between the present form of government and the future which a DLP government can offer, since the DLP is "on course".

Besides the tension between visual images, the caption is contrasted with the balloon text to suggest that leadership is an important aspect of the campaign. The suggestion is that the BLP government lacks character and integrity and does not consider them important in a leader. There is a direct contradiction between the actions of the BLP and its words – leadership matters most. This cartoon goes beyond merely commenting on the state of the economy and the quality of leadership provided by the current government to invite a contrast between the poor performance of the BLP as government and the promises of a new DLP government. It does not leave it up to readers to judge the extent to which the leadership of the BLP has failed but presents all the ways in which it has failed, such as an endangered economy, rising crime, and cost overruns, and invites the public's condemnation of the BLP.

Figure 8.10 also demonstrates contrast as an organizing principle. The contrast between the visual and the caption invites not mere agreement with what is imaged but invites the reader to condemn Owen Arthur for his introduction of the idea of a Taiwanese connection with the DLP campaign. In figure 8.12, the contrast of graphic directions is also used with significant effect. The ship that represents the BLP is sailing in one direction while M.I.A, (an allusion to Mia Mottley, deputy leader of the party), who

Figure 8.12. Leadership Issues

has been given the boot by the captain is going in another direction. M.I.A. also draws on the military use of the abbreviation MIA to refer to members of the armed forces who do not return from a military operation but who are not known to been killed or captured by the enemy. MIA stands for "missing in action". This again draws on the metaphor that frames politics as war. This cartoon alludes to the rumoured separation in the leadership of the party and the replacement of the deputy leader by another and emphasizes the idea that the leadership of the BLP is divided. This cartoon draws on the readers' knowledge of the campaign incident in which the leader, Owen Arthur, was said to have introduced Clyde Mascoll to a political meeting as his "second man" as its source.

Figure 8.11 shows contrast in line and form on the visual plane. There are two clear directions for the eye to follow: one, presumably, on the right track (moving to the right on a horizontal plane) and the other (moving to the left) clearly not on the right track. The contrast in directions again invites readers to decide which path they want to follow.

According to Medhurst and DeSousa (1981, 212), there are at least six stylistic elements available to any graphic artist: "the use of line and form to create tone and mood; the relative size of objects within the frame; the exaggeration or amplification of physiognomical features; placement within a frame, relation of text, both caption and balloon, to visual imagery; and rhythmic montage within the frame which arises from the interaction of invention, disposition and stylistic elements." Each cartoonist may also employ idiosyncratic elements of style. For example, Guy-O uses "Willi Worm" and the unknown cartoonist on figure 8.12 uses a bird to make critical comments on the situations expressed in the frame.

The relative size within the frame is manipulated to good effect in figure 8.10, where the fish is portrayed as much bigger and heavier than Mr Arthur, who is carrying it on his shoulders. Arthur's relative size also suggests that he is not big enough for the job. In figure 8.9, size is again used as part of the visual rhetoric of the cartoon; Mr Arthur is portrayed as a baby, complete with diaper and rattle. The large size and long reach of the arms of the electorate which remove Mr Arthur from his seat suggest not only the power of the electorate to effect change, but also the extent of that power and suggests further, that no politician is beyond its reach. It reminds voters that they can indeed effect change by their vote.

As Medhurst and DeSousa (1981, 216) theorize, "physiognomic exaggeration is one element of visual style which clearly invites value judgements". They point out that aspects of physical appearance of candidates are often caricatured to the point that they become completely identified with the persons. Mia Mottley's size, hairstyle, glasses and nails were often the elements exaggerated by cartoonists. In the figure 8.13, they seem to take on symbolic significance creating a portrait of the wicked witch. These signs, as Medhurst and DeSousa explain, structure our perceptions and invite us to "know" the candidates.

Owen Arthur's size was often the object of caricature in cartoons. He was portrayed as diminutive, with a large head out of proportion to his body. This is thought to allude to his sense of self-importance or "swell-headedness." David Thompson's height was often emphasized, suggesting his capacity for the job of leader of the country. Other elements caricatured were his glasses, smile, and the patch of grey hair at the front of his head. David Comissiong, the leader of the left-wing People's Empowerment Party (PEP), one of the other political parties which

Figure 8.13. Abandon Ship

contested the general elections, appeared once in the cartoons for the period. He was portrayed in the classic African dashiki shirt and sandals, alluding to his association with the Pan Africanist movement and perhaps making a subtle comment that this is where he is most effective. His role in the cartoon is the same as Willi Worm, to comment on the events. By this, the cartoonist suggests that he does not have a significant role to play in the elections.

The placement of an object within the frame, as Medhurst and DeSousa proffer, may "indicate the attitude or value judgement which the cartoonist offers the reader". For example, in figure 8.11, the DLP's plane is in the upper portion of the frame, and it is in the sky, suggesting hope and integrity above the muddle created by the BLP. The invitation is for the audience to see David Thompson, the leader of the DLP, as above the fray, focused on maintaining the right course and offering the hope of a new dawn. His position "above" suggests visionary and leadership ability.

Another important stylistic element in the rhetoric of cartoons is the relationship between the verbal text (caption or dialogue) and the visual images (Medhurst and DeSousa 1981, 217). Two types of texts are identified: "the words attributed to actors within the cartoon world and labels provided by the cartoonist to help explain his creation. Labels may appear as a part of the scene or as commentary above or below the image. All texts serve three major functions: commentary, explanation, and revelation. "The text may comment on the graphically-rendered scene, it may explain or unpack the meaning in the images, or it may reveal some "truth" about the portrayed character or scene".

Some cartoonists use a character who functions as a sort of third-person omniscient narrator to comment on, explain or reveal the truth of the scene. This character is a constant in the cartoons and the audience looks here for clarification or confirmation of attitudes expressed in the cartoon. Guy-O's signature character is "Willi Worm", and the other featured cartoons use a bird as the omniscient narrator.

In figure 8.14, Willi Worm is dressed as the court jester and his words are meant as a comment on the campaign season in general and in particular refers to the scene depicted in the cartoon in which the BLP candidate for St Michael South constituency, Mr Noel Lynch, in a slip of the tongue

Figure 8.14. Silly Season

expresses gratitude to the DLP instead of the BLP. It had been rumoured before the elections were announced that he was going to cross the floor to represent the DLP and the readers would be well aware of this. The text in the poster held by the candidate is also a comment on his tenure as parliamentary representative for the St Michael South constituency. This candidate served as the minister with responsibility for tourism. The poster alleges that he has taken good care of the tourists and the hoteliers but has "forgotten" his constituents in much the same way that he has momentarily forgotten the name of the party which he represents. This tension also causes the audience to question his integrity, since he is wearing a BLP shirt and carrying a poster which reads, "Vote Dems". In this figure, Willi Worm's words also serve as explanation of what is going on in the scene. It helps the readers to make sense of what they see; without it the meaning may be lost or at least harder to find.

Texts also serve the function of revelation. In figure 8.15, the "dialogue" reveals the "truth" about the alleged Taiwanese connection with the DLP; it is a concoction of the leader of the BLP designed to discredit the DLP. In the inset, the dialogue expresses concern as to whether the tactic will work. The "meaning" of the cartoon for any reader, Medhurst and DeSousa (1981, 217–19) suggest, lies in "the clash of the constituent

Figure 8.15. The Taiwan Connection II

parts to form a coherent whole – the clash of distinctive elements which, in their conflict, invite the reader to perceive an idea that is greater than the sum of the parts". This is what these authors define as "montage". The meaning a reader gets from a cartoon depends in part on their interpretive skills, their political orientation and their background knowledge. Therefore, the way a cartoon works for readers will depend largely on readers playing their part in contributing to the argument. The overall style of the cartoon depends on each of these elements.

The full meaning of the cartoon in figure 8.15 is arrived at by consideration of all the elements involved: *political commonplaces* of an incumbent in office; *character traits* such as a propensity for dissembling; *temporal context* such as the 2008 general election platforms; visual contrasts between two or more verbal texts; placement and commentary as organizing principles; the *exaggeration* of physiognomic characteristics such as grey hair, diminutive stature, and the heart-shaped face; the relation of text to visual information as commentary on events, explanation of the visual message and revelation of the "truth" behind this particular campaign event.

This cartoon, composed as two frames within one, deals with the subject of the Taiwan's support for the DLP's campaign. Again, Mr Arthur's portrayal, reading a book of fairy tales titled "Arthur's Fairy Tales" and written by O. Arthur, an allusion to "Uncle Arthur's Bedtime Stories", suggests that he is dealing in imaginings. His explanation, "Dis "Taiwan Connection" is de best story I come up wid so far! (This Taiwan Connection is the best story I have come up with so far)" is a verbal commentary reinforcing the visual. In the second smaller frame, Mr Arthur sits at the end of a dock fishing. He is using bait from a tacklebox labelled "Red Herring" and comments to himself, "Ah boy . . . Ah wonder if dis bait gine work (I wonder if this bait will work)?! The cartoonist's visual repetition of the idea for emphasis works much like repetition in a verbal argument to emphasize the main point.

Medhurst and DeSousa (1981, 219–20) propose that memory as an element of persuasion works differently in graphic persuasion from the way it works in oral persuasion. They posit that for the cartoonist, memory is "primarily an art of evocation" whereas for the oral persuader, it is "primarily a productive art". The cartoonist selects an idea from the universe of discourse, compresses it into a frame and relies on the readers to unpack the layers of cultural meaning available to them as part of the available communal cultural consciousness which they both share. These authors theorize that "it is the compressing and condensing function of memory as practised by the cartoonist, that accounts for the enthymematic nature of caricature identified by previous researchers".

Readers may therefore draw conclusions to the arguments in the cartoons as they rely on the different layers of cultural memory evoked by the visual message. The cartoonist must select familiar visual backgrounds to evoke specific memories in the reader. These backgrounds are taken from cultural resources such as literary archetypes, cultural heroes, and socio-political commonplaces, but the cartoonist also draws upon communal consciousness to form visual backgrounds which draw on root metaphors through which readers can interpret the artistic ideas. One such metaphor is that of the political process. These authors suggest that cartoonists draw on communally sanctioned metaphors such as: politics is a battle; politics is a race, politics is a gamble; politics is a circus; politics is a beauty contest, and so on. Some of the metaphors of the 2008 electoral campaigns include: politics is a battle (figures 8.7 and 8.8); politics is a voyage (often in dangerous seas) (figures 8.12 and 8.13); politics is a gamble (figure 8.15); political office is a job (figure 8.16).

Figure 8.16. Elected to Office

The graphic counterpart of oral delivery can be seen as the presentational aspects of cartooning (Medhurst and DeSousa 1981, 226). In this respect, the authors consider image placement to be the most important component of the editorial "voice". The editorial cartoon in the upper half of the editorial page gets the readers' attention. Size is also an important part of voice. Most of the cartoons intended as political advertisements occupied the lower half of a page in the main section of the newspaper; some of them were full page advertisements. These large drawings command the readers' full attention and say to them, "This is important".

CONCLUSION

The cartoons analysed here carry several layers and levels of meaning which were impossible to explore fully, given the parameters of this paper. Therefore, I focused on the aspects that best illustrate the cartoon as argument and a means of communicating attitudes and ideas which could influence popular sentiment. The effectiveness of the graphic persuader lies in the ability to use the tools at his disposal in the best possible manner to achieve his purpose. The cartoonists of the general elections campaign of 2008 were able to use their cartoons to evoke and reinforce public perception of candidates and of the political parties. The coverage of parties in the cartoons also served to reinforce the popular perception Barbadians have of the island as a two-party (BLP and DLP) state. Of the three other parties in the election race only one (PEP) was featured once in the cartoons of the general elections. This neglect, evident in the treatment of the other parties in the press and especially of their candidates, seemed to have been mirrored by the electorate. Candidates of the two other parties, the Peoples' Democratic Congress (2) and the Peoples' Empowerment Party (4), and two independent candidates together polled a mere 425 votes.

The major issues of this campaign were integrity or lack thereof, leadership and the cost of living. Over 80 per cent of the cartoons published in this period addressed the issues of leadership and corruption. It seems that the DLP platform was the more convincing of the two main platforms. Cartoons published as electoons were paid advertisements. Although there was nothing concrete to tie them to a particular party's campaign, these same cartoons were shown on the big screens at the start of DLP political meetings and they were often criticisms of the government and the BLP, so it is reasonable to conclude that they were the DLP's. The DLP's adept use of cartoons as public advertisements in the printed press, along with the broadcasting of these cartoons on their nightly platforms, seemed to have shaped or reinforced public opinion, which led in part to their success at the polls.

To the point that the public shared in the Barbadian communal cultural memories, the cartoons reinforced images of dishonesty, lack of integrity and arrogance on the part of the incumbent government and may have been the source, along with newspapers articles and radio call-in programmes, from which many young voters formed their impressions of candidates and parties in the electoral campaigns. The DLP was seen as "better for Barbados" since their team under the leadership of David Thompson was seen as those who offered integrity, had good character and were capable of leading the country. The fact that the DLP was victorious in the 15 January election, winning twenty of the thirty seats contested, seems to suggest that the electorate did identify, and to a large extent, agree with the attitude and sentiments expressed in the cartoons.

REFERENCES

Alimi, Shina and Michael Olusegun Fajuyigbe. 2016. "A Thematic and Contextual Analysis of Boko Haram in Selected Editorial Cartoons". *Africa e Mediterraneo* 85 (Dicembre): 54–60.

Baumgartner, Jody C. 2008. "Editorial Cartoons 2.0: The Effects of Digital Political Satire on Presidential Candidate Evaluations". *Presidential Studies Quarterly* 38(4): 735–58.

Buell, Emmet H.,Jr. and Mike Maus. 1988. "Is the Pen Mightier than the Word? Editorial Cartoons and 1988 Presidential Nominating Politics". *Political Science and Politics* 21(3): 847–58.

Bush, Larry. 2013. "More than Words: Rhetorical Constructs in American Politic al Cartoons. *Studies in American Humor* New Series 3, no.27: 63–91.

Conners, Joan L. 2007. "Popular Culture in Political Cartoons: Analyzing Cartoonists Approaches". *Political Science and Politics* 40 (2): 261–65.

DeSousa, Michael A., and Martin J. Medhurst.1982. "Political Cartoons and American Culture: Significant Symbols of Campaign 1980". *Studies in Visual Communication* 8 (1): 84–97.

Denton, Robert E., Jr. ed. 2005. The 2004 *Presidential Campaign: A Communication Perspective"*. Lanham, MD: Rowman and Littlefield Publishers.

Dewey, Donald. 2007. *The Art of Ill Will: The Story of American Political Cartoons*. New York: New York University Press.

Edwards, Janis L. 1997. *Political Cartoons in the 1998 Presidential Campaign: Image, Metaphor, and Narrative*. New York: Garland Publishing.

Fisher, Lawrence E. 1976. "Dropping remarks" and the Barbadian Audience". *American Ethnologist* 3(2): 227–42.

Johnson, Isabel Simeral.1937. "Cartoons". *Public Opinion Quarterly*1(3): 21–34.

Koetzle, William, and Thomas L. Brunell. 1996. "Lip-reading, Draft-dodging, and Perot-Noia: Presidential Campaigns in Editorial Cartoons". *International Journal of Press/Politics* 1(4): 94–115.

Kotzé, Dirk. 1988. "Cartoons as a Medium of Political Communication". *Communication Theory and Research* 14(2): 60–70. https://doi.org/10.1080/02500168808537742.

Linus, Abraham. 2009. "Effectiveness of Cartoons as a Uniquely Visual Medium for Orienting Social Issues". *Journalism and Communication Monographs* 11(2):117-65.

Medhurst, Martin J. and Michael M. DeSousa. 1981. "Political Cartoons as Rhetorical Form: A Taxonomy of Graphic Discourse". *Communication Monographs* 48 (3): 197–236.

Mulanda, Oliver M., and Michael Ndonye. 2015. "Audiences' Interpretation of Editorial Cartoons and Cartoonists Intentions in the Run-up to the 2013 General Election in Kenya". *International Journal of Research in Social Sciences* 4 (2): 91–104.

Norris, Pippa. 1997. "Choosing Electoral Systems: Proportional, Majoritarian and Mixed Systems". *International Political Science Review* 18 (3): 297–312.

O'Neill, Morna. 2015. "Cartoons for the Cause? Walter Crane's The Anarchists of Chicago". *Art History* 38 (1):106–37.

Patterson, Thomas E. 1980. *The Mass Media Election: How Americans Choose Their President* (American Political Parties and Elections). New York: Praeger.

Press, Charles. 1981. *The Political Cartoon*. London: Associated Press.

Richardson, John E. 2007. *Analysing Newspapers: An Approach From Critical Discourse Analysis*. London: Palgrave Macmillan.

Sani, Iro, Mardziah Hayati Abdullah, Afida Mohamad Ali and Faiz Sathi Abd ullah. 2012. "Linguistic Analysis on the Construction of Satire in Nigerian Political Cartoons: The Example of Newspaper Cartoons". *Journal of Media and Communication Studies* 4 (3): 52–59. https://doi.org/ 10. 5897/JMCS11.129

Wekesa, Nyongesa B. 2012. "Cartoons Can Talk? Visual Analysis on Cartoons of the 2007/2008 Post-Election Violence in Kenya: A Visual Argumentation Approach". *Discourse & Communication* 6 (2): 223–38. https://doi.org/10.1177/1750481312439818.

Appendix A

Table 8.1. Voter Turnout and Election Results 1994–2008

Year	Registered Voters	Voters	Percentage Vote Garnered		
		Number & Percentage	DLP	BLP	Incumbent Party
1994	206,000	124, 121 (60.25%)	38.75%	48.77%	DLP
1999	203, 621	128,484 (63%)	35%	65%	BLP
2003	218,811	124, 463 (57%)	44.09%	55.80%	BLP
2008	235, 510	149, 633 (63.54%)	67%	33%	BLP

Source: Inter-Parliamentary Union

CHAPTER 9

Language Rights and the Inter-American Human Rights System

A Preliminary Examination

ALISON IRVINE-SOBERS

INTRODUCTION

The United Nations (UN) Declaration on the Rights of Persons Belonging to National or Ethnic, Religious and Linguistic Minorities asserts that: [linguistic minorities] *have the right to use their own language, in private and in public, freely and without interference or any form of discrimination.* In addition, and in keeping with other UN resolutions, the Organization of American States (OAS) has declared the second week in August each year as the Inter-American Week for Indigenous Peoples: *in order to promote their traditions, recognize the value of their languages, transmit their history, and draw attention to their contributions in different fields.*

There are hundreds of indigenous languages and scores of contact languages now spoken in the Americas.[1] For reasons of history, the ecologies in which this linguistic diversity exists are all dominated by a handful of colonial languages – most notably Spanish and English. Given the linguistic complexity of the hemisphere, and the growing assertiveness of historically marginalized groups in demanding inclusion, the organs of the OAS that primarily concern themselves with issues of human rights and the protection of minorities in the Americas must be central in addressing this demand.

My main focus will be on the kinds of cases brought to one institution in the OAS – the Inter-American Court of Human Rights. My interest here is on litigation that specifically engages any aspect of language use or has resulted in judgments that seek to recognize language rights. I will discuss how and why these cases demonstrate competing ideologies in the Inter-American System, about the very notion of cultural rights, issues of economic development and the tension between the two. I will also suggest that a lack of diversity in an organization like the Inter-American Commission on Human Rights (the Commission), that tries to address access to cultural and human rights in the hemisphere, may contribute to the perception that cultural rights – including language rights – are desirable, but not central to its mandate.

THE INTER-AMERICAN HUMAN RIGHTS SYSTEM

The Inter-American System is composed of two principal entities: the Inter-American Commission on Human Rights (the Commission) and the Inter-American Court of Human Rights (the Court). The Commission was created in 1959. Every independent country in the Americas – including nearly all Caribbean countries – subscribes to and funds the Commission and has agreed, to varying degrees, to be bound by its recommendations and resolutions. A decade later, the American Convention on Human Rights (the American Convention, hereafter) was adopted by the then member states of the OAS; the American Convention came into effect in 1978. Apart from articulating a set of rights, obligations and freedoms, the American Convention established the Court, currently headquartered in Costa Rica.[2]

The purpose of the Commission is twofold: to promote and protect human rights in the American hemisphere; and to provide recourse to any citizen of a member state who has suffered human rights violations. The work of the Commission rests on three main pillars: a) the individual petition system; b) monitoring of the human rights situation in the member states; and c) attention to priority thematic areas. My data for this chapter comes from the first of these – the petition system and the subset of cases that eventually end up at the Court for adjudication.

In brief, petitions to the Commission may be submitted by individuals, groups of individuals, or organizations that allege violations of the human rights guaranteed in the American Declaration of the Rights and Duties of Man (hereafter, the American Declaration – 1948), the American Convention, and other inter-American human rights treaties. These petitions are analysed at the Commission for admissibility, that is, whether a *prima facie* case can be made that violations did occur and that the petitioner has followed certain procedural requirements before submitting the petition. Chief among these requirements is the attempt to exhaust all domestic judicial remedies available to deal with the matter. If deemed admissible, the Commission will then proceed to a final determination of the merits of the petitioner's case. If the Commission concludes that the State has committed violations, it will make recommendations for remedial actions to be taken by the State. In cases where the Commission considers that the State is non-compliant, or if the State thinks the requested remedy is unfair, the case may end up before the Court for adjudication.

All member states of the OAS do not have the same level of commitment to the Inter-American System. The weakest level of commitment is reflected in those states that have only sought membership in the OAS. While there is an obligation to adhere to the rights set out in The American Declaration, these countries have not ratified the American Convention, nor have they acceded to the jurisdiction of the Court. A second set of countries has ratified the American Convention, a more specific set of regional obligations, but they too have not acceded to the jurisdiction of the Court. Finally, the countries that have fully committed to the Inter-American System have ratified the American Convention and have agreed to be governed by and comply with the judgments of the Court. Table 9.1 lists all the member states and indicates their relationship with the Inter-American System.

Effectively, it is the non-Anglophone countries that have fully engaged the regional human rights system. Indeed, Barbados is the only English-speaking member state that has done so.[3]

Although the American Declaration and the American Convention do not mention linguistic human rights specifically, they do protect the following rights, *inter alia*, that conceivably will impact language rights:

Table 9.1. Member States and Their Relationship to the Inter-American System

Member State	OAS member	Ratified American Convention	Accepts jurisdiction of the Court
Antigua & Barbuda	×		
Argentina	×	×	×
The Bahamas	×		
Barbados	×	×	×
Belize	×		
Bolivia	×	×	×
Brazil	×	×	×
Canada	×		
Chile	×	×	×
Colombia	×	×	×
Costa Rica	×	×	×
Cuba	—	—	—
Dominica	×	×	
Dominican Republic	×	×	×
Ecuador	×	×	×
El Salvador	×	×	×
Grenada	×		
Guatemala	×	×	×
Guyana	×		
Haiti	×	×	×
Honduras (suspended 2009)	×	×	×
Jamaica	×	×	
Mexico	×	×	×
Nicaragua	×	×	×
Panama	×	×	×
Paraguay	×	×	×
Peru	×	×	×
St. Lucia	×		
St. Vincent & The Grenadines	×		
St. Kitts & Nevis	×		
Suriname	×	×	×
Trinidad & Tobago	×	denounced	
United States	×		
Uruguay	×	×	×
Venezuela (suspended 2018)	×	denounced	

The American Declaration
Chapter I, Article II – *All persons are equal before the law (. . .) without distinction as to race, sex, language, creed or any other factor*
Article IV – *Every person has the right to freedom of investigation, of opinion, and of the expression and dissemination of ideas, by any medium whatsoever*

The American Convention
Article 1 – Obligation to Respect Rights -*without any discrimination for reasons of race, color, sex, language,*
religion, political or other opinion, national or social origin, economic status, birth, or any other social condition
Article 8 – Right to a Fair Trial
Article 13 – Freedom of Thought and Expression[4]
Article 23 – Right to Participate in Government[5]

Additionally, the Commission has a number of thematic Rapporteur-ships, special mechanisms to gather and disseminate information on how different groups of people or different rights are being protected. Of particular relevance here are the Rapporteur on the Rights of Afro-descen-dants; the Rapporteur on the Rights of Indigenous Peoples; the Special Rapporteur for Freedom of Expression; and the Special Rapporteur on Economic, Social, Cultural, and Environmental Rights.

A TYPOLOGY OF CONSTITUTIONAL ARRANGEMENTS

In order to discuss any litigation in the Inter-American System, it is useful to understand the two legal traditions that separate the member states into distinct groupings.

Broadly speaking, the Anglophone countries follow a *common law* tradition; all the others – including Suriname and Haiti – are *civil law* countries. At the heart of the latter framework lies a belief in codification as the means to ensure a consistent application of the law. As such, par-liamentary legislation is the principal source of law and includes codes, separate statutes and ancillary legislation. According to O'Connor (2012), within civil law countries, there is a hierarchy of laws, with the Constitu-tion at the very top; and below there will be legislation, executive decrees, regulations, and local ordinances. Custom, as a rare source of law, sits at the bottom of the pyramid and is rarely relied upon in court (11).

In contrast, the judge in the common law tradition occupies a central role and judicial opinions were historically the primary source of law. The development of case law as source of law in this tradition lead to the creation of precedents, and it is this that primarily ensures that similar cases are approached in the same way. In essence, in the civil law tradition judges are tasked with applying the law only; in the common law tradition judges can also be tasked with setting precedent that becomes law.

Given the information in table 9.1 above, it is not surprising that the Court in Costa Rica is dominated by practitioners who come out of the civil law tradition and who look first to what is codified when determining the obligations of the member state. It would be useful then, to sketch out the extent to which the domains of use for language are codified in the hemisphere.

The types of arrangements individual countries have made to recognize the languages spoken in their respective societies will be briefly discussed for necessary context: contrasting places like Bolivia and its constitutional provisions, with those of places like Belize and most of the Caribbean territories. The thirty-five countries of the OAS have various constitutional arrangements that outline the status and functions of the languages used within their borders. Here I will discuss only the contemporary situation, as several of the member states have replaced constitutions that were enacted during the colonial period or at independence.[6]

Generally speaking, the recognition of language rights has been relatively late, given the cultural and linguistic diversity in the hemisphere (Colón-Ríos 2011, 375). Language policies have moved from what can be termed a *"norm-and-accommodation model"* (Colón-Ríos, 375), to one that recognizes the many languages spoken in a region or particular area as official, and tries to guarantee to speakers of those languages, certain rights. In the former, the orientation is tolerance of ethnolinguistic diversity in a context of Spanish or English hegemony – typified by the acceptance of private, individual actions to promote minority languages (community newsletters, locally organized literacy classes). In the latter, speakers have specific language rights in, say, public institutions or in education that the State pledges to uphold.

The main distinction that can be made in the thirty-five member states is between those that have *de jure* official language(s) and those that do not.

A further distinction can be made between those States that have some provision that recognizes the other language(s) spoken in the society and those that acknowledge the existence of only the colonial language, either directly (for example, Costa Rica) or indirectly (for example, Dominica).

In table 9. 2, I set out the various provisions that are commonly found in the constitutions of the various States of the OAS: prohibitions on discrimination, language requirements for political participation (naturalization, membership in the legislature), and any recognition given to non-European languages used in the society.

Explicit recognition of language rights moved through three distinct phases, each available to us in the types of constitutions that now function in the various member states. The first phase acknowledged only the European language of the particular colonizer – an arrangement still found in many Caribbean and Central American territories. Article 6 of the constitution of Honduras, for example, makes Spanish the sole official language of the nation and requires the State to "*protect its purity and increase its learning*". A number of Caribbean territories have explicitly discriminatory sections that require English language proficiency for membership in the legislature.[7] St Lucia, for example, specifies English language proficiency (spoken and written) as necessary for members of the Senate or House of Representatives, even though French Creole is the first language of many and is widely spoken and understood (St. Hilaire 2008, 62).[8]

The second phase – typically in the late 1980s – recognized the multilingual and multicultural nature of societies in the hemisphere and specified the need to tolerate and protect minority linguistic rights. Typical wording for such provisions in constitutions is:

> The native languages that are spoken in the national territory form part of the cultural patrimony and shall be the object of preservation, dissemination and respect (El Salvador).

In general, this respect for Indigenous languages tends to be largely symbolic, typically confined to either the promotion of folklore, or to the creation of Indigenous language academies or institutes. Moreover, the wording used, which includes verbs such as, "*preserve*" (Mexico), and "*encourage*" (Ecuador); or phrasing such as, "*Aboriginal languages shall be*

Table 9.2. Constitutional Provisions for Language in the Member States

Member state	De jure official (nation)	Provisions for use of languages (education, regional govt.)	Language requirement for political participation	Prohibition on language discrimination	General recognition of Indigenous Peoples/heritage to be preserved	No real mention of language
Antigua & Barbuda			x			
Argentina		x			x	
The Bahamas						x
Barbados						x
Belize						x
Bolivia	x	x				
Brazil	x	x				
Canada	x	x				
Chile	x	x				x
Colombia	x	x				
Costa Rica	x		x			
Cuba*	x					
Dominica			x			
Dominican Republic	x			x		
Ecuador	x	x		x	x	
El Salvador	x	x				
Grenada			x			

Table 9.2 continues

Table 9.2. Constitutional Provisions for Language in the Member States (cont'd)

Member state	De jure official (nation)	Provisions for use of languages (education, regional govt.)	Language requirement for political participation	Prohibition on language discrimination	General recognition of Indigenous Peoples/heritage to be preserved	No real mention of language
Guatemala	x	x			x	
Guyana			x			
Haiti	x	x				
Honduras	x					
Jamaica						x
Mexico		x		x	x	
Nicaragua	x	x	x			
Panama	x				x	
Paraguay	x				x	
Peru	x	x		x		
St. Lucia			x			
St. Vincent/Grenadines			x			
St. Kitts & Nevis						x
Suriname				x		
Trinidad & Tobago						x
United States		x				
Uruguay						x
Venezuela	x				x	

the object of special study, conservation and dissemination" (Panama), both point to a lack of binding force and a deliberate vagueness about issues of implementation (Haboud, Howard, and Cru 2016, 214).

The third and most recent phase (through to the late 2000s) recognizes multiple linguistic identities and conceives of one territory, consisting of several nations with their own language variety, coexisting with an over-arching official language of wider communication. So the constitution of Venezuela specifies: *"The use of native languages also has official status* [along with Spanish] *for native peoples . . ."* and Bolivia recognizes Spanish as official, as well as *"all the languages of the rural native Indigenous nations and peoples".*⁹ It is not always clear, however, that these arrangements are any less symbolic than the ones discussed above, as some of the wording itself, clearly still reflects the norm and accommodation attitude described by Colón-Ríos (2011). Indigenous languages are, after all, typically official only for Indigenous peoples and are generally not given national scope; and Creoles have generally not been constitutionally recognized at all (but see Paraguay and Haiti as exceptions). Moreover, issues such as access to adequate resources, the capacity and training of teachers, attitudes of speakers to mother-tongue education, development of materials are all complicating factors in the implementation of language policy (King 2005, 6). Implementation, however, and whether, more generally, official multilingualism has actually affected the day-to-day lives of minority language speakers are beyond the scope of this paper.

LANGUAGE RIGHTS CASES BEFORE THE INTER-AMERICAN COURT

Data for this paper comes from two primary sources: The web page of the Inter-American Court itself and The Inter-American Court of Human Rights Project run by Loyola of Los Angeles International and Comparative Law Review.¹⁰ My analysis here concerns some 161 judgments given by the Court between 1988 and 2014. Of the 161 decisions, the majority deals with human rights violations that resulted in loss of life, loss of liberty or inhumane treatment and torture (70 per cent). However, some fifteen cases (roughly 9 per cent) involve issues that have some relevance to the question of language rights (see Blommaert 2001; Wright 2007 for discussions on those rights generally and their development). This is significant, as it represents a very high proportion of the litigation before the Court that engages second and third generation human rights (Vasak 1977). Significantly, the Commission did not raise the specific matter of language rights in any of these fifteen cases, even when the Petitioners (or their agents) did bring up examples of linguistic discrimination or linguicide before the Court.

These fifteen cases can be broadly divided into those that do not specifically engage a claim to use/recognition of particular language(s) and those that do. In this chapter, I have highlighted a few examples of each. In the first set, the Court has made no direct reference to language rights in the relevant judgments. Indeed, the petitioners themselves did not include recognition of their language(s) in their pleadings. However, because safeguarding the rights of Indigenous Peoples necessarily has a cultural component to it, language has been indirectly featured in cases that engage protections for Indigenous peoples and their territory.

A Right to a Juridical Personality

This first set of cases establishes the idea that certain ethnolinguistic groups, like Indigenous Peoples and Maroons, also have the right to a juridical personality and the right to be seen and treated in law as a collective – in the way they see themselves. This issue becomes crucial in delineating the way the State is charged with interacting with these groups. Moreover, in its judgments, the Court can be seen grappling with cultural practices and belief systems that are typically not acknowledged in the post-colonial jurisprudence of many member states. In *Aloeboetoe et al. v. Suriname* (1993), for example, financial compensation for victims had to take into account the polygamous nature of Saramaka society, even though this was not recognized by the Surinamese government as a legal family arrangement. Notably, all the cases discussed in this paper bring into sharp relief the tension between notions of national development, the State's imperative to maximize resources for economic growth, and more recently articulated ideas of human rights within multicultural and multiethnic societies. The common thread that runs through the petitioners' appeals to the Inter-American System is encroachment on communally owned ancestral territory by agents of the State, or licensees given authority by the State, to mine, log, farm or develop tourist attractions. In all of these cases, one generally held position advanced by States is that national development and the national imperative for pursuing economic growth demands development of resources, some of which are to be found in territory claimed by Indigenous/Maroon groups.

As Kibbe (2008, 105) discusses, this is a contentious matter, with sometimes seemingly contradictory determinations in international law. How, for example, do Indigenous populations differ from any other colonized and oppressed ethnic group? Does the distinction serve to perpetuate, without using the terms, now outdated ideas of "primitive" and "civilized"? As he points out, "sometimes the reference is made almost explicit, using the term 'tribal', which carries its own heavy baggage". The focus on Indigenous Peoples suggests that groups so categorized are acknowledged to have specific, distinct concerns and characteristics that call for treating them apart from minority groups *per se* (Anaya 2004, 21).

A number of petitions have come before the Court that involve Suriname Maroon/Indigenous communities and their right to a collective identity and communal property (1993,[11] 2005,[12] 2007,[13] 2015).[14] In 2007, representatives of the Saramaka people argued before the Court that they were entitled to compensation from the government of Suriname as it had violated their people's rights to property, cultural integrity, and due process. The Saramaka asserted the following:

1. Land rights were crucial to their existence;
2. Control over their territory was vital;
3. A historical claim to their territory;
4. Equivalence with Indigenous groups;
5. The need to live as free people in Suriname

Moreover, the delegation at initial hearings before the Commission in Washington, DC, representing some twelve clans and sixty-one villages, chose to make their presentation in Saramakan, even though it was clear that there were persons in the delegation who could speak Dutch and/or English.[15]

The Court ruled in 2007 that its jurisprudence regarding Indigenous Peoples' right to communal property applied to the Saramaka people because they share distinct social, cultural, and economic characteristics, and have a special relationship with their ancestral territories. The Court further ruled:

The State shall grant the members of the Saramaka people legal recognition of the collective juridical capacity, pertaining to the community to which they belong, with the purpose of ensuring the full exercise and enjoyment of their right to communal property, as well as collective access to justice, in accordance with their communal system, customary laws, and traditions.[16]

As Price (2012) points out, this was a landmark decision, as other Maroon communities throughout the Americas would be treated as equivalent to Indigenous Peoples in international law and subject to the United Nations Declaration on the Rights of Indigenous Peoples (2007).[17]

Because the Saramaka are a people with communal rights that the State must recognize, the judgment further required communication of the outcome of the litigation in Saramakan, specifically the financing of radio broadcasts accessible to the Saramaka people. This aspect of reparations to the petitioners is particularly interesting, because it is not routinely demanded in all cases.

In *Kaliña and Lokono Peoples v. Suriname* (2015), for example, the Court ruled that, "... *official summary of the judgment must be translated and published in Dutch and Surinamese in a newspaper of general circulation.*"[18] Presumably "Surinamese" refers to Sranan, but it was not made clear in the judgment; there was no requirement for communication of the Court's ruling in the mother tongue of the petitioners. Similarly, reparations for the Ndjuka, in 2005, did require that the State issue a public apology and publicize this apology ceremony through the national media, but no specific language of broadcast was named.[19]

A Recognition of the "Indigenous Cosmovision"

In a case that involved a violation of the right to freedom of expression, the Court issued a judgment in the case of three apuche men who had been arrested and convicted in Chile under anti-terrorism provisions[20] that arbitrarily prolong detentions, and prohibit the individual from engaging in any political activities or holding public office for a period of fifteen

years. The three men in question held particular positions within the
Mapuche culture. As the judgment noted:

> The *Lonkos* are the foremost leaders of their respective communities for both
> administrative and spiritual matters; they are considered to be the depositaries
> of ancestral wisdom and head the decision-making processes as well as presid-
> ing [over] important religious ceremonies. The *Werken*, whose name signifies
> "messenger," assist the Lonkos and play a complementary leadership role; they
> are spokespersons on diverse issues, such as political and cultural matters,
> before other Mapuche communities and before non-Mapuche society.[21]

Apart from the general human rights violations in the arrest, detention
and treatment of the men in question, in adding ancillary punishments
such as the prohibition on holding public office for fifteen years, the
government of Chile was effectively silencing dissent and protest in the
community generally by silencing its spokesperson. Further, for fifteen
years, the petitioners (including particularly the *Werken*) were disqualified
from public use of social media, from administration of a social media
platform, or from *"performing functions related to the emission and diffusion
of opinions and information."* The State had, by its actions, restricted the
possibility of the *Werken* taking part in the dissemination of information,
and this was a violation of *"the social dimension of freedom of expression"*
and an *"indirect violation of* [the right to] *the freedom of expression of the
Mapuche people."*[22]

Here again, we see the Court attempting to recognize the relationship
between the social organization of the Mapuche, its importance in the
way the group communicates formally as a people, and the philosophy of
language in Mapuche culture (Course 2012; Richard 2013, 176).[23] Moreover, by insisting that the judgment be broadcast in Spanish as well as
Mapudungun, there is an implicit recognition given to the language of
the petitioners that is not found in the Constitution of Chile. Crucially,
this recognition by the Court is, arguably, symbolic rather than necessarily
in the service of ensuring understanding of the judgment. According
to Lagos, Arce and Figueroa (2017, 198), during Mapuche community
ritual activities, Spanish is often used as a tool for explaining what is
happening to the wider audience, as many do not understand what is
going on when Mapudungun is used.

Access to Justice

The examples in this section, unlike those above, discuss cases before the Court that explicitly mention issues of discrimination against speakers of specific languages and seek remedies that involve the right to use one's language in some institutional context. A number of the cases brought to the Court, that specifically mention language rights, relate to the use of language in the justice system and whether there can be true access to justice if one's language is not accommodated in the process.

The head of a number of organizations in the Honduran Garifuna community (Black Fraternal Organization of Honduras, Confederation of the Autonomous Peoples of Honduras, Committee for the Defense of the Triunfeñas Lands) was arrested for drug possession and illegal trafficking in 1997 and held at the Criminal Centre of Tela. Notably, the Criminal Centre banned members of the Garifuna population from speaking in their native tongue at the beginning of 2000. More particularly, the director of the Criminal Centre of Tela prohibited the Garifuna population from speaking Garifuna with the other inmates they knew and with the people that visited them. As such, among other reasons, Honduras was found to have violated the American Convention in its treatment of the petitioner. Mr López Álvarez, though initially sentenced to fifteen years, was eventually acquitted and released in 2003.[24]

The Court heard that in the prisons and the centres of public detention in Honduras, persons of Indian and African descent are often beaten when they speak in their own language, because it is assumed that they are plotting something. Further, they are "advised" to speak in Spanish. The State of Honduras has argued security reasons to justify this restriction.

In its judgment, the Court made a number of interrelated points on the issue of language rights. Firstly, the State did not prove – as it needed to – that the prohibition on languages like Garifuna was *"evidently necessary"*. To do so, it would have had to show that the use of Garifuna among prisoners could have implied problems for national security, public order, health, rights of third parties, or the common good. In fact, the President of the Court quipped, "It is not even necessary to say, but I will mention it, that we are referring to a language established in a social group, not a code of voices used by criminals to trick or distract

State agents."[25] The prohibition, therefore, violated Articles 1 and 24 of the American Convention and the general prohibition of discrimination for reasons of language.

Secondly, the right to speak and the right to use one's language of choice when speaking are one and the same and any restriction on these rights is a restriction on the right to freedom of expression. The Court found that the prohibition further violated Mr López Álvarez's right to speak and express his thoughts, his personal dignity, and his right to identify as Garifuna.

Thirdly, the Court held that prohibiting the Garifuna language discriminated specifically against the Garifuna, in violation of the American Convention. Indeed, as was noted, the principles of a right to equal protection and non-discrimination are *jus cogens* obligations. Further, the arbitrary prohibition of the use of the Garifuna language in the Criminal Centre of Tela was a discriminatory act and a violation of the Constitution of Honduras.[26]

While recognizing that the official language, Spanish, may have to be used in certain judicial contexts, representatives of the Garifuna petitioners asked the Court to order Honduras to implement the measures necessary so that the Indian and Black populations may have complete access to justice. They especially requested that this order include the provision that they be allowed to use their mother tongue in all procedural actions and in the detention centres. The Court, however, sidestepped the matter and instead required Honduras to implement, within a reasonable period of time, a training programme on human rights for the officers that work in the penitentiary centres.[27] Notably, the Commission itself did not directly argue for a violation of Mr López Álvarez's right to use his own language; rather, the Commission presented a case for violations of freedom of expression and of prohibitions against discrimination.

However, in a later judgment (2008) the Court noted in a matter from Guatemala that,

> This Tribunal considers that in order to guarantee the victims' right to a fair trial – as members of the Maya indigenous community – (. . .) the State must ensure that they understand and are understood in the legal proceedings started, thus offering them interpreters or other effective means for said purpose.[28]

In its submissions to the Court, the Commission outlined the deficiencies in the Guatemalan justice system and attributed them, in part, to a lack of intercultural training of justice operators and the use of a single language (Spanish) in the development of judicial processes.[29]

The petitioner, a speaker of Maya K'iché, described the fear she felt in approaching the authorities, the contempt with which people like her tend to be treated by the authorities, and the lack of interpretation/translation available to her. Similar issues were raised in a petition from Mexico (2010) where, in order to interact with the authorities and obtain information about her case, a Me'paa speaker was forced to rely on a personal acquaintance who spoke some Spanish. In that judgment, the Court ruled that the State did not comply with the obligation to guarantee, without discrimination, access to justice.[30]

DISCUSSION

Linguistic human rights can be described as a series of obligations on the State and its representatives that relate to the recognition of, the use of and the support for certain languages in a variety of contexts. States ideally should not interfere with the linguistic choices and expressions of private parties; should recognize and support the use of languages of minorities or indigenous peoples; should adopt language policies that increase inclusion and access to participation in the institutions of government. Arguably, while many states have attempted to create more inclusive legal frameworks and recognize the multiethnic nature of their societies, the recognition of linguistic rights remains patchy.

The organs of the OAS that do deal with human rights, tend to defer to the State when it comes to determining matters of internal regulation as long as there is no violation of what are largely first generation human rights. To illustrate, the constitutions of St Lucia, Grenada and Guyana, for example, have the provision that excludes non-English speakers from full political participation. While Kwéyòl speakers in St Lucia need to be bilingual to be in the legislature, there is no such reciprocal requirement for English speakers; there is also no consideration for even oral proficiency in Kwéyòl, assuming a desire to reach the widest audience possible when governing. However, the American Convention allows the

State to set exceptions to the right to participate in government, "on the basis of age, nationality, residence, language, education, civil and mental capacity, or sentencing by a competent court in criminal proceedings."[31]

Generally, as Colón-Ríos (2013, 10) shows,

> Under that approach, language rights are seen as capable of protection through basic liberal freedoms. For example, the right to freedom of speech would be seen as enough to protect the right to choose one's language of expression in social contexts, and the right to privacy as giving people the ability to choose the language to be used at home.

The Court in recognizing that Mr López Álvarez's rights had been violated by the ban on speaking Garifuna, for example, opted to suggest human rights training as a remedy to the situation, rather than create an affirmative right to use one's mother-tongue in the criminal justice system. In essence, governments should attempt to increase tolerance for minority languages among its agents, but it will not be compelled to include them formally in its institutions. This is, of course, not surprising given that instruments like The American Convention are the result of negotiation and compromise among many sovereign states.

Without the active protection of minority languages, the almost inevitable language loss discussed above for Mapuche communities, is the fate of numbers of languages in the hemisphere (May 2006, 259). This issue of language shift and loss has been directly addressed in comments made by at least one judge of the Court (Judge Cançado Trindade of Brazil). In his Separate Opinion in the case of the *Moiwana Community v. Suriname* (2005), Judge Trindade advanced "uprootedness as a human rights problem confronting the universal juridical conscience."[32] When peoples are uprooted from their homes, it ultimately affects their right to cultural identity, which is integral to the right to life itself. Moreover, uprootedness creates multiple sources of loss, including the loss of the native language. Implicit in this Opinion is the hope that Inter-American human rights jurisprudence will come to recognize the State's obligation to protect vulnerable communities from the conditions that exacerbate language shift specifically.

However, without an accompanying insistence on increasing the domains in which minority languages are used, particularly in spaces sanctioned by government and given the imprimatur of authority that comes with institutional inclusion, issues of linguicide will persist. In the cases discussed in this paper, that necessarily means safeguards against encroachment on territorial integrity and recognition of the "*indigenous cosmovision*" in crafting reparations. But it also means an Inter-American Human Rights System willing to recognize an affirmative right to some aspects of mother tongue use – in the justice system, in education, and in information from the State.

Two examples of reparations ordered by the Court can be used to illustrate the point. The Court considered it appropriate that the State publicize a judgment in a matter from Ecuador in "Spanish, Kichwa and other indigenous languages."[33] Representatives of the petitioners asked the Court to order the State to disseminate the judgment in national media. The Commission did not make a similar request in its presentation to the Court; and the State did not refer at all to the representatives' request. The Court decided that the judgment should be given, with the relevant translations, through a radio station with coverage in the "southeastern Amazonian region only". This effectively relegates Kichwa to being less than, regional and only useful for intragroup communication. Ironically, the constitution of Ecuador recognizes Kichwa as an official language "for intercultural ties."[34]

In a similar vein, despite requests from Mr López Álvarez's representatives that the Court affirm the use of Garifuna in the justice system, that is, to broaden the institutional reach of the language, the Court would not do so. One aspect of the reparations ordered by the Court, however, was to encourage the government of Honduras to fund a community radio station for the use of the Garifuna. If the recognition of minority languages persists in being tokenism, instead of being a safeguard for the languages concerned, shift to official languages/languages of wider communication like Spanish, or English, or Sranan may, instead, be the likely outcome.

Preliminary data from members of staff at the Commission suggest that there are really no speakers of non-European languages there, and many are not aware of "linguistic human rights."[35] However, nearly all are aware that groups in their respective countries are discriminated against because of the language that they speak. It is very likely that greater attention to the issue of language discrimination and the rights of speakers of minority languages might come from persons who have themselves experienced said discrimination and recognize the impact seemingly neutral language policies can have on communities. The discussion in this paper does suggest that in the Inter-American Human Rights System, safeguarding language rights– to the extent that they are thought of at all – are not really seen as an integral part of its mandate.

NOTES

1. According to Mithun (2011), during first encounters with Europeans, around 300 distinct, mutually unintelligible languages were spoken in North America, another 350 in Middle America, and perhaps as many as 1,500 in South America. The information in Smith (1994), suggests some 100 Creoles and Pidgins also existed in the Americas at one time.
2. The history of the Inter-American Human Rights system and both the American Declaration and the American Convention can be found at the web site of the Organization of American States http://www.oas.org/en/iachr/mandate/what. asp.
3. It should be noted, however, that Canada and the United States provided roughly 60 per cent of specific funds to the OAS in 2017 (Annual Report of the Secretary General 2017, page 48). Arguably this also reflects a type of commitment to the system.
4. Excepting *Any propaganda for war and any advocacy of national, racial, or religious hatred (. . .) against any person or group of persons on any grounds including those of race, color, religion, language, or national origin.*
5. Excepting – *The law may regulate the exercise of the rights and opportunities referred to (. . .) only on the basis of age, nationality, residence, language, education, civil and mental capacity, or sentencing by a competent court in criminal proceedings.*
6. In 1987, for example, Nicaragua adopted a new constitution that redefined the country as multiethnic. This has resulted in regional official status to languages like Miskitu and Sumu-Mayangna where before only Spanish was constitutionally recognized (see Section 1, Article 7 of the 1950 constitution). Similarly, the 1961 constitution of Boliia says nothing about language; the present constitution recognizes over 30 official languages.
7. The exact wording of the provision in all the relevant countries is: "*is able to speak and, unless incapacitated by blindness or other physical cause, to read the English language with sufficient proficiency to enable him to take an active part in the proceedings of the Senate.*" Constitution of St Lucia, Chapter III, Part I, 25 (c).

8. In the Report of The Saint Lucia Constitutional Reform Commission, March 2011, the status of Kwéyòl is raised, as is the inclusion of language as one of the heads of discrimination. The majority of Commissioners were of the view that the status of Kwéyòl was not a constitutional matter and was something that could be dealt with through ordinary legislation. The Commissioners were amenable to a constitutional provision prohibiting discrimination on the grounds of "language". As the Commissioners did not address the discriminatory clause specifying proficiency in English as necessary for membership in the legislature, inclusion of such a provision might be an area for challenging the clause in the future. Similar stipulations are found in the constitutions of Antigua and Barbuda, Dominica, Grenada, Guyana, and St Vincent and the Grenadines.

9. The exact wording of Article 5 is: (I) The official languages of the State are Spanish and all the languages of the rural native Indigenous nations and peoples, which are, Araona, Baure, Canichana, Cavineño, Cayubaba, Chácobo, Chimán, Ese Ejja, Guaraní, Guarasu'we, Itonama, Leco, Machajuyai-kallawaya, Machineri, Maropa, Mojeño-ignaciano, Moré, Mosetén, Movima, Pacawara, Puquina, Sirionó, Tacana, Tapiete, Toromona, Uruchipaya, Weenhayek, Yaminawa, Yuki, Yuracaré and Zamuco (II) The Pluri-National Government and the departmental governments must use at least two official languages. One of them must be Spanish, and the other shall be determined taking into account the use, convenience, circumstances, necessities and preferences of the population as a whole or of the territory in question. The other autonomous governments must use the languages characteristic of their territory, and one of them must be Spanish.

10. The Court publishes all Decisions and Judgments at http://www.corteidh.or.cr/index-en.cfm Loyola's Human Rights Project can be accessed at https://iachr.lls.edu/

11. *Aloeboetoe et al. v. Suriname* (massacre of 20 Saramaka in Atjoni).

12. Moiwana Community v. Suriname (massacre of 40 Ndjuka in Moiwana).

13. *Saramaka People v. Suriname* (construction of a hydroelectric dam/granting of mining and logging rights).

14. Kaliña and *Lokono Peoples v. Suriname* (mining and sale of land).

15. The official languages of the OAS are English, French, Portuguese and Spanish. The day-to-day working languages for staff in the various organs of the OAS are Spanish and English.

16. I/A Court H.R. Case of the *Saramaka People. v. Suriname*. Preliminary Objections, Merits, Reparations, and Costs. Judgment of 28 November 2007, Series C No. 172. VIII Reparations, 194(b).

17. In essence, Indigenous individuals are entitled to all human rights recognized

in international law; Indigenous Peoples possess collective rights; Indigenous Peoples have the right to autonomy, and the right not to be forced to assimilate to a wider majority culture. The following OAS member states voted against the UN Declaration – Canada, USA; Colombia abstained.

18. I/A Court H.R., Case of the Kaliña and Lokono Peoples v. Suriname. Merits, Reparations and Costs. Judgment of November 25, 2015. Series C No. 309. VII Reparations, 312

19. I/A Court H.R., Case of the *Moiwana Community v. Suriname.* Preliminary Objections, Merits, Reparations and Costs. Judgment of 15 June 2005. Series C No. 124. XIII Reparations, 216

20. See a brief discussion of the history between the government of Chile and the Mapuche in Richards, P. 2005. The Politics of Gender, Human Rights, and Being Indigenous in Chile. *Gender and Society* Vol. 19, No. 2:199–220.

21. I/A Court H.R., Case of *Norín Catrimán et al. (Leaders, members and activist of the Mapuche Indigenous People) v. Chile.* Merits, Reparations and Costs. Judgment of May 29, 2014. Series C No. 279. VI Facts, B, 78

22. Supra VII, paras. 367, 373 and 375.

23. See for example this public declaration (2003) signed by the heads of three Indigenous NGOs, on the issue of an agreement between Microsoft and the government of Chile to develop a Windows OS using Mapudungun: *"El mapudungun es el idioma del Pueblo Mapuche y la protección de este patrimonio de vida no solamente compete a una organización en particular sino al conjunto, porque debemos ser los propios mapuche quienes decidamos sobre la administración de nuestros conocimientos y a quienes nos deben consultar y nos referimos tanto a los mapuche del gulumapu (Chile) como a los del puelmapu (Argentina) ya que somos un solo Pueblo y un solo idioma. Por eso hacemos un llamado a preservar y controlar la comercialización de las propiedades culturales e inmateriales en dominio público de nuestro Pueblo. No nos olvidemos que así como nuestros recursos naturales se encuentran desprotegidos y sobre explotados como el agua, los bosques, el subsuelo, las riberas, las que están inscritas a nombre de grandes empresas locales, transnacionales y particulares, Hoy quieren comercializar con nuestro idioma."* http://www.mapuche.nl/espanol/cybermapuche.htm (16 October 2018).

24. I/A Court H.R., Case of *López Álvarez v. Honduras.* Merits, Reparations and Costs. Judgment of February 1, 2006. Series C No. 141.

25. Supra VII, para. 47.

26. Article 173 – The State shall preserve and promote the native cultures as well as authentic expressions of national folklore, popular art and handicrafts.

27. Supra paras. 205 (iv) and 210.

28. I/A Court H.R., Case of *Tiu-Tojín v. Guatemala.* Merits, Reparations and Costs. Judgment of 26 November 2008. Series C No. 190. REPARATIONS – VII, C. Pg. 35, Para. 100.

29. Supra Pg. 33, Para. 92.
30. IA Court. Case of *Rosendo Cantú et al v. Mexico.* Preliminary Objection, Merits, Reparations and Costs. Judgment 31 August 2010. Series C No. 216.
31. American Convention On Human Rights (Adopted at the Inter-American Specialized Conference on Human Rights, San José, Costa Rica, 22 November 1969) https://www.cidh.oas.org/basicos/english/basic3.american%20convention.htm
32. I/A Court H.R., Case of the *Moiwana Community v. Suriname.* Preliminary Objections, Merits, Reparations and Costs. Judgment of June 15, 2005. Series C No. 124. Separate Opinion of Judge A.A. Cançado Trindade, I, para. 2; III, para. 14.
33. I/A Court H.R., Case of the Kichwa Indigenous People of Sarayaku v. Ecuador (Merits, Reparations, Costs) IACtHR Series C No 245 (27 June 2012) – paragraphs 303 & 304, page 82.
34. Title 1, Article 1, Chapter 2.
35. I have initial data from 12 members of staff – 8 are unfamiliar with the term or the concept.

REFERENCES

Anaya, S. 2004. "International Human Rights and Indigenous Peoples: The Move Toward the Multicultural State Arizona". *Journal of International & Comparative Law* 21 (1): 13–61 https://ssrn.com/abstract=1485138

Blommaert, J. 2001. "The Asmara Declaration as a Sociolinguistic Problem: Reflections on Scholarship and Linguistic Rights". *Journal of Sociolinguistics* 5 (1): 131–55.

Colón-Ríos. J. 2011. "Law, Language and Latin American Constitutions". *Victoria University of Wellington Law Review* 42 (2), Issue 2; Victoria University of Wellington Legal Research Paper (367–386).

———. 2013. "Law, Language and the New Latin American Constitutions". *Victoria University of Wellington Law Review,* 3 (4); Victoria University of Wellington Legal Research Papers No. 16/2013 (1–20).

Course, M. 2012. "The Birth of the Word: Language, Force, and Mapuche Ritual Authority".*HAU: Journal of Ethnographic Theory* 2 (1): 1–26. https://doi.org/10.14318/hau2.1.002

Haboud, M., R. Howard, J.Cru, and J Freeland. 2016. "Linguistic Human Rights and Language Revitalization in Latin America and the Caribbean". In *Indigenous Language Revitalization in the Americas,* edited by, 201–23. New York: Routledge

Kibbee, Douglas A. 2008. "Minority Language Rights: Historical and Comparative Perspectives." *Intercultural Human Rights Law Review* 3:79–136.

King, Kendall A. 2005. "Language Policy and Local Planning in South America: New Directions for Enrichment Bilingual Education in the Andes". In *Bilingual Education in South America*, edited by Anne-Marie De Mejía, 1–14. Clevedon, UK: Multilingual Matters.

Lagos Cristian, Felipe Perez de Arce, and Veronica A. Figueroa V. 2017. "The Revitalization of the Mapuche Language as a Space of Ideological Struggle: The Case of Pehuenche Communities in Chile". *Journal of Historical Archaeology and Anthropological Sciences* 1(5):197–207. https://doi.org/10.15406/jhaas.2017.01.00031 May, Stephen. 2006. "Language Policy and Minority Rights". In *An Introduction to Language Policy*, edited by , 255–72. New York: Blackwell.

Mithun, Marianne. 2011. *Indigenous Languages of the Americas*. Oxford Bibliographies. https://doi.org/10.1093/OBO/9780199772810-0004 (Accessed June 30, 2019)

O'Connor, Vivienne. 2012. "Practitioner's Guide: Common Law and Civil Law Traditions". INPROL – International Network to Promote the Rule of Law, March 2012. https://www.fjc.gov/sites/default/files/2015/Common%20and%20Civil%20Law%20Traditions.pdf

Price, Richard. 2012. "Saramaka People v Suriname: A Human Rights Victory and Its Messy Aftermath". Cambridge, MA: Cultural Survival. https://www.culturalsurvival.org/news/saramaka-people-v-suriname-human-rights-victory-and-its-messy-aftermath

Richards, Patricia Lynne. 2013. *Race and the Chilean Miracle: Neoliberalism, Democracy, and Indigenous Rights*. Pittsburgh: University of Pittsburgh Press.

Smith, N. 1994. "An Anotated List of Creoles, Pidgins and Mixed Languages". In *Pidgins and Creoles: An Introduction*, edited by J. Arends, P. Muysken and N. Smith, 331–74. Amsterdam: John Benjamins Publishing Company.

St. Hilaire, Aonghas. 2008. "Postcolonialism, Identity, and the French Language in St. Lucia". *New West Indian Guide* 81(1/2): 55–77.

Vasak, Karel. 1977. "Human Rights: A Thirty-Year Struggle: The Sustained Efforts to give Force of Law to the Universal Declaration of Human Rights", *UNESCO Courier* 30 (11): 28–29,32. Paris: United Nations Educational, Scientific, and Cultural Organization.

Wright, Sue. 2007. "The Right to Speak One's Own Language: Reflections on Theory and Practice". *Language Policy* 6: 203–24.

CHAPTER 10

"Don't Say a Word"

Interpreting Jamaican Idioms in a Toronto Murder Case

CLIVE FORRESTER

INTRODUCTION

On the night of 24 November 2013, Mr Reshane Hayles-Wilson was in attendance at a basketball tournament at the North Kipling Community Centre in the Greater Toronto Area (GTA). During the tournament, MrNeko Mitchelle arrived at the tournament and while there, exchanged a greeting with Hayles-Wilson. Shortly afterwards Hayles-Wilson pulled a firearm and fired eight shots at point blank range hitting Mitchell who subsequently succumbed to his injuries some time later. The entire incident was caught on a closed-circuit surveillance camera. Hayles-Wilson fled the scene and remained in hiding for ten months before he was arrested and sentenced to first degree murder (CTV Toronto 2014).

The Crown argued that Hayles-Wilson carried out a targeted hit against Mitchell and sought the maximum penalty of first-degree murder under Canadian law – life imprisonment without the possibility of parole before twenty years. The defence, however, argued that Hayles-Wilson acted pre-emptively, assuming, as it were, that Mitchell came to murder him on the night in question. The defence presented evidence that Hayles-Wilson had owed Mitchell, an alleged drug dealer, a substantial amount of money for the purchase of narcotics prior to the night of 24 November. Hayles-Wilson, who was unable to repay what he had owed in the specified time, felt that his life was in danger based on a text message he had received from Mitchell who, he alleges, issued a veiled threat. The defence maintains Hayles-Wilson felt that on the night in question he fired his gun at Mitchell to prevent Mitchell's attempt on his own life. The decision faced by the jury was determining whether Mitchell's murder was premeditated (first-degree murder) or Hayles-Wilson killed Mitchell in an act of self-preservation (second-degree murder). A central concern of the case in question is the fact that the language of the involved parties displays features of Jamaican Creole alongside Afro-Canadian Vernacular English which would involve the interpretation of several different idioms as captured in text messages as well as wiretapped conversations. Correctly interpreting these idioms is particularly important for the defence since a large part of their strategy is premised on what their client argues was a death threat.

There are two events prior to the night in question which might explain why Hayles-Wilson felt his life was threatened; a text message he received from Mitchell, and a following warning he received from his cousin.

A Threatening Text Message

To understand the self-defence rationale presented by the counsel for Hayles-Wilson, a series of events and communication leading up to the night of the incident have to be taken into consideration. Though not captured on the surveillance camera, nor the wiretap audio used as the data for this study, it helps to construct the threatening atmosphere Hayles-Wilson alleges caused him to act in self-defence on the night of 23 February. The details of the communication between Hayles-Wilson and Mitchell preceding the night of Mitchell's murder were provided by Hayles-Wilson's legal counsel as additional information to assist with the language analysis.

Both Hayles-Wilson and Mitchell are alleged to have been involved in illicit activity prior to the night of the incident, specifically, Mitchell is said to have sold a quantity of narcotics to Hayles-Wilson, and received partial payment with an understanding that the full amount would be settled at a later date. Hayles-Wilson seems to have agreed to this arrangement initially, but avoided subsequent attempts to settle the balance. Additionally, he skipped a meeting with Mitchell to repay the outstanding amount. After the skipped meeting, Mitchell sent a text message to Hayles-Wilson in which he says; *"Keep the change, and when I see you, you know what time it is."*

Sometime afterward, Hayles-Wilson was speaking to his cousin who informed him that the debt he owed to Mitchell was becoming well-known in some parts. The cousin is alleged to have said; *"He's telling people that you owe him money and when he sees you, it's a ting."*

There is no indication either from Mitchell's text message or what the cousin later related to Hayles-Wilson what the exact intentions of Mitchell were. It is possible however, given the context of the utterances, to analyse Mitchell's text message in terms of Speech Act Theory. Mitchell's utterance appears to have the perlocutionary structure typical in a conditional threat. Salgueiro (2010) states that, ". . . certain perlocutionary effects seem to be intrinsic to threats. For an act to count as a threat, it would seem to be necessary for its purpose to be to intimidate or cow the person threatened, which raises the question whether it is an illocutionary or perlocutionary act."

The prevailing context for the interaction between the two men is that of a demand by Mitchell that Hayles-Wilson pay the agreed sum:

1. De(R d a)
   Where *De* is "demand," R is "receiver," and "*d a*" means *does action*. Essentially, the prevailing context of interaction between the two is that Mitchell has demanded that Hayles-Wilson (R) repay him the outstanding amount owed (*d a1*). Speech acts which count as direct or elementary threats usually have the following structure:

2. Th(S d a)
   Where *Th* is "threaten," and *S* is "speaker." The action in (2) above is an action which the receiver would not want to be carried out. The subsequent threat in the text message could be understood in the following format by combining (1) and (2) above:

3. De(R d a1) **if** ¬(R d a1) **whenever** (*S* sees *R*) **then** Th(S d a2)
   The exact nature of a2 is of course masked by the idiomatic expression "you know what time it is" which conjures up the image of an action destined to take place at an appointed time. The fact that Hayles-Wilson's cousin is also relaying the threat second hand further inten-

sifies the perlocutionary force, since, it could be argued, that threats sent via proxy are an attempt to increase the level of intimidation. Whatever the perlocutionary effect of Mitchell's utterance, there is linguistic grounds on which to establish that it structurally resembles a conditional threat. As Kissine (2014, 162) points out, "the probability of a threat being fulfilled has to be with respect to the situation on which it is conditional".Given the context for the threat – a drug deal gone awry – it is reasonable to take the threat seriously as Nesse (2001) suggests that persons who issue a threat are under no less commitment than when making a promise. While I do not take this approach to threats, preferring instead to see them as intimidatory rather than as strictly commitments, there is little doubt that it was within Mitchell's capacity to cause harm to Hayles-Wilson.

A Cousin's Warning

Some time after Hayles-Wilson had received the text message from Mitchell containing the threat, he spoke with a cousin of his who appears to be reinforcing the threat issued by Mitchell. The cousin says to Hayles-Wilson: "Why is my bwoy looking for you? He's telling people that you owe him money, and when he sees you, it's a ting."

The Jamaican colloquial expression "my bwoy" simply acts as a space filler for a name which both participants in a discourse would be familiar with. A direct parallel in English would be saying "Why is *you know who* asking for you?" The name is ellipsed as an act of discretion especially given the nature of the message – a threat being issued by a drug dealer to his debtor. What is critical at this point is the revelation by the cousin that "he's telling people that you owe him money" suggesting that Hayles-Wilson's failure to repay his debt is now a known transgression among common associates.

The cousin ends his message with what appears to be a restatement of the initial threat issued by Mitchell; "when he sees you, *it's a ting.*" Whether this latter portion of the message is being relayed verbatim or paraphrased is unclear, but it essentially captures the sentiment and speech structure of the conditional threat outlined previously and restated in a modified format below in (4):

4. De(R d a1) & ¬(R d a1), (S tells A) **whenever** (S sees R) → Th(S d a2)

In this configuration, the element A is introduced to stand in for "associates" to complete what could be seen as a second-hand threat; the speaker (S), tells several associates (A) that the next time (S) encounters the receiver (R) an unpleasant action (a2) will occur. In this construction in (4) above, "it's a ting" serves as the idiomatic guise for a2.

Request for Expert Witness Testimony

As stated earlier, the main line of defence for HW was not whether he killed M – this was caught on camera and is therefore incontrovertible evidence – but rather the motivation for the homicide (which consequently determines if the conviction is first or second – degree murder). During the trial, I was contacted by the defence team for HW with a specific request; 1. determine whether the text message sent from M to HW could be interpreted as a threat, and 2. listen to a wiretap conversation between HW and his cousin JD while HW was incarcerated awaiting trial to determine whether JD instructed HW to be uncooperative with the prosecution and withhold crucial information My assistance would subsequently take the form of a written analysis of the idioms as they appeared in the context of the conversation as well as an appearance on the witness stand to explain to the courtroom what would be the most natural interpretations of a number of these idioms when uttered by someone who is using Jamaican Creole.

THE DATA

The data for this study comes primarily from two sources; (i) a text message exchanged between the accused and the victim, and (ii) a wiretapped conversation between the accused and a family member. The text message, discussed in the introduction, was used to establish HW's claim that he felt threatened by NM and subsequently had to act preemptively against that threat. It served as the primary piece of evidence to argue against a premeditated homicide. The wiretapped conversation on the other hand contained a very specific idiom, "don't say a word," which the prosecution argued was an instruction for HW to be uncooperative during the investigation.

The audio transcript of the conversation between HW and his cousin, JD, is facilitated through a third party (an unnamed woman) since the call originated from the jail at which HW was stationed awaiting his trial. The call was made to a woman jointly known to the participants, and she connected them in a conference call. Her contribution ended shortly after it was established that both HW and JD could hear each other clearly.

The conversation is casual in nature; the men catch up on past events, focusing primarily on HW's predicament and its impact on him and his family. JD expresses interest, and even concern, about HW's legal representation throughout the conversation, and both men spend time discussing the challenges of getting lawyers to treat their cases with the urgency it deserves. The men talked for close to twenty minutes and concluded with JD indicating he plans to get in touch with a mutual friend on behalf of HW.

Transcript Excerpts

The specific token, "don't say a word," occurs twice in the nineteen- minute long audio recording. The first appearance is early in the conversation, occurring shortly after JD enquires about HW's mental state on account of being on lockdown for 23 hours per day. The second appearance happens close to the end of their dialogue around the time when JD expresses concern about the quality of the legal representation HW is receiving. The excerpts below are numbered 1 and 2 to show the context of the conversation in which the idiom occurs.

HW = accused, calling from jail

JD = cousin to HW, and alleged leader of the gang to which HW belongs

UK = unknown woman who facilitated the call

(Hhh) = laughter

Excerpt 1

1. 00:00:03:	(Phone ringing)
2. 00:00:11: JD:	Hello?
3. 00:00:13: UK:	Hold on, hold on. Come Emily! Hold on talk, talk.
4. 00:00:17: JD:	Hello?
5. 00:00:19: HW:	Yow.
6. 00:00:21: JD:	Yeah. Yeah cuzzy. You hear me?
7. 00:00:26: HW:	Yeah I can hear you, how you doin?
8. 00:00:27: JD:	Yeah I'm here man, I was just at court man tryin to get some a dese conditions changed.
9. 00:00:27: HW:	Court? [unintelligible]
10.00:00:35: JD:	No I caught a charge di other day boom.
11.00:00:39: HW:	What?
12.00:00:40: JD:	Fuck bro, I'm out here boom (hhh) I'm out here, they have me on house arrest cuzzy.
13.00:00:40: HW:	Yes? [(Hhh)
14.00:00:49: JD:	[(hhh) Naa bro (hhh) I'm fuckin – they taking it off today right.
15.00:00:57: HW:	Yeah.
16.00:00:59: JD:	Yeah they taking it off today. Nothing serious though. You done know, little works.
17.00:01:05: HW:	Ok.
18. 00:01:06: JD:	You know how it is. Wa you dealing with dog, how you doin dog? How you feeling? You good? How's your [unintelligible]?
19.00:01:11: HW:	Just working on reading my bible you know.
20.00:04:23: JD:	So how they dealing with you in there?
21.00:04:27: HW:	Where I am, I'm locked down everyday right. I

don't come out. I only come out to shower and use the phone.

22.00:04:33: JD:	How long they give you, like an hour?
23.00:04:35: HW:	Yeah.
24.00:04:37: JD:	Ook. So how you doin just readin your books and shit?
25.00:04:41: HW:	Yeah just read my bible and some books, my mom sent me books and stuff.
26.00:04:45: JD:	Ok. Don't put too much pressure on your brain now. Just gwaan hold it, yu zeet?
27.00:04:51: HW:	[Unintelligible]
28.00:04:53: JD:	Just gwaan hold it. Don't say a word.

Excerpt 2:

1. 00:13:59: HW:	Talk with your lawyer, and get him to link with my lawyer and see what a pop.
2. 00:14:05: JD:	Ok. Oh yeah I know. I'm gonna give him a call now. I'm gonna tell him – I just want him to know exactly like you know, you're in good hands and they have to know, I have to let them know that you're my family. Like, they better know what it is.
3. 00:14:20: HW:	He sounds like he wants to fight, but then he sounds like he wants to roll over at the same time.
4. 00:14:26: JD:	Ok, ok, ok, ok. Naa, ok, I'm gonna have a little word with the L still. I'm gonna call my lawyers.
5. 00:14:34: HW:	Yeah.
6. 00:14:35: JD:	You know what it is too? So much sussu boom. Everybody talking, even in that little lawyer world? It's all a big drama for them too, it's like a movie for them, you know what I'm saying?

7.00:14:43: HW: Yeah.

8. 00:14:45: JD: Yeah like, like there just like everybody sussu and sussuing. I have to go tell my lawyer you guys don't play with my cousin's life eh. Like real talk. Cause I don't even know boom. I'm just gettin goosebumps even talk to you right now. These people just cheese me off bro. Yow. (2.0) Crazy (3.0). Crazy (4.0).

9.00:15:21: HW: The way I'm lookin at it, even if these guys can't [unintelligible]

10.00:15:31: JD: Crazy.

11.00:17:03: JD: The only thing they can be talking is if there's no letter with it (3.0). No letter with the number, you get what I'm saying.

12.00:17:10: HW: Yeah, yeah, I hear you.

13.00:17:13: JD: Yeah that's the only thing they could be talking about. Like what else could they be talking about. Shit it's not even making sense. Cause if they're saying, like a little kinda steep number with no letter with it, then yeah we have to think about that right?

14.00:17:29: HW: I'll go knock out a number no problem fam.

15.00:17:31: JD: Yeah come on you don't have to tell me cuzzy. It's just like yeah, but . . . that must be what he's talking about. Cause nothing else makes sense.

16.00:17:42: HW: Yeah that's what I'm saying but –

17.00:17:43: JD: Don't say a word, don't say a word. I'm gonna go, gonna go talk to him. I was just with him last night too. I was just with my lawyer last night too.

ANALYSIS

The analytical method I believe best suits this data is conversation analysis (CA). With a CA approach it allows for analysis of the text to occur along "neutral" lines, that is, without assuming any motives of the conversants based on their statuses as known gang members. The prosecution further argues that it is well within JD's power, being the leader of the gang, to order a subordinate to withhold information and in doing so become uncooperative with investigations. Using CA means the relative status of each person involved in the interaction becomes irrelevant and instead the text serves as both the locus of analysis and the primary basis upon which any conclusions about intentions can be drawn. The analysis which follows is divided into six "topics" corresponding with conversational topic changes occurring between HW and JD.

Topic 1: "house arrest"

The first topic is introduced roughly thirty seconds into the audio recording when JD mentioned his ongoing court case;

00:00:27: JD: Yeah I'm here man, I was just at court man tryin to get some a dese conditions changed.

This is new information for HW which indicates that JD's current legal problems started after HW was incarcerated. It is also clear that this is the first time the two cousins are interacting since HW was charged for first-degree murder. JD, perhaps sensing the surprise by HW after getting the news, diffuses the severity of his house arrest by assuring him that it was not serious and it was just a "little works" – meaning it was a minor infraction which led to the house arrest. Both men share a quick laugh about the irony of the situation; one cousin calling from inside a jail to talk about his legal problems, only to find out his cousin on the outside is himself facing legal problems of his own.

Topic 2: "how they dealing with you in there?"

The second topic occurs shortly after the first when JD asks about how HW is coping while in lock up;

00:01:06: JD: You know how it is. Wa you dealing with dog, how you doin dog? How you feeling? You good? How's your [unintelligible]?

There is some indication that this topic is the purpose of the entire interaction, that is, the reason for the call was for HW to tell JD how he was doing. The first indication is that the topic occurs fairly early in the conversation and is expanded on several times throughout the exchange. The other, and more important indication, is that both men return to this topic even when other topics interject in their conversation. Essentially, HW's well-being is the one topic which lasts the entirety of the conversation while the other topics are subordinate. It serves as both the segue for other topics as well as the landing place for when the alternate topics have become exhausted.

HW's response doesn't so much explicate how he's being treated in the jail as much as it gives a dire assessment of his current day to day affairs:

00:04:27: HW: Where I am, I'm locked down everyday right. I don't come out. I only come out to shower and use the phone.

HW explains that he is locked down every day, with only a short window to have a shower and make phone calls. He reveals that this break from lock down lasts all of one hour, nineteen (19) minutes of which he spent on the phone talking with JD. Sensing the abject boredom of a 23 hour daily lockdown, JD enquires if HW is at least able to read his books, to which HW replies in the affirmative, stating that his mother had secured the reading material. This is actually the second time HW's mother is being mentioned; in one of the subordinate topics – not transcribed above – JD tells HW that he will send him some money so that he will be able to purchase food at the commissary since HW's mother shouldn't have to bear this additional burden while her son is incarcerated. JD tries to console his cousin the best way he knows how;

00:04:45: JD: Ok. Don't put too much pressure on your brain now. Just gwaan hold it, yu zeet?

He advises HW about undue "pressure on the brain" which is an idiomatic expression used to talk about stress and depression. JD encourages his cousin to continue to "hold it" and not be overcome by the desperation of his current predicament.

Token occurrence #1: "don't say a word"

It is within the context of the aforementioned that HW finally tells his cousin:

00:04:53: JW: Just gwaan hold it. Don't say a word.

The token idiom "don't say a word" serves two purposes here. First, it acts as a rhetorical device signalling the completion of the topic which JD had raised earlier (how he's being treated in lock up) and a transition into a new topic (the quality of the legal representation). The second function of this idiom is a culturally situated speech act used to console another person. One of the most common ways to express comfort in a Jamaican speech community is to tell the grieving party "hush" or "no say nothing" and more recently "don't say a word" all of which are various denotative methods of saying *shut up*. Within the context of intra-cultural communication, however, the idiom is understood as a display of sympathy, and this is how JD intended it at that point in their conversation. He was, as best as he could, offering his cousin a measure of emotional support. Ascribing this meaning to the utterance goes back to one of the main paradigms of conversation analysis, that is, the meaning of an utterance and the action it performs in a conversation depends on its sequential position in the interaction (Ten Have 2007).

Topic 3: "talk with your lawyer"

As soon as JD closes the previous topic dealing with HW's well-being, he self-selects the next topic on the legal representation. JD sounds particularly invested in this topic as he is wary of the pitfalls of lackluster legal representation. He believes that HW's lawyer may need some assistance so he advises his cousin;

00:13:59: HW: Talk with your lawyer, and get him to link with
                       my lawyer and see what a pop.

JD is insistent that he needs to get his own lawyers to intervene in the legal representation of HW since this is more than the legal defence of a friend, this is *family*, and as such the defence needs to be airtight. HW himself is skeptical about the effort from his lawyer: he makes it clear that his lawyer's zeal is sporadic even bordering on "rolling over" and giving up.

Topic 4: "everybody susu and susuing"

JD believes he knows the reason for HW's listless defence;

00:14:35: JD: You know what it is too? So much sussu boom. Everybody talking, even in that little lawyer world? It's all a big drama for them too, it's like a movie for them, you know what I'm saying?

As far as JD is concerned, it all comes down to gossip. He uses the Jamaican expression "sussu" which means gossip/gossiping to suggest that lawyers can be distracted from doing serious legal preparation because they descend into the mundane business of idle talk. He further complains that the dilemmas faced by clients serve as fodder for the "big drama" that lawyers make of it from time to time. JD is audibly agitated at this point and doesn't mince words in demanding that the lawyer takes this matter seriously:

00:14:45: JD: Yeah like, like they're just like everybody sussu and sussuing. I have to go tell my lawyer you guys don't play with my cousin's life eh. Like real talk. Cause I don't even know boom. I'm just gettin goosebumps even talk to you right now. These people just cheese me off bro.

He stops short of uttering an ultimatum when he says "Cause I don't even know boom" in reference to the prospect of the legal defence being so poor as to be comparable to *playing with my cousin's life*. JD makes it clear he is both angered and unnerved by the entire ordeal. JD is handling most of the conversational work at this point, while HW chimes in usually to agree with JD's assertions. Both men transition into a sub-topic having to do with – based on what I could decipher – the length of the potential prison sentence that HW would have to serve.

Token occurrence # 2:"don't say a word"

The second and final time the idiom in question appears, it occurs shortly after both men have introduced the matter of the prison sentence. Just as HW begins to expand on the topic his turn is interrupted by JD;

00:17:42: HW:	Yeah that's what I'm saying but –
00:17:43: JD:	Don't say a word, don't say a word. I'm gonna go, gonna go talk to him. I was just with him last night too. I was just with my lawyer last night too.

Just as in the first occurence of the token, the idiom serves as a rhetorical mechanism to signal topic closure. JD brings closure to the topic by agreeing to complete an action item – get in contact with his lawyer – that could bring a resolution to their concerns. The second function of the idiom this time around however, is not to console, but instead to reassure HW that nothing more need be said on the issue; it will be handled. JD has essentially closed the current topic and committed to its resolution beyond the scope of their conversation; indeed, there is nothing else that warrants saying on the matter.

DISCUSSION

During the cross-examination in the trial, the counsel for the Crown wanted to know whether a possible interpretation for "don't say a word" could be an instruction to keep quiet, specifically, to withhold information and cooperation from the judicial system. The simple answer to this is yes, it could conceivably mean such a thing. However, not in this context highlighted in the transcript excerpts above. Whether JD wanted HW to withhold evidence from the authorities is not a matter which can be directly extrapolated from the data nor could it be inferred from anything which was said during the conversation. JD's utterance only looks like an instruction to remain silent in form, but it's substance – as indicated in the analysis – is something entirely different.

Idioms such as these pose a particular kind of difficulty for cross-linguistic interaction, and not just for witnesses who have a Jamaican background. Coulthard (2007) describes the twofold challenge the linguist faces after having done an analysis – conveying the "linguistic insight" to the lay audience on the jury panel, and then navigating the interactional rules of cross-examination if called on to give oral evidence at court.

At any point in time in an Ontario courtroom, it is possible to have an individual on the witness stand who is using a blend of non-standard English, a hybridized form of a heritage language, and urban slang to a courtroom which operates in Standard (Canadian) English. In the case used for this study, the wiretap audio at the centre of the trial also has a blend of three codes: Afro-Canadian Vernacular English, a hybrid Jamaican Creole which exists in the GTA, and urban colloquialisms used among members of a particular demographic. The judge, both the defence and Crown counsel, as well as about half of the jury were white and likely spoke predominantly in English. It wouldn't be unusual for those individuals to surmise that an utterance which looks like English, and sounds like English, should be interpreted like English. If anything, this case should demonstrate that such conclusions are at best problematic for clear communication, and at worst detrimental to the delivery of justice.

CONCLUSION

HW was ultimately convicted of second-degree murder, which I have come to understand was what the defence team had wanted, since the alternative would have been first-degree murder which is a considerably longer sentence. HW's lawyer, who contacted me to do the analysis, said he believes that my testimony likely played a large part in moving the jury to understand that HW reasonably felt his life was under threat, and that he was not in fact instructed by his cousin to be silent and withhold information. If anything could be said about the outcome of this case it would be that the verdict was not based on an instance of misinterpretation – the use of linguistic expertise mitigated against this outcome.

Serving as an expert witness for the defence was certainly a learning experience. Though my CV was submitted to the court days before I took the witness stand, my expertise on this matter still had to be established to the satisfaction of the Crown during cross-examination. And while I could confidently talk about my expertise on the analysis of the language in the courtroom setting in general, my experience with testimony was admittedly non-existent – this was my first time. The counsel for the defence was quick to re-examine me after the cross to ensure any doubt about my expertise to speak on this matter was removed (or at least reduced). A fruitful endeavour for further research lies in this area of delivering complex linguistic information to lay jurors.

I was pleasantly surprised by the attentiveness of some of the jurors while I tried to explain some of the subtle differences between the structure of Jamaican Creole and that of English. Both the judge and members of the jury seemed genuinely intrigued, since I imagine this was the first time they had heard an academic exposition of the ubiquitous Jamaican speech. This, along with the fact that individuals can register as court interpreters of Jamaican Creole, makes it clear that the Ontario court system isn't afraid to look beyond notions of "substandard language" to ensure that justice is carried out.

After the case had concluded I spoke with the defence team along with another lawyer who happened to be in the vicinity just on the outside of the courtroom. Out of curiosity I asked how many times do they imagine this sort of service would be needed – that is, analysing and interpreting Jamaican language for the courts or giving expert testimony. While neither could give an exact number, I was assured that it was more than most people would imagine. What was worrying was that because the existence of experts is either unknown or sourced by serendipity, it means that on more than one occasion no expert analysis could be given or an ad hoc "expert" had to be retained. Such experts, I was told, could simply be a Jamaican mother of someone on the police force. All three of those lawyers now have my contact and since that time I've gotten one more paid referral. I expect more to come in the years ahead.

REFERENCES

Coulthard, Malcolm. 2007. "The Linguist as Expert Witness". *Linguistics and the Human Sciences* 1(1). https://doi.org/10.1558/lhs.2005.1.1.39 (6 August, 2019).

CTV News Toronto. 2014. "Man charged with first-degree murder in November 2013 shooting case". *Toronto.* CTV News. https://toronto.ctvnews.ca/man-charged-with-first-degree-murder-in-november-2013-shooting-case-1.2020803 (21 August, 2019).

Kissine, Mikhail. 2014. *From Utterances to Speech Acts.* Cambridge: Cambridge University Press.

Nesse, Randolph M., ed. 2001. *Evolution and the Capacity for Commitment.* New York: Russell Sage Foundation.

Nicoloff, Franck. 1989. "Threats and Illocutions". *Journal of Pragmatics* 13 (4): 501–22. https://doi:org/10.1016/0378-2166(89)90038-6 (20 September, 2019).

R. v. Hayles-Wilson. 2018. Vol. 4337 (CanLII). http://canlii.ca/t/ht15d (21 August, 2019).

Salgueiro, Antonio Blanco. 2010. "Promises, Threats, and the Foundations of Speech Act Theory". *Pragmatics. Quarterly Publication of the International Pragmatics Association (IPrA)* 20(2). 213–28. https://doi.org/10.1075/prag.20.2.05bla (9 August, 2019).

Ten Have, Paul. 2007. *Doing Conversation Analysis.* Los Angeles: Sage Publications.

Contributors

SANDY ABU EL ADAS is a postdoctoral researcher at the Basque Center on Cognition, Brain and Language (BCBL). Her work focuses on how variability in the input (talker) and output (speech production) is manifested in clinical and non-clinical populations.

KORAH BELGRAVE, lecturer in linguistics and communication studies, taught in the University of the West Indies' Use of English programme at Cave Hill, and was Coordinator for the Foundation Language Programme for over 10 years. Dr Belgrave is also a trained teacher with over 15 years' experience.

RENÉE A. BLAKE is an associate professor in the Departments of Linguistics and Social and Cultural Analysis at New York University. She also serves as a Faculty Fellow in Residence at New York University. She received her PhD in linguistics from Stanford University in 1997.

NICKESHA T. DAWKINS is a lecturer at the University of the West Indies. Her research focuses on Phonetics and Phonology, and Language and Gender. She recently translated the Universal Declaration of Human Rights into Jamaican Creole for the United Nations. She earned her PhD from the UWI (Mona) in 2016.

CLIVE FORRESTER, PhD, is a faculty member in the Department of English Language and Literature at the University of Waterloo where he teaches courses on academic writing, technical writing, linguistics, and Caribbean language and culture. He is currently the president of the Society for Caribbean Linguistics.

SHELOME GOODEN is Professor of Linguistics and Assistant Vice Chancellor for Research for the Humanities, Arts, Social Sciences, and Related Fields, at the University of Pittsburgh. She researches language contact, intonation and prosody in Caribbean Creoles.

ALISON IRVINE-SOBERS is an adjunct faculty member at the University of the West Indies Open Campus. She teaches courses on Discourse Analysis, Sociolinguistics and the History and Development of Tertiary Level English Language Courses. Her PhD from the UWI (Mona) focussed on ideologies of language and Standard Jamaican English.

JANICE E. JULES has been a teacher in the Primary School System for over thirty years. From 2000 until 2005, she worked at The University of the West Indies, Cave Hill Campus as a Part-time Tutor of the Foundation Language Programme in the Faculty of Humanities and Education. Presently, Dr. Jules is assigned duties as a Lecturer/Coordinator in the discipline of Linguistics in the Department of Language, Linguistics and Literature at the UWI.

TARA MCALLISTER is an Associate Professor of Communicative Sciences and Disorders at New York University. Her work aims to understand how speech is acquired in typical and clinical populations and measure the efficacy of technology-enhanced treatment for speech sound disorder.

ELIZABETH MONTOYA-STEMANN is Voice and Speech and Acting Lecturer at the Edna Manley College of the Visual and Performing Arts in Kingston, Jamaica. She received her BFA in Drama at the Teatro Libre de Bogotá Escuela in Bogotá, Colombia. She is currently a PhD candidate at the UWI (Mona). Her research analyses issues that future Jamaican performers display when presenting a poetic text written in Standard English.

EWART THOMAS, a Guyanese-born graduate in Mathematics from UWI, earned his PhD in Statistics from Cambridge University in 1967. He has developed mathematical and statistical models in many areas of Psychology and, more recently, in the study of Creole languages. He is now Professor of Psychology Emeritus at Stanford University.

LISA TOMLINSON is a Lecturer at the University of the West Indies, Mona Campus, in the Department of Literatures in English. She teaches African Diaspora and Caribbean film, as well as World Cinema.

KARLA N. WASHINGTON is an Associate Professor in the Department of Speech-Language Pathology, University of Toronto. Her work focuses on characterizing speech productions, expressive language, and functional communication in monolingual and multilingual children in the context of their environment.

Index

Printed in the USA
CPSIA information can be obtained
at www.ICGtesting.com
CBHW021047070624
9586CB00001B/8